Eric '09

D1567337

Jim Otis and Woody

1968

THE YEAR THAT SAVED OHIO STATE FOOTBALL

BY DAVID HYDE

Orange Frazer Press
Wilmington, Ohio

Additional copies of *1968* may be ordered directly from:
Orange Frazer Press
P.O. Box 214
Wilmington, OH 45177

Telephone 1.800.852.9332 for price and shipping information.
Website: *www.orangefrazer.com*

Design and cover: *Jeff Fulwiler & John Baskin*

Jacket photo of Woody Hayes by kind permission of Donna Brockway
from The Chance Brockway Collection.
Other photographs: the Ohio State University archives—pages iv, x-xi, xvi, 3,
43, 97, 109,195, 213. The *Columbus Dispatch*—pages viii, 119, 251.
All others, which are most of the unusual closeup action shots, are by OSU grad
Malcolm W. Emmons, a well-known sports photographer of the midcentury.
Special thanks to Matthew Emmons.

Library of Congress Cataloging-in-Publication Data

Hyde, Dave, 1961-
  1968 : the year that saved Ohio State football / by David Hyde.
     p. cm.
  Nineteen sixty-eight
  Includes bibliographical references and index.
  ISBN 978-1-933197-60-9
  1. Football--Ohio--History--20th century. I. Title. II. Title:
Nineteen sixty-eight.

  GV938.H93 2008
  796.332'630977157--dc22

                                    2008036489

For Warren and Janet Hyde,
who started this book in 1961

ACKNOWLEDGEMENTS

Most of the information for this book came through interviews with players, coaches, and others involved with the 1968 Ohio State season. The interviews were done over a period of several months in the first half of 2008. Some lasted minutes. Dozens took more than an hour. Some involved several hours with repeated follow-up interviews as more information was gathered and better questions could be asked. Especially since most interviews took place over the phone, virtually everyone was gracious with their time, thoughts, and memories.

I would like to acknowledge the help of Jennifer Kirchner of the Ohio State Sports Information Department in retrieving media guides, game play-by-play and any other details that arose in the writing; Bertha Inhat of the OSU Archives for her research help; Ellie Haydock, who once again came through when help was needed; Connie for putting up with everything and Alec, Casey and Abigail for having no choice but to do so.

The interviewees: Tim Anderson, Tom Backhus, Tom Bartley, Ed Bender, Mike Bordner, John Bozick, John Brockington, Earle Bruce, Dave Brungard, Paul Caldwell, Ross Carlson, Larry Catuzzi, George Chaump, Dave Cheney, Jim Coburn, Jim Conroy, Pete Corey, Steve Crapser, Mike Dale, Mark Debevec, Brian Donovan, Ray Dyson, Gerry Ehrsam, Dave Foley, Jim Gentile, Ray Gillian, Bill Hackett, Randy Hart, Leo Hayden, Glenn Hodge, Ralph Holloway, Lou Holtz, Marv Holman, Rudy Hubbard, Paul Huff, Chuck Hutchinson, Alan Jack, Bruce Jankowski, Jim Jones, Rex Kern, Kaye Kessler, Gerald King, Dick Kuhn, Ted Kurz, Ed Lapuh, Ed Linser, Bill Long, Ron Maciejowski, Bill Mallory, Jack Marsh, Carole Moorehead, John Muhlbach, Jim Opperman, Jim Otis, Mike Polaski, Bill Pollitt, Ted Provost, Larry Qualls, Mike Radtke, Jim Roman, Gary Roush, Kevin Rusnak, Mike Sensibaugh, Joe Sinkowski, Bruce Smith, Butch Smith, Bob Smith, Mark Stier, Jim Stillwagon, Vic Stottlemyer, Phil Strickland, Jerry Tabacca, Jack Tatum, Bob Trapuzzano, Rich Troha, Jan White, Dave Whitfield and Dirk Worden.

Woody and the elements

TABLE OF CONTENTS

The boys of 1968

Front row from left: Jim Roman, Gary Roush, Jay Bombach, Gerald Ehrsam, John Muhlbach, Mark Stier, Dirk Worden, Nick Roman, Rufus Mayes, Dave Foley, Vic Stottlemyer, Bill Long, Bob Smith, John Stowe, Ed Bender, John Sobolewski.

Second row from left: Woody Hayes, Dan Aston, Butch Smith, Mike Polaski, Alan Jack, David Whitfield, Paul Schmidlin, Chuck Hutchinson, Ted Provost, Bill Urbanik, Brad Nielsen, Paul Huff, Jim Otis, Art Burton, Dave Brungard, Kevin Rusnak.

Third row from left: Bruce Jankowski, Bill Hackett, Jim Gentile, Ray Gillian, Mike Radtke, Steve Crapser, Tom Backhus, Randy Hart, Bill Pollitt, Jan White, Leo Hayden, Ted Kurz, Horatius Greene, Bob Trapuzzano.

Fourth row from left: Jim Stillwagon, Mike Sensibaugh, Larry Zelina, Larry Qualls, Rex Kern, Jim Conroy, David Cheney, Charles Aldrin, Brian Donovan, Dick Kuhn, Jim Oppermann, Richard Troha, Gerald King, John Brockington, Tom Ecrement.

Fifth row from left: Steve Page, Mike Dale, Vince Suber, Bruce Smith, Ralph Holloway, Tim Anderson, Charles Waugh, Ron Maciejowski, Ed Lapuh, Rick Hausman, Jack Marsh, Mark Debevec, Jim Coburn, Denny Law.

Sixth row from left: Dick Merryman, Jack Tatum, Phil Strickland, Doug Adams, Tim Wagner, Hugh Hindman, Bill Mallory, Lou McCullough, Earle Bruce, George Chaump, Lou Holtz, Rudy Hubbard, Tiger Ellison.

P r o l o g u e

Laughs spill. Drinks flow. Yesterday is alive again and aging men
are young for a night inside the Hall of Fame Café in Columbus. At one table,
Rex Kern and Ron Maciejowski are trading Woody Hayes stories. At another,
Jim Oppermann and Richard Troha joke about bumping into each other while
practicing that 50-Trap play.

"Know which way you're going yet?" Opperman asks, as he has
for decades.

"Got it figured out yet?" Troha says.

Dave Cheney is channeling the Southern high pitch of defensive coordinator
Lou McCullough and saying, as McCullough did one day to Bill Hackett: "Ah'd
play a billy goat be-fuh ah'd play yew!"

Their faces are loosening and their joints have stiffened. Bellies have grown.
Knees have been replaced. John Brockington has one kidney. Judge William
Pollitt is here from Courtroom 12A. Lou Holtz is here on videotape, because he
is busy working the sideline at the University of South Carolina.

All across the room, like some secret buffalo-lodge greeting, one of them will
occasionally purse his lips, jut his chin, and drop a Woody on his teammates.

"Mmm-hmmm, sons-of-bitches, mmm-hmm," he'll say, as their coach
once did.

Most of them are here, most of the Boys of '68, for this thirty-fifth reunion
of their Ohio State championship season, though Jim Roman and Mike Polaski
have plans for one who isn't.

"You about ready, Ski-bee?" Roman says.

"All set, Pork," Polaski says.

For decades, they've called each other by these names. Polaski initially was
called, "The Polack" by his teammates. But Hayes considered that offensive and
made them stop. From then on, he was just "Ski," which Roman mutated
to "Ski-bee."

And Pork? Well, the winter of his freshman year in 1965, Roman was sitting in his dorm room in a pair of gym shorts. He had entered school weighing 215 pounds. Now, a few months later, he was a hefty 245. Hayes entered the room on one of his casual check-ups and said, "Jesus Christ, you're fatter than Porky Pig."

Roman became "Pork," ever after. He didn't care. Not that he had much choice in the matter. Not with these teammates. And now, as the beer flows at this reunion in September of 2003, as the clock ticks, as they rekindle the camaraderie of that season, Pork and Ski-bee are about to fulfill the final wish of one of their fallen teammates, Nick Roman, Jim's cousin.

Nick had died earlier that year when the heart that took him from Ohio State to the Cincinnati Bengals and Cleveland Browns gave out. He had wanted some of his ashes to be spread in Wyoming on an Indian reservation that he enjoyed visiting. The rest he wanted put on the field at Ohio Stadium. That's where he had enjoyed some of the finest days of his life.

It was a simpler time in sports. Freshmen were ineligible, so they could acclimate themselves to college life. Games didn't start until late September so most players spent extended summers with their families. Ohio Stadium kickoffs were always at 1:30 p.m., meaning the temptress of television hadn't hijacked starting times with dollars. Nor were the pros yet tossing millions at players, so there was a greater emphasis on education.

The Big Ten championship was the goal, not the mythical national title. There were four bowl games, not a few dozen. Teams could play only ten regular-season games a year, though Ohio State played nine games to appease vocal faculty who didn't want their school viewed as a football factory.

Weights? Nutrition? Year-round training? Only those on the cutting edge were involved in any of that. And if there was any talking on the field, it was generally limited to something like Polaski said after one play to Southern Methodist receiver Jerry Levias in the 1968 season opener: "Nice catch."

That era is long gone. As is their mentor, their teacher, the man who perhaps—outside their fathers—shaped most of the Boys of '68 with his passion and pride. On nights like this reunion, they don't have to praise or explain or defend or excuse or certainly apologize for Woody Hayes. They all knew him. They loved him. Some also hated him. Woody was complex that way.

Ultimately, they came to embrace their years with him, hearing him talk of his heroes in history, explain the intricacies of the off-tackle play, scream how he would fight the opposing coach at midfield, roar that no one could outwork him, or just say how they could count on each other forever.

The mission of Pork and Ski-bee this night is evidence of the latter. At 2 a.m., just after leaving the restaurant, these two men in their mid-50s drive down Olentangy Road and walk up to the stadium. Each carries a Ziploc bag filled with their teammate's ashes.

A policeman stops them. They explain who they are, why they are here, what they hope to do. The policeman considers their odd request.

"You been drinking?" he asks.

Then he waves them forward to the stadium security. Bomb-sniffing dogs are just finishing their work for the game later that day. Again, they explained their mission to the security director. He looks, too, closely at them.

He, too, asks, "You been drinking?"

But he waves them in. From there, they know the way. And in the dark and quiet of the stadium that defined their youth, they walk to midfield and begin sprinkling the ashes of their teammate.

"Nick, we miss your big goofy Polish ass," Polaski says as the ash scatters in the night air.

"We wish you were around, Nick," Jim Roman says.

Then in the dark, each man walks to an opposing end zone. And from one end zone, as he scatters the last of his teammate, Polaski looks to the sky and shakes the night with a yell:

"HEY! YOU SONUVABITCH! I HOPE YOU DO A BETTER JOB KEEPING THEM OUT OF THIS END ZONE NOW THAN WHEN YOU WERE PLAYING HERE!"

The following night, as they tell that story at the reunion dinner, their teammates laugh and cry and applaud and say, once again, The Old Man was right. Hayes had told them long ago, when they all first met, how they'd become each other's best friends through life, the ones they would bond closest with, the ones they always could count on.

Four decades later, it still held true.

This is their story.

Jim Stillwagon

1968

Best class
ever

$\mathcal{I}$n the cold, in the quiet, in the beauty of a midwestern winter snowfall, a high school senior named Jim Stillwagon stood in the open end zone at Ohio Stadium. The stadium was empty, save for a couple of inches of new-fallen snow. Lou McCullough, Ohio State's defensive coordinator, told Stillwagon to imagine playing here before a full house turned to full volume.

"Your parents are sitting right over there, watching you play," McCullough said, pointing to a spot. "Wouldn't that be special for you?"

It was a recruiting line McCullough had used a thousand times, and it still touched Stillwagon somewhere inside. His parents hadn't seen him play much since his collision with Catholic-school discipline landed him in a Virginia military school. In fact, he had made this recruiting visit not so much to see Ohio State but for a free trip home to see his parents in Mount Vernon, just up the road from Columbus.

After a few more minutes standing there, imagining, Stillwagon and McCullough walked over to St. John Arena. They stamped the snow off their shoes and went upstairs to the second floor football offices. Upon entering, a voice called out.

Jim Stillwagon

"You're the boy from the military school?" Woody Hayes said, walking over.

"Yes sir," Stillwagon said.

"I like that," Hayes said. "I like that, 'Yes sir.' "

Stillwagon was 18 years old in January of 1967 when he caught a bus from the Virginia backwoods to Columbus for this first face-to-face encounter with Hayes, who was 55 and a coaching legend, but one whose star had dimmed considerably of late. Stillwagon recognized Hayes immediately. Growing up in Mount Vernon, he saw Hayes every football season peeking out from billboards, in newspapers, even in 8x10 glossy photos taped up at the local stores. All this had opposite the usual effect on Stillwagon. He disliked everything Ohio State. His father was a Notre Dame man. Stillwagon had grown up wearing Irish players' jerseys, and South Bend was where he always dreamed of playing. But on his recruiting trip to Notre Dame, he couldn't get beyond the veneer of arrogance covering everything. He had told his father he couldn't go there. Much to his relief, his father didn't balk. The question became where he *would* go.

"What's the last novel you read?" Hayes asked in the lobby of the football offices.

Stillwagon's mind reeled. He wasn't a book person. He had never read a novel in his life. But recently he had watched a movie on television and his quick mind reached for that.

"*Moby Dick*," he said.

Hayes's face lit up. "Come in here and let's talk about that," he said, leading Stillwagon to his office.

It was just another room, like all the others in a line down the hall. The furniture in Hayes's office consisted of an industrial-steel desk, a couple of chairs and a red-vinyl couch where he sometimes slept during long nights. A wall was covered with framed documents, scrolls, and the signed pictures of U.S. generals Lewis Walt, Creighton Abrams, and William Westmoreland, whom Hayes had befriended on goodwill trips to Vietnam.

For the next forty-five minutes, Hayes conducted a seminar on *Moby Dick*, lecturing on the lessons of Ahab and the symbolism of the Great White Whale. Stillwagon sat silent, offering only an occasional, "Yes sir." He wavered between being bewildered by the discussion and transfixed by this man giving it.

All the other schools Stillwagon had visited talked only football, a language in which he was fluent. They had asked what football meant to him, told him how he fit in their plans, and argued why their program was right for him. They saw Stillwagon exactly as he saw himself: six feet and 220 pounds of football ambition. At the end of his college career, his height became such an issue that he slipped corn plasters on his feet to appear an inch taller for an excited Dallas Cowboys scout. But Stillwagon's size caused no such concern among college recruiters. On film, they saw his immense strength. They saw his fury when he started the first three plays of every game by ferociously head-butting the opposing center. There was also his remarkable speed. As big as he was, Stillwagon ran 100 yards in 10.5 seconds.

The only problem Stillwagon had to this point was getting colleges to see him. The man who had been responsible for filming his school's games that fall was shipping out for Vietnam after that football season. So he often put the camera on his two young daughters to have a keepsake of them while he was overseas. Occasionally, he shot a play. Rarely was Stillwagon in it. But enough of his game film got into the hands of Ohio State assistant Bill Mallory, who discovered this Virginia kid actually was from Ohio. That's how Stillwagon found himself listening to Hayes lecture on *Moby Dick*. Finally, the conversation meandered as close to football as it would.

"Can I ask you a question?" Hayes said. "Can I see your ankles?"

Stillwagon looked to see if Hayes was joking, and not seeing a smile, pulled up his pants legs. Hayes bent down a bit to get a better look.

"Aw, yes, you *are* fast," Hayes said. "All fast horses have skinny ankles, and it's the same for people."

Hayes considered inspecting the goods part of the recruitment process. A few years later, for instance, a chiseled recruit named Champ Henson sat in this same office. Hayes asked to see his legs. Henson pulled down his pants. Hayes stared for a few seconds, then softly marveled, "Look at those quadriceps. Look at those hamstrings."

But sitting here, having the great Woody Hayes talk about *Moby Dick* like an English professor and his ankles like a genetic engineer, Stillwagon felt a thaw in his thinking. For some reason, he was drawn to this odd and passionate man. He could actually see himself playing for Ohio State. It was as if some fundamental tenet of his youth was all wrong. Ohio State *wasn't* the Evil Empire, after all.

"I can only promise you two things," Hayes told him as they walked out of the office. "If you're good enough, you'll make it. If you're not, you won't."

Hayes offered Stillwagon a scholarship. That caused a commotion among his staff, since all the available scholarships were spoken for. Many had been accepted. But late that spring, in what would be one of several good twists of fortune for a program that needed some, a scholarship opened for Stillwagon. He signed on, the last member of what Hayes later pronounced his "best class ever."

(2)

The talent hunt began that winter amid a swirl of doubts in Columbus. Hayes was coming off only the second losing season he would have as a coach. Sports writers were criticizing him. A plane had circled Ohio Stadium carrying the banner, "Goodbye Woody." On game days, pennants bearing the same message were sold on the Oval at the center of campus. Fans sang to the tune of the alma mater, "Carmen, Ohio":

> *Oh, come let's sing Ohio's praise,*
> *And say goodbye to Woody Hayes.*

Booster donations, always a barometer of a coach's future, were down $500,000 that year. Hayes was hanged in effigy, and at one rally players attended, the effigy was burned.

As if this weren't unsettling enough, there were volatile behind-the-scenes issues, too. Hayes's famous temper had erupted in the Iowa game during the 1966 season. He hit an Iowa player on the sideline. Or grabbed him. Or something. It wasn't captured on television or film. It didn't make the newspapers. It happened so quickly many inside the team didn't even know about it, or think anything of it, because everyone on the inside knew Hayes's fists could be fast.

It was news, however, to prominent university officials. Athletic director Dick Larkins entered the football office the following Monday morning and met with much of the coaching staff. He didn't bother to take off his coat. He was shaking, he was so nervous.

"Woody," Larkins said, "the Athletic Council has met and asked for your resignation."

Hayes didn't flinch. "Is that all you have?" he asked.

Larkins nodded.

"Okay, you go back to the Athletic Council, tell them I'm not resigning and that they're wasting my time," Hayes said.

Larry Catuzzi, a young assistant, observed the give-and-take across the table that morning in silent shock. But what happened after Larkins left and apparently took the news back to the Athletic Council was even more stunning: Nothing. No firing. No resignation. No mention of it again to the staff. Nothing but business as usual.

Still, no one felt comfortable at the direction of the program. Mallory, who had arrived as an assistant for that 1966 season, thought by this next winter that he had made a mistake in taking the job, and he wasn't alone. Earle Bruce arrived on the coaching staff at the same time as Mallory and was surprised by the team's low level of talent. He thought he'd left better players behind at Massillon High School. It all came back, Bruce figured, to the lifeblood of any program: recruiting.

Some of the recruiting problems stemmed from a 1961 Rose Bowl bid that Ohio State turned down because its faculty committee feared the school was becoming a football factory. Hayes was irate after that vote. Protests were held. The *Columbus Dispatch* even printed the addresses and phone numbers of the faculty committee members who promptly found loud segments of the city shouting in their yards.

"That hurt us for years," Hayes once said. "All the recruits from other schools had to tell a boy was, 'Go to Ohio State and you'll never play in the Rose Bowl.'"

Another problem was more practical: Ohio State's recruiting was a mess of tactical disorganization and lost opportunity. Esco Sarkkinen, for example, recruited the fertile football ground of Cleveland's Catholic league. Sarkkinen was a good coach and legendary Ohio State name. But he wasn't Catholic. And he didn't drive a car. Graduate assistants picked him up for work each morning at his home and drove him into the office. Either his wife drove him on recruiting trips or he took a plane and taxis. Needless to say, Sarkkinen neither soothed some parents' faith-based concerns nor spent enough time working the area.

In 1966, Lou McCullough, who headed Ohio State's recruiting, proposed four fundamental changes that had an immediate effect: *1)* He would schedule Woody Hayes's recruiting visits to organize his time and take full advantage of his presence; *2)* The recruiting base would be expanded beyond Ohio for special players; *3)* He would move Sarkkinen to the more driver-friendly central Ohio region; and *4)* He would hire Catuzzi.

Catuzzi was the kind of coach this staff lacked, McCullough knew. At 26, he was young, smart, and carried himself well. He had the eastern contacts of a New Jersey native and a Catholic-family background that no other assistant did. When McCullough brought up the idea, Woody Hayes shouted, "Catuzzi, Catuzzi, what the hell kind of name is Catuzzi?"

"A good, Italian-Catholic boy," McCullough said.

Catuzzi had been marked as a rising star in the coaching universe, so much so that he was the only assistant retained from Indiana's fired staff that winter of 1966. Still, Notre Dame was trying to hire him away from Indiana when Hayes called him. They set up an 11:30 a.m. meeting at the football offices in St. John Arena. Catuzzi arrived at the arena with five minutes to spare but couldn't find an unlocked door. He began walking around the arena, looking at his watch, trying not to panic.

"Jee-zus H. Christ, you want to coach my quarterbacks and you can't find an open door!" Hayes said, lightheartedly, when Catuzzi walked into the football office just before noon.

Catuzzi was given a piece of chalk and told to draw up some plays on the chalkboard. A few hours later, he was the newest member of the staff. He was put in charge of the quarterbacks. But it would be recruiting New Jersey, New York, and Cleveland where he would make his biggest impact.

He discovered new lands. He brought home riches.

He became the program's Christopher Columbus.

(3)

Coming out of the locker room one day at Lancaster High School, Rex Kern couldn't believe who was walking out of the principal's office toward him. He looked more closely just to be sure. And he was right! It really was Woody Hayes!

Kern swelled at the thought of Hayes driving to this southern Ohio town for one reason: to recruit *him*. Never mind that Notre Dame was recruiting him hard for football and places like UCLA and North Carolina were recruiting him for basketball. Never mind that he was good enough in baseball to be drafted by the Kansas City Royals. This was Woody Hayes! In his school! To see him! As the two approached each other, Kern wondered what to say.

"Hello," Kern said.

"Hello," Hayes said.

And that was all. Hayes said nothing more. He didn't look at Kern again. He just kept walking. Kern was confused. What had just happened? Wasn't he the reason Hayes was here? Didn't the coach want to stop and talk with him? He was just walking away down the hall.

Kern stood there with the sinking idea that Hayes didn't want him. That was okay, he tried to tell himself. Basketball was his first love anyhow. It was true, too. Like many Ohio boys his age, Kern grew up wanting to be the next Mel Nowell or John Havlicek, players on the 1960 Ohio State national championship basketball team and runners-up to Cincinnati in 1961 and 1962.

So as Hayes disappeared down the hall, Kern thought to himself, "Well, I'll go to Ohio State and play basketball."

The truth was something else entirely. Hayes didn't just want Kern. He had circled Kern and Larry Zelina, a Cleveland running back, as his two must-have recruits. Each was an Ohio boy, first of all, and Hayes considered the state his fiefdom. Each was seen as a game-bending talent, too. They were the kind of homegrown stars, Hayes told his assistant coaches, that could change the program.

So, while he didn't talk to Kern that day in the hallway, Hayes had carefully plotted his courtship. He was late to the party, considering all the other schools in the mix. Even Ohio State basketball coach Fred Taylor had been wooing Kern for more than a year by the time Hayes came on the scene. But Hayes was performing his due diligence in the manner he did with any recruit. He had gone to the principal's office to check on Kern's grades and character. When he met Kern in the hall, he was on his way to the football office to talk with the coaches.

Later that night, when Kern came home after practice and was talking with his father, a barber, he had nearly forgotten about the nonmeeting with Hayes.

"You'll never guess who I had in the chair today," Trenton Kern said. "Who do you suppose it was?"

"I have no idea," Rex said.

"Coach Hayes was down. I cut his hair."

So began the wooing of the player who eventually would lead The Best Class Ever. There were meetings, conversations, the recruiting trip to Columbus. One night, Kern went to jump center on his basketball team and there was Hayes sitting alone in the crowd. And it was a memorable game, if only because Kern missed a free throw to lose it. He sat afterward in the locker room, distraught. He even grew more so when thinking Hayes was waiting for him.

But when he walked out of the locker room, Hayes had left. His parents said the coach had talked with them, saying, "Rex probably isn't in a good mood and wouldn't want to talk to anybody. I know how he feels. I hate losing, too."

That struck an appropriate note with Kern. So did Hayes and Taylor, who constantly talked about education. No one in Kern's family had attended college. As the winter lengthened, as his decision narrowed, Kern felt the tug of not just Ohio State, but of both football *and* basketball. He had settled on his school, it seemed. He just couldn't settle on his sport.

"I'd really like to go to Ohio State, if they'd let me play both," he told his high school basketball coach, George Hill.

"Is that the only reason you aren't telling them you want to go there?" Hill said.

"Yeah, that's the only reason," he said.

The coach called Taylor and explained the situation. Taylor talked with Hayes. It was agreed Kern could play both sports. Sharing him, the coaches decided, was better than not having him at all.

At halftime of an Ohio State-Illinois basketball game on March 6, 1967, Kern announced in an interview with television announcer Jimmy Crum that he was committing to Ohio State. Immediately afterward, Hayes gave him a list of recruits to call, most notably Zelina.

"We've got to get him," Hayes said. "Tell him you're going to Ohio State and we've got the best group of freshmen the school's ever had." He looked at Kern. "But that depends on us getting Zelina."

Kern looked at the name and phone number on the paper. He had just signed. He had never met Zelina. And now the fate of this class's worth rested on his phone call?

Minutes into his Buckeye career, he was already being asked to deliver.

(4)

Jack Tatum was playing basketball with some friends one afternoon in the concrete jungle of Patterson, New Jersey, when a friend came running up with some news.

"Tate, I think that sweeper salesman went to your house and your mom let him in!"

Tatum took off running. Across their neighborhood, a con game had been operating. A white salesman was selling vacuum cleaners for $10 down and $5 a month into eternity. Some people never even got the vacuum. And now this guy was at Tatum's house? Talking to his mom?

Tatum ran through gaps in fences, down a couple of alleys, and was home in the time it took his adrenaline to rise. He planned to do some talking to this salesman. Or maybe his fists would do it, if necessary. As he stormed through the front door, ready for battle, his juices up, he heard his mom say from the kitchen, "Well, there's John David now."

Tatum turned the corner into the kitchen, looking for the vacuum salesman, ready for battle.

There sat Woody Hayes.

This was always the trick, getting the coach to this very seat in a recruit's life. Catuzzi had done the legwork on Tatum for months, talking with his coach, visiting with his father, always showing Ohio State had everyone's interests in mind. Then he scheduled Hayes to make the full-court sell.

Tatum stopped in the kitchen, surprised. Hayes looked at him from a table chair. Tatum quickly recovered and traded the angry-son look for his star-recruit mask, the nonchalant one that said every coach in the land wanted him.

"Hi," he said.

"Hi," Hayes said, then turned back to Tatum's mom. He looked down at the piece of banana cream pie on his fork. "This is the best pie I've ever tasted. I've got to get the recipe for my wife."

His mom smiled. "It's made with a special crust and . . . "

For the next five minutes, as Tatum stood silently by, his mom and Hayes discussed how she made that banana cream pie. Hayes acted as if it contained the secret to life. It did, too, at least to Hayes. Because therein lay a secret of his success.

Dick Kuhn, another recruit that winter, later became a graduate assistant and one of his chores was to drive Sarkkinen to work each morning. One morning, Sarkkinen told a story that had become part of the Hayes lore among his staff. It began with Anne Hayes opening a bedside drawer where her husband emptied his pockets each night. She found it was filled with inscribed watches from appearances he made, $50 and $100 checks that he never had cashed from speaking engagements, and dozens upon dozens of cards with women's handwriting. Upon seeing these, she became enraged. She got in her car, drove the couple of miles to St. John Arena, and charged into her husband's office. She slammed the door and began screaming so everyone in the football office heard.

Who were all these women writing him? What was going on here? Why was he hiding this?

Finally, when Hayes could get a word in, he asked, "Did you read the cards?"

No, she just saw all women's handwriting, she said.

"Go back and read them," he said.

She went back. She read them. They were recipes.

"My wife, I love her dearly," Woody would tell a recruit's mother, "but she just can't make an apple pie like you can."

Or cherry pie. Or chocolate cake. Or, in Tatum's case, a banana cream pie.

When Woody was recruiting, he knew there was one person who could sway the deal—a parent. Often, it was the mother, though not always. Jan White's father, for instance, had a Penn State decal on the front door of their Harrisburg, Pennsylvania, home. When he heard Hayes was visiting them, he asked, "Why's he coming here?"

"I want to hear him out," Jan said.

"Why? You're going to Penn State, right?" his father said.

"We might as well listen to him," the son said.

After Hayes spent two hours at the Whites' dinner table discussing education, family, and philosophy—talking to the parents, that is, as Jan wondered why he was being excluded—the father turned to the son immediately upon Hayes's leaving.

"If you don't go to Ohio State," he said, "I will."

That was how Hayes could be. He had an intangible aura about him, an indefinable magnetic force that put people under his spell. The scouting report on him read: *If you want to dislike him, you must never talk with him or hear him make a speech.* As he discussed his bedrock beliefs—education, family, integrity—he seemed more like part of the family than a famous visitor.

Not every parent talked football, Hayes knew. But in an era when pro football wasn't a winning lottery ticket, they all talked education. Rarely did recruits see Hayes's inexplicable side, the schizophrenic one they'd see on the field, ripping hats, smashing glasses, and throwing fists. It was there, somewhere below the surface, of course. And sometimes he couldn't hide it. One recruiting class earlier, in the spring of 1966, Catuzzi was talking on the phone with a recruit from Cleveland named Frank Titas. Titas intended to be a doctor and was considering Michigan, too. Catuzzi put Hayes on the phone.

"Well, Frank, don't forget we run the fullback better than anyone in the country," Hayes said. "And you want to be a doctor. We have the best premed program in the country."

He listened.

"Uh-huh," he said. "So you're thinking of going to Michigan then?"

Pause.

"Well, Frank, you're not being patriotic," Hayes said. "You're not doing the right thing as an Ohio boy. This is where you belong!"

His voice was rising now.

"You don't belong up there! Not with them! Not with *that* team!"

He slammed down the phone.

"I hope he breaks his goddamned leg!"

That was Woody, too. But what Tatum saw that afternoon in his Patterson home was the rich personality of Hayes at work. After listening to the banana-cream-pie conversation, Tatum left the room, figuring he wouldn't be missed. Evidently, he wasn't, either. When he returned an hour later, Hayes was telling his mom about General Patton and World War II. His mother began telling the story of her grandfather, who rode with General Grant in the Civil War.

After Hayes left the Tatum home that day, she said, "Jack, I kind of like that Mr. Hayes."

Oh, Lord, Tatum thought to himself, *I'm going to Ohio State.*

Tatum knew all about Hayes and Ohio State. His high school coach, John Federici, was a Hayes disciple. He ran Hayes's three-yards-and-a-cloud-of-dust offense. That was a fine high school offense, Tatum figured, because he played the featured position of fullback.

But Tatum saw himself following to Syracuse the famous black running backs such as Jim Brown, Ernie Davis, and Floyd Little. He even befriended a girl there on his recruiting trip and made plans to see her. Or maybe she had befriended him. Because later, on a recruiting trip to Michigan State, Tatum was talking with another recruit named John Brockington, and they made a startling discovery. They had met the same girl at Syracuse. She acted the same way with each of them. She had said she hoped to see each of them play there. And, well, their eyes were opened a bit.

Then again, nothing surprised Tatum too much. Not by this point in the game. He was educated on the streets and found recruiting to be one life lesson after another. He counted five new girlfriends at different schools from his recruiting trips. From some schools, he came home with hundreds of dollars in his pocket. He had been promised jobs and cars and gifts for his parents if he signed with the proper school.

Tatum was enjoying the bidding war for his services when he walked into Hayes's office on his visit. So far, nothing had been offered by Ohio State. He figured this is where it would happen.

"I don't know what the hell the other schools promised you," Hayes said, "but I'll make you only two promises. And I'll keep both of them."

They were the same promises he made in some form to everyone: To get a diploma and to become a better football player. That was it. No money. No cars. No girls. No grades. Nothing that Tatum had come to expect was a regular part of the recruiting process.

Tatum was surprised. He wasn't completely sold on the school. Ohio State's coaches, for the first of many times, couldn't get a read on his thoughts. But in the end none of that mattered. His mom had been won over since that first meeting in Patterson. She said how wonderful Hayes was. She said her son would get his degree there. She said how the holes in the soles of the coach's shoes showed he was a genuine person they could trust.

"I think you should go to Ohio State," she told him.

That settled it. He committed. Still, Catuzzi wasn't ready to celebrate until the national signing day on May 17. That spring, he was in New Jersey at a track meet in which Tatum ran the 100-yard dash. It was a slow cinder track. Tatum stumbled out of the blocks, but he quickly caught his stride and won the race in 9.9 seconds.

"Who's that?" Arizona State coach Frank Kush said.

Catuzzi looked at Tatum as if he had never seen him before.

"I don't know," he said.

(5)

To grasp the regional phenomenon that was Ohio State football at this time, there was the story of Matt Snell, a heralded high school star from Long Island, New York. In 1960, he could have gone to any school he wanted. But Snell's high school coach, Joe Coady, was a Woody Hayes fan, and one day he called Ohio State to say he had a great player who might want to go there.

He was asked to send some film of the kid.

Click.

That's how Ohio State operated. Snell became the first star recruit to come from the East. He went on to be an All-American player and later, a fullback for the New York Jets. But he didn't exactly open the notion of brave, new football worlds beyond the Ohio border.

When Bill Urbanik arrived from Donora, Pennsylvania, as a freshman in 1965, the varsity roster had three out-of-state players. Each was from western Pennsylvania, just like Urbanik.

"Going to a Big Ten school at the time was like going to the other side of the world," Urbanik said. He estimated more than a hundred college players had played in his high school program. He was the first to attend a Big Ten school. And he did so primarily because he wanted to take a separate path from his older brother, who had played at Penn State.

This is where Catuzzi entered. Others would help. Earle Bruce, for instance, recruited Jan White. But in his first recruiting season of 1966, Catuzzi went east, using his name as an All-New Jersey quarterback and spreading the name of Ohio State. He signed a couple of New Jersey talents that first year, Kevin Rusnak and Mike Radtke.

Then he waded into New York, where he set up a meeting with a fullback at Brooklyn's Thomas Jefferson High. The first time Catuzzi saw John Brockington was across the high school gymnasium. Brockington was walking toward him in a too-small suit jacket. The sleeves approached his elbows.

"Don't say anything about the coat," the high school coach, Moe Finklestein, whispered to Catuzzi. "It's actually *my* coat. He wanted to dress up and make a good impression."

Thus began the long courtship of Ohio State and Brockington. Catuzzi liked him from the start. How could he not? Brockington cared about making a first impression, which was the first step toward making a good one. Catuzzi knew Brockington was a great talent, too. But Brockington's grades were a question, as was his interest in Syracuse. When Brockington went to a New York prep school called Manlius Pebble to improve his grades and, as he remembers, Syracuse paid the tuition, that deal seemed sealed.

Catuzzi was busy enough the following year, anyhow. There was the Cleveland area. There was Tatum. There was a lineman at Matt Snell's high school named Joe Sinkowski. There was also another tailback from Fairlawn, New Jersey, who presented an unusual sale. Bruce Jankowski's parents weren't sports fans. His father, who owned an interior decorating business, never played sports. His mother didn't attend any of Bruce's high school games and wasn't impressed when schools from across the country flocked to her doorstep. She thought sports were foolish and wanted her son to attend either Princeton for the academics or West Point as a patriot.

Bruce was a natural athlete. His weakest sport was basketball, where he merely started on a team directed by future NBA coach Hubie Brown. He was All-New Jersey in baseball and a third-round pick of the Philadelphia Phillies as an outfielder. He considered attending Arizona State, because its climate and program were known to produce pro baseball players.

But in an area that spat out football talent, Jankowski stood out in that sport, too. The All-New Jersey backfield in 1966 consisted of Jankowski and Tatum at running back and Joe Theismann at quarterback. Theismann didn't want anything to do with them, or Ohio State, but Jankowski and Tatum became friendly and would joke at some of the banquets they attended.

"Why don't we both go to the same school?" Jankowski would say.

"We could be the two starting running backs," Tatum would say.

In high school, Jankowski scored 26 touchdowns as a senior halfback and wanted to attend a school with a running back tradition. Ohio State fit that model. He saw himself as a fullback type who could catch balls out of the backfield. He liked the friendly and genuine manner of Catuzzi. But Ohio State was just one of the many top programs he visited, and he didn't discuss his intentions even inside his family for fear of repercussion with his mother until Hayes visited his home. At the end of that evening, Jankowski stood up, shook Hayes's hand and said, "Coach, I'm coming to Ohio State."

"My mother about had a heart attack," he said. "My dad said, 'It's his decision, Doris, let him do what he wants to do.' But my mother couldn't believe I was going to do this."

Catuzzi, playing his New Jersey card, offered himself as proof things would be fine. He vowed to take care of her son. For weeks, he tried to soothe her mind. Then, one night, with Bruce and his father at track practice, Catuzzi sat at the kitchen table alone with her.

"Please don't worry," he said.

"Believe me, Bruce is in good hands," he said.

"We'll have a good support system for him," he said.

Finally, she cracked. She gave her blessing. Jankowski was in. The Best Class Ever was taking numbers.

(6)

Across the state line, up the steep mountain, down the dirt road, seemingly at the end of civilization, he stood on a doorstep in the wilderness delivering his pat opening line:

"Hi, Mrs. Anderson, my name is Woody Hayes, and I want to talk to you about your son coming to Ohio State and getting an education."

The Andersons were getting ready for church and eating a bean dinner that Wednesday night. Hayes sat down to eat with them. Throughout this winter, he would sit with patrons in Ed Lapuh's family bar, get a haircut from Kern's dad, and talk the Bible with various families. But no setting was more unique than this mountaintop.

Tim Anderson's mother was African American. His father had an American Indian father and a white mother who sidestepped a society with some serious interracial issues in Follansbee, West Virginia, and moved up this nearby mountain. They called it Anderson Hill. This was 1915, and Tim's grandfather began a successful coal mining company. He started a church. He brought in a professor from Texas to run a school. The Andersons founded and operated a successful business and vibrant family community for several decades where as many as fifty-five Andersons lived.

Through the years, however, the company was lost, the Ku Klux Klan burned the schoolhouse, and most of the family land was taken over by white people. Not that there were many other kind. Tim, the thirteenth of fourteen children, didn't have a date for his senior prom because there were no black girls in his high school.

His older brothers and sisters had integrated the public schools, as well as some minds in the area. It wasn't easy. There were fights. There was name-calling. There were scars left on them. Everything that went on in the 1950s and 1960s across America was conducted in an isolated manner in this small West Virginia town just across the Ohio River. As a youth, Tim figured there must be an easier way. He wanted to reverse this process and tried to befriend white kids rather than always fight with them.

He reached out to whites in his classes. He made friends around town. Even in the seventh grade, a young white couple he knew offered him a job in the town's Dairy Queen. Since he was black, they said, he'd have to work in the back. But what sold him on the idea was that he could have all the ice cream he wanted. He gained twenty-five pounds that summer and, immediately, became a sports star.

Sports, he soon concluded, lowered the temperature on the town's sketchy race relations. Anderson found his skin color didn't matter so much on the sports fields. In a game, any skin color was cheered. That carried over into regular life, too. He wasn't just a star on Follansbee's football and baseball fields. He was elected class president every year in high school. And now, as if to underline his special qualities, colleges all over the country were recruiting him. He had more than a hundred scholarship offers.

McCullough had done Ohio State's groundwork in recruiting Anderson, but over that bean dinner Woody moved the deal forward. Anderson's father had died three days after he was born, so his mother got all Hayes's attention. None of her children had a college education, and Hayes hit that idea hard. He invited her to a college class at Ohio State so she could observe one. He learned she had always wanted to attend the opera and ballet. When she came to visit Columbus on her son's recruiting trip, Hayes said, he'd make sure she got tickets to both. He followed through, too.

Finally, in a statement Tim never forgot, Woody said, "I don't believe in any swearing on the football field."

And so the truth may have tilted a little.

But watching it all unfold, Tim figured his mother had never been recruited so hard in her life. She loved the attention, too. He came to realize it really didn't matter what he thought. He was going to Ohio State.

He'd become part of The Best Class Ever.

(7)

Ring. Ring.

Kern had dialed Zelina's phone number. Now, as he listened to it ring, he wondered what to say.

Ring. Ring.

He didn't feel especially comfortable doing this. But when Zelina answered, he began.

"Hi, my name is Rex Kern and . . . ."

They talked a few minutes. Kern talked about the freshman class they might have at Ohio State. Zelina was friendly but noncommittal, just as Hayes had expected. Every little bit helped. As a junior, Zelina had scored 20 touchdowns as a halfback at Cleveland St. Benedictine. As a senior, he had scored 26 in just eight games because of injury. He could run, catch, even kick. Now he was seeing how coveted those talents were. One coach offered him a new car to sign with his college. Another, a new wardrobe. A third coach said he prayed every morning at Mass for him.

"I know he never saw the inside of a church," Zelina said in the book, *I Remember Woody.*

At one point Catuzzi thought Zelina seemed signed, sealed, and all but delivered to Notre Dame in the kind of Catholic-player-to-Catholic-school transaction Ohio State had bumped against in the Cleveland area for years. But Catuzzi kept making all the necessary calls, scheduling all the necessary visits, and investing all the necessary time in befriending players as well as their parents.

Catuzzi and Larry's father, Red, a steelworker, spent a few evenings in the Zelina home drinking a beer and discussing the world. During those chats Red talked about his love of racehorses. Red didn't just enjoy making a $2 bet. He knew horses and followed the biggest races. It was the kind of information a smart recruiter like Catuzzi could use to his benefit. Armed with it, Catuzzi reached for his trump card to pry Zelina from Notre Dame: John W. Galbreath.

By the spring of 1967, Galbreath was 70 years old, a world-renowned Columbus businessman and a full-statured sportsman. He owned the Pittsburgh Pirates. He ran thoroughbred horses at the biggest races. He was also an enthusiastic member of a select Ohio State booster club called the Athletic Committee. This group once went by the name "Frontliners," but the Big Ten had demanded a name change to something more collegiate. Its mission didn't change, though. It was the pumping heart of Ohio State's athletic machine. Its 300 members—alums, ex-jocks, businessmen, friends-of-the-program boosters—provided financial, personal, and recruiting support in any way possible.

Ohio State's coaches would make a list of players in an area they wanted checked out. The committeemen in that area would divvy up the list to make the best fits. For linebacker Doug Adams of Xenia, for example, the committeeman was Jimmy Hull. He was a dentist, just like Adams wanted to be. He had also been captain of Ohio State's 1939 basketball team, making him the athletic success Adams hoped for himself. He took Adams to Ohio Stadium for a game, answered questions about the university, and was generally the wingman for assistant Tiger Ellison's recruitment of Adams.

There were a dozen committeemen in the Dayton area alone. One was Paul Moody, owner of the Imperial House hotels. Another was Dave Albritton, a 1936 Olympic silver medalist who had attended Ohio State with Jesse Owens. Will Johnston, a dentist, played basketball at Ohio State in 1946 and helped recruit several football players, including Bill Long, the starting quarterback in 1966 and 1967. Johnston figured Long was too small for Ohio State and contacted Wisconsin to help him find a scholarship. Then Ellison called one day.

"It's your job to make sure Long comes here," he told Johnston.

No one was a better friend of the athletic department—or more involved—than Galbreath. He found players summer jobs in an era when the NCAA allowed it, assured that athletic coffers were full, and was best of friends with Woody Hayes. Galbreath also had a standing policy of helping with top recruits. It was Galbreath who helped Ohio State sign Heisman Trophy winner Vic Janowicz by taking him and his date—along with movie star Bing Crosby—to see a Pirates game. He helped recruit basketball forward Jerry Lucas by letting him catch a six-pound bass off a bridge on his 4,400-acre Darby Dan Farm, which was just outside Columbus.

"If I can fish here every spring all four years, I'll go to Ohio State," Lucas said.

In the spring of 1967, Galbreath got Zelina on Darby Dan Farm, too. To call it a farm was to undersell it. Darby Dan was a natural embodiment of Galbreath's rich personality, full of rolling hills, feeding birds, and exotic animals. Bison. Zebra. Rhinoceroses. Thompson gazelle. And horses. Not just any horses, either. Galbreath was a thoroughbred breeder and owner of Kentucky Derby champions.

Catuzzi knew all this. He convinced Woody Hayes that this match—the famous horseman with the horse-loving father—could close the Zelina deal. So a tour of Darby Dan Farms was set up for the Zelina family. After seeing some of the wild animals, Galbreath took the Zelinas down to the horse stables. He asked if Red wanted to see the 1963 Kentucky Derby winner, Chateaugay.

"Red almost fell to his knees," Catuzzi said.

Galbreath then asked if Red wanted to walk the horse.

"I thought Red was going to pass out," Catuzzi said.

As Red walked Chateaugay around the paddock area, Catuzzi watched the smile on the father's face and thought to himself: *If we don't get this kid now, there's nothing else I can do.*

Zelina became the latest, biggest catch.

(8)

"Where you going to school, Leo?"

Leo Hayden stood at a urinal in the bathroom at the Jai Lai Restaurant. He looked to see who had asked the question. Down the line of urinals, several other players on their Ohio State recruiting trip were looking at him. *Jack Tatum. Jan White. Dave Cheney. Tim Anderson.* This was their official visit to Columbus, during their official big meal at the unofficial Ohio State football restaurant. The Jai Lai was pink, with oddly Middle Eastern architecture and a life-sized, black-and-white photo of Hayes, which greeted people as they walked in. He wore his trademark block "O" baseball cap, an Ohio State shirt, a whistle around the neck, and he had written on the photograph: "TO THE JAI LAI, IN ALL THE WORLD, THERE'S ONLY ONE."

Now, at the urinals—of all places in the world—Hayden answered the question by saying, "I think I might be going to Ohio State."

"I think I am, too," Tatum said at the next urinal.

"Me, too," Cheney said, at the next one.

"Me, too," White said at the next one.

"Me, too," Anderson said at the very next one.

They all laughed. But this moment, Hayden figured, was revealing. Not just because each of these players was highly recruited. Not just because they could form a stellar recruiting class by themselves in this bathroom. It was revealing because, Cheney excluded, they were all African American. And African American players didn't exactly flock to Ohio State at this time.

Only three African American players would be on the team when this recruited class became eligible to play as sophomores. While Ohio State had broken the color barrier long ago—in 1930—and while it had famous black players like Bill Willis, Jim Marshall, and Paul Warfield, it wasn't seen as friendly a place for African Americans as some other schools. Hayden heard the whispers: "Marshall didn't get his degree." "Warfield left with people saying he couldn't catch." "It's just not a good place for you, if you know what I mean."

Hayden attended the all-black Dayton Roosevelt High School and was Ohio's Player Of The Year and a *Parade* magazine All-American as a senior. He'd never had a white teammate in his life but he embraced the idea, although not so much from a black-and-white issue. It was a green issue. His high school field was a dirtball. The joke was that it grew rocks, not grass. But programs with white players, he saw, had money. They had nice fields. Good equipment. The best uniforms.

Playing in a college program, Hayden, figured, would be like heaven.

Even with the nagging questions of how blacks fit in, Hayden always felt the recruiting pull of Ohio State. His high school coach was an Ohio State fan. Tiger Ellison, the Ohio State assistant who recruited the area, was a legend in nearby Middletown. Moody, one of Dayton's committeemen, took him to Ohio State games. They stayed in one of Moody's Imperial House hotels in Columbus.

"Let's go inspect the place," Moody told him during the stay. Hayden, raised with no money, thought it eye-opening to walk amid the kingdom of such a successful businessman. He remembered Moody's counsel, too: "If you're going to live in Ohio, you might as well play at Ohio State."

Still, Hayden wavered. *Michigan State? Iowa? Indiana? Where would he go? Which was the best fit?* And then came that night at the Jai-Lai. He looked down the row of urinals at all the faces staring back at him. All the *black* faces. Ohio State had been talking about a new spirit in the football program, a new era. Maybe they meant it. Maybe these players, right here, could be the start of it.

Hayden's deciding was done. Ohio State was his pick, too.

(9)

As a high school senior, Mike Sensibaugh secretly graded on a curve the colleges that were recruiting him: The farther away from his hometown of Lockland, Ohio, the better. *Maryland. Florida State. Georgia Tech. The University of Florida.* He visited them all.

Sensibaugh never felt nervous playing before 80,000 people on a football Saturday. But sitting in the first pew at Lockland Christian Church was more than he could take. His father, Hugh, was the preacher, and he felt the eyes of the congregation glued to him each Sunday morning. Any move, he thought, was noticed. Every action, he sensed, was graded. Just to sneak an M&M, he perfected a fake cough that brought his hand to his mouth to deposit it. He was a regular member of the "52 Club," meaning he attended each Sunday service in that calendar year. He did Sunday School. He often did a midweek service. He wanted to go to Florida.

Or Maryland.

Anywhere far away.

His athletic talent always stood out, especially against the backdrop of his high school class of sixty-nine students. In a game, he never left the field. Quarterback, safety, kicker, punter, return man—he did it all. He played it all, too. In baseball, he competed in the Ohio All-Star Game. In basketball, he was good enough to play on the Ohio State freshman team. But football was the sport at which he excelled. It's the one that could pay his way through college. Recruiters kept calling. He kept looking at schools far away. And then one day, sitting in class, he saw this man with a buzz cut peeking around the door at him.

Who is this guy? Sensibaugh thought.

It was McCullough. Sensibaugh was about to get the full-court press from the home state team. McCullough kept calling. A committeeman from the Cincinnati area checked in. Woody attended a Lockland basketball game, visited his family, and—on Sensibaugh's recruiting trip to Columbus—didn't just have him talk with football coaches. Knowing Sensibaugh was interested in math, he sent him to talk with a math professor. No other school did this. *Score one for Woody*, Sensibaugh thought.

Still, there was a fundamental problem with Columbus: it was close to the front row pew. He didn't tell anyone his plan. It wasn't too hard to figure out.

"I know what you're doing," his high school coach told him one day. "One hundred miles is far enough away."

More and more, Sensibaugh found himself falling back on that expression. He had gone to Ohio State games regularly as a kid. He had an uncle in Canton who was a big sports fan and said a star named Kern was going there.

Yes, he ultimately decided, *a hundred miles would be far enough.*

(10)

One day that recruiting season, the committeemen in northwestern Ohio sent word that Michigan was making inroads on an All-Ohio lineman from Bluffton. Hayes swung the full power of the machine into action.

This time, it wasn't Galbreath or a dentist or an Olympic medalist who called the player.

"Hello, Jim," Jim Oppermann heard over the phone one night. "This is Governor Rhodes."

The Ohio governor invited the Oppermann family to dinner at the governor's mansion. Jim wasn't going to go. He was deciding between Michigan and Florida State at the time. But his family and everyone in town kept pushing him until one night he was sitting next to James Rhodes over a filet mignon dinner, wondering what to say. He was a 17-year-old farm boy. He never felt more like one, either.

Finally, watching the table being served, Oppermann blurted out, "Boy, it must be hard getting help here."

"Not at all," Rhodes said. "We get them from the state penitentiary. The man serving your dinner is in for killing his wife."

This full-court gubernatorial press didn't always work. Just a year earlier, Rhodes had dropped into the family bar of Solon standout Jim Mandich, who was considering Michigan as well. Mandich's father wasn't overly impressed.

"What are you doing at a bar in Solon when there are so many pressing problems around the state?" he asked the governor.

Mandich, due more to Ohio State's run-happy offense, signed with Michigan. The governor's magic worked on Oppermann, though. He signed with Ohio State. There were other networks to tap that winter, too, and Hayes wasn't bashful about using them. One March afternoon the principal of Lima High School called a student into his office.

"Do you know why you're here?" the principal asked.

"No, but I haven't done anything bad or wrong," Dave Cheney said.

"What do you think you're doing?" the principal said.

"I'm not sure," Cheney said. "What do you mean?"

The principal looked at him squarely and asked, "Why haven't you told Coach Hayes you're going to Ohio State?"

Cheney, an All-Ohio lineman, said he wasn't sure, that he probably would commit to Ohio State. The principal said Hayes would call him that night and Cheney should tell the Ohio State coach. Lima High, after all, had been a pipeline to Ohio State and it had worked out well for both sides. Cheney's parents already had been won over by Hayes. So that night, when Hayes called, Cheney committed. The Ohio State network had another score.

Sometimes it wasn't that complicated. The Big Ten allowed only a couple of games to be televised. Ohio State games were televised across the state. So players didn't see the Saturday sights and the spectacle of faraway places unless it was, say, the Rose Bowl. That got Phil Strickland. He saw the California sun and wanted to play in the Rose Bowl. Ohio State, he figured, was the best way to do that.

As recruits signed, as the class grew, as the news spread, something new bloomed in the Ohio State football offices, which cut through the hangover of 1966's losing season: Hope. With each successive signing, the assistants felt it. It positively surged through the office when Jan White, Jack Tatum, and Bruce Jankowski signed within a few days of each other.

For whatever reason, the planets were aligning this recruiting year. Catuzzi was working miracles. Hayes was on fire. It seemed wherever they turned, they bumped into another recruit. One day during the state high school wrestling championships, Hayes walked out of his office in St. John Arena and sat down to watch. He began talking with a man. His son happened to be wrestling. Jim Coburn played football, too, and after his match that day his father met him with a surprising question.

"Would you consider going to Ohio State?" his dad asked. "I just met Woody Hayes and . . . ."

Coburn signed. Everyone did. Hayes would tell them later he was hoping to sign a few of them, just get part of the talent they'd gone after. But every top recruit they wanted signed on. By early spring, when Hayes sat down in the home of Mark Debevec in Geneva, Ohio, he added a new talking point to his recruiting spiel. "Within two years, you'll be playing for a national championship," Hayes said.

Those were big words for a coach whose goodbye banner had been flying over the stadium a few months earlier. But Debevec didn't laugh. He saw the All-Everything players signing up. Lots of people saw them. Opposing recruiters, especially. And they tried to use Ohio State's suddenly bulging talent to their own purposes.

(11)

Ron Maciejowski took a phone call one day that spring from an assistant coach at the Naval Academy named Lee Corso. Maciejowski was a heavily recruited quarterback from Bedford, Ohio. Corso knew he was leaning to Ohio State, though he wanted to test that thought. They had already signed Kern and Sensibaugh, after all.

"Aren't you concerned about playing there?" Corso asked.

"No, not at all," Maciejowski said.

"Why not?" Corso said.

"Well, didn't you just have Roger Staubach there a few years ago?" Maciejowski said.

"Well, yeah," Corso said.

"What if you have the next Roger Staubach in your recruiting class now?" Maciejowski said.

Maciejowski's grandparents were European immigrants from Poland and Croatia. His parents learned to speak English in grade school. His mother dropped out of school in the tenth grade to help support her family. His father made it through the eleventh grade before quitting school for a full-time job.

So like many second-generation Americans, he lived a childhood far different from relatives immediately before him. The old world's language was lost. The new world's sports became a passion. College, through sports, became a probability. Like Kern, Maciejowski enjoyed basketball more than football and was a big fan of the Ohio State basketball teams of the early 1960s.

In fact, it was Maciejowski's talent as a 6-2 guard on Bedford's basketball team that winter that accelerated his decision to sign with Ohio State. Weekend recruiting trips kept cutting into his final high school basketball season. Games were Friday and Saturday nights. Why would he want to miss any of that fun for football recruiting trips?

One day, Maciejowski simply had seen enough, went to his coach's office, and said he was signing with Ohio State. They called Hayes, who had visited Maciejowski and afterward written his mother for her chocolate cake recipe.

Hayes congratulated him, then suggested he cancel his scheduled visit to Virginia. "That wouldn't be right for you to do," Hayes said.

So that was that. Talent was stacking on top of talent at the all-important quarterback position now. And not just there. Because a year after meeting Brockington in a Brooklyn high school gymnasium, Catuzzi was talking with him at the New York prep school. Brockington seemed more than interested, too. He wanted to visit.

(12)

The land, John Brockington marveled. *Look at the Ohio land!*

The first time he got on an airplane was to visit Ohio State, and the first thing that struck him as he stepped off the plane was this wide, open, clean-aired land. It went on forever. He'd never seen anything like it.

Brockington was born in Manhattan and raised in Brooklyn. His world was bordered by crowded streets and subway stops. A few years later, he would ride home from Columbus with Kevin Rusnak, who lived in northern New Jersey. It would be early in the morning by the time they crossed the George Washington Bridge into New York City.

"Okay, John, where do I go now?" Rusnak asked.

"I don't know," Brockington said. "I've always just taken subways."

Rusnak had to stop at a bar in the general vicinity of his friend's neighborhood and call out if anyone knew where John Brockington lived. Someone directed them to drive three blocks this way and another couple of blocks that way.

As Rusnak drove, Brockington suddenly recognized the buildings. "That's where I live right there!" he said.

His family was stacked in Brooklyn's Bayview Projects, though when people heard this they immediately got the wrong idea. He didn't grow up poor in some New York ghetto. The Brockingtons were a middle-class family. His father worked in the post office. Bayview was 95 percent Jewish. There were just six black families among the thirteen buildings. Thomas Jefferson High had Jews, African Americans, Cubans, Puerto Ricans—a veritable melting pot smack dab in the melting pot of America. So early on Brockington gained an appreciation that there were good and bad people in any group, not good or bad groups of people.

But his New York experience fit the stereotype in this regard: There was no space. His high school didn't have home games because it didn't have a real field. The team practiced the width of it. If it had worked the length of the field, players risked ending up in gravel end zones that doubled as parking lots. The field was all dirt, too. It was watered down before each practice so players wouldn't choke on the dust. A train ran over the meeting room where the team watched film. The projector would be stopped whenever a train passed because players couldn't hear coaches talk.

So upon touring Ohio State, Brockington found the open-space difference startling and wonderful. He was taken to an empty Ohio Stadium, told to spin slowly around 360 degrees and imagine a packed stadium. Then imagine playing behind an offensive line of players bigger than he was.

He had arrived knowing so little of the Ohio State culture that he asked, "What are the colors, red and gray?"

But after this trip, he wanted to attend Ohio State. It didn't matter that Syracuse had paid for his prep school, he figured. Syracuse was slow on the trigger in offering a scholarship, anyhow. As Brockington suddenly put out the idea he was ready to sign, Catuzzi found himself with a new issue. The problem wasn't selling Brockington on Ohio State.

It was selling Hayes on Brockington.

Brockington's grades remained shaky, and by now he was a father. Hayes recognized the talent. He just wasn't certain that Brockington—so far from home—was a recipe for success.

"I'm not sure about this one," Hayes said.

"He's a great kid," Catuzzi said.

"I don't know . . . ." Hayes said.

And so Catuzzi would tell the story of that first meeting and the jacket. How it showed Brockington wanted to do right. And he explained that this was a great kid. Back and forth they went, Catuzzi understandably pushing, Hayes understandably hesitating. It was a two-step they performed for a couple of weeks. Finally, as the signing deadline neared, Hayes gave in. Brockington would be a Buckeye.

(13)

There was no national recruiting guru saying Ohio State had the Number One class in the country that year. No ESPN to come on live from Columbus to show Hayes talking about signing this fine class of student-athletes. No hotline. No chat room. Nothing at all to get excited about, considering these incoming freshmen weren't even eligible for another year.

The signing date wasn't an event on the national sports calendar.

It was just May 17.

"This is the best recruiting job in years," the Associated Press quoted a source as saying in a story that ran on April 27 under a small headline in a handful of Ohio papers. It was the kind of gibberish every team might say about their recruits every year, as if to verify their hard work. Why get too excited?

So in the greater sports kingdom, people didn't realize what Ohio State's coaching staff had just pulled off. Aside from Kern announcing his decision at an Ohio State basketball game, no one took more than local notice. A picture of Dave Cheney and his high school coach, for instance, graced the front of the

Lima News on the day he committed to Ohio State. Mike Sensibaugh was a story in the Cincinnati papers. Tatum and Jankowski were All-New Jersey, and a story there.

But who in Ohio knew how that translated? And who knew who would survive until the sophomore year? Just in this class, John Dombos broke his hip, Chuck Aldrin tore up his knee, Ed Lapuh had grade problems, and Joe Sinkowski got hit over the head with a bottle of Gordon's vodka at home in New York and lost the use of his speech and an arm for a while.

So the full story couldn't be told because it hadn't happened yet. And it wouldn't be fully told for years. In 2003, at the thirty-fifth reunion of the 1968 team, Brockington gave a speech on his Ohio State days. He asked Catuzzi to stand up.

"I want to thank you for all you did in recruiting me and getting me into this school," he said. "It changed my life."

Everyone in the audience began to applaud. None applauded louder than the coaches on hand. Right from the start, they knew what kind of talent was coming into the program. Five players in that recruiting class would be taken in the first twenty-nine picks of the 1971 NFL draft.

That didn't include Kern or Sensibaugh, who became All-American players, or Stillwagon, who also became the first Outland Trophy winner as college football's top lineman. It didn't include Doug Adams, who was a second-round NFL pick, or Ron Maciejowski, who would become so valuable in coming years. In all, thirteen players from this class would be drafted in the NFL. Some would play professionally in Canada. All that lay far ahead, though.

In the spring of 1967, The Best Class Ever was coming like cavalry over the horizon.

The coaches just hoped to survive until they arrived.

In the
beginning

"Look around at everyone in the room."

It was September of 1967, and Woody Hayes stood at the front of a meeting room in Smith Hall. School hadn't started. The hall was empty except for the thirty-one freshman football players who had just arrived. This was their first meeting, and if there was one speech Woody Hayes knew how to make resonate, it was this one.

"Goddammit, I said look around the room at everyone!" he said.

The freshmen started looking at each other.

"The people here in this room will be your best friends in life," Hayes said. "You'll see, that's how it will be. You'll keep one or two friends from high school. That's just how it is. But right here, in this room, are the people who will be your best friends through your life."

He let that sink in, because this was the point at which, every year, he began to lose some of them. This class was no different. Some players had met on recruiting trips or during high school all-star affairs. But for most of them this meeting was the first chance to match faces with names they had heard about or read in the newspapers.

Jack Tatum

In some cases, the initial impressions were staggering. The first player John Brockington saw from his class was Doug Adams. Brockington thought Adams looked like a Greek god. He had never seen anyone so chiseled. *No one looked like that on my Brooklyn team*, he thought. No one lifted weights because there were no weights. In the first seconds of meeting his first player, Brockington thought how hard he'd have to work if he wanted to make an impact at Ohio State. Leo Hayden had a similar impression of Jim Stillwagon. *He must be a senior*, Hayden thought. For many of them, for the first time in their lives, they stood in a room with players of similar athletic ability.

Each year, the first few days provided an awakening. The year before, for instance, 5-10, 170-pound cornerback Mike Polaski walked in for his team physical and stood next to 6-3, 230-pound Paul Huff. He figured Huff was an offensive tackle.

"I'm a fullback," Huff said.

Polaski then talked to Jim Otis, a 6-0, 208-pound barrel.

"I'm a fullback," Otis said.

Polaski realized he would have to tackle these masses of muscle. *What the hell did I get myself into?* he thought to himself.

Now, a year later, in the dorm where Hayes was giving this first talk, most of the freshmen wondered the same thing as the coach made their life plans. *What did he say? We'd become each other's best friends? These strangers and me? Huh?*

"Okay, now, let's talk about the word, 'apathy,'" Hayes said.

The freshmen had arrived to the meeting carrying, as ordered, a small book they had received in the mail that summer. It was called *Word Power Made Easy*, by Norman Lewis. Hayes, the son of an English teacher, used it to build vocabulary among his players, even demanding they mail him a chapter quiz each week of the summer. The ones who hadn't completed the quizzes would sit with him after practice to do so. That book would have been the first tip-off—if they knew how to recognize such things—that nothing was to be quite what they expected from Hayes over the next four years.

Hayes waited for them to look up "apathy." Then he read the definition: "'Lack of feeling or emotion. Impassiveness,'" he said.

"Let me tell you, apathy defeats teams," he said. "Apathy brings down nations. You want to avoid apathy like the plague."

He looked at them fiercely.

"By god, we're not going to let apathy into our team."

He continued on that theme, telling them what he expected over the next four years. Then he returned to his first point, about the players in this room becoming each other's best friends for life. This, they soon discovered, would be Hayes's regular topic. The next time they heard it, the entire team would be listening, and the thought would expand from the members of their individual class becoming best friends, to everyone on the roster.

"These are the guys you will count on for the rest of your life," Hayes said at this first meeting, picking his words slowly and deliberately. "They'll be with you forever. If you need help, they'll be there for you. If you can give help, you'll be there for them."

He paused and looked around the room.

"Take another look at who they are today."

The differences were startling. Most of the freshmen were white, but the nine African Americans represented the largest class of minorities in Ohio State football history. Most were Ohio boys, but the six represented states that cut as wide a geographical swath as the program ever had.

And whatever these differences were, they threatened to become more pronounced as the players stepped onto a college campus at this most volatile time in history. Their college experience would involve a world rocked by anti-war demonstrations, race riots, and assassinations. Some wouldn't last the four years. Some would quit football. That first night most of them thought, as Jack Marsh did, that the coach's talk didn't apply to them. The only player Marsh knew well at that meeting was Ralph Holloway, whom he had grown up near in northern Ohio. Marsh also had met Stillwagon and Ron Maciejowski on their recruiting trip to Ohio State. But that was it. Everyone else was a stranger. And now the man who recruited him, this coaching legend, the biggest name in the state of Ohio, was saying these guys would become his best friends for life?

He couldn't believe it. None of them could.

It became the first time that, years later, the players realized how smart the Old Man was.

(2)

On their first day of practice in the fall of 1967, Lou McCullough, the defensive coordinator with a squeaky voice still rooted in Georgia, held an index card in front of the freshman defensive players.

"Here, look at this," he told them.

All across campus the leaves were turning and so was a page symbolizing a college ritual. Freshmen were about to be introduced to the next chapter in their life. *Books. Classes. Dorms. Bars. Sex. Alcohol.*

And at practice this first day, the freshmen discovered their new world order. On this index card was a defensive scheme showing them where to line up and what to do in a certain alignment. But McCullough held the card up so briefly the players couldn't see their individual assignments.

"Okay, get into position," he said.

No one lined up properly. No one followed his assignment. They went the wrong way and bumped into each other or just took a couple of steps and stopped. It was nothing like what they were supposed to do. This, of course, was exactly as McCullough had intended. At every corner of the practice field, in fact, came the first steps of putting the freshmen in their proper place. As grunts. Fresh meat. Cannon fodder.

"ARE Y'ALL IDIOTS?" McCullough shouted to the freshmen defensive players. "IS THIS GONNA BE THE DUMBEST FRESHMAN CLASS EVER?"

He had them line up 10 yards from the chain-link fence bordering the field. He told them to run as hard as they could into the fence, telling them to hit with their head down.

They did so, too. What choice did they have? They couldn't tell the coach how crazy this was on their first day, could they? They had such little standing their names were taped across the front of their helmets so everyone knew who was who.

Several players did think this was stupid. And dangerous. Especially when they bounced off the fence in a dazed lump. Richard Troha remembers feeling humiliated. But they did it, because they understood the natural order in football: Coaches ordered. Players obeyed. No questions were asked.

"DO IT AGAIN!" McCullough shouted.

And so they did it again. And then again. And by the time they had run full speed into the fence a third time, some players were moaning softly on the ground. Again, this is what McCullough intended. This was a normal first practice for freshmen. This is the way it had been done since 100-yard fields were invented.

The upperclassmen knew how they felt. Guard Jim Roman, now a senior, spent the first twenty-five minutes of his college career being pounded by the first team defense in a goal line scrimmage. He left that practice with his eye closed, lip bleeding, forehand mangled, and one overriding thought, which he immediately relayed to his dad by phone.

"Come and get me or I'm hitchhiking home," he said.

All normal.

All expected.

Freshmen couldn't play varsity anyway, not in this era when they were actually expected to spend the first year ingraining themselves in the collegiate atmosphere, concentrating on the added academic strain, and exploring campus life without the big time pressures of big time sports.

In other words, they were allowed to be student-athletes.

Not athlete-students.

So, if a few freshman bodies or egos were bruised on the first day of practice, that was okay. They had time to learn. Besides, this was the norm for how teams operated. Just as it was normal for Roman's father to talk his son into staying in school.

But six days after the freshman class's first practice in 1967, something happened that was decidedly *not* normal.

It happened a week before the Ohio State opener against Arizona. Hayes wanted a dress rehearsal for his varsity, something to create game conditions, and, at the same time, build team confidence. The best way to do this, he decided, was to have the varsity maul the freshmen.

So on a hot September afternoon, the varsity ran out of the locker room to one sideline and the freshmen to the other in what had the look and feel of an actual game. The clock was running. The refs were whistling. The coaches were snarling. And, well, the freshmen were at every disadvantage you could imagine. Younger. Less experienced. Having played together not even a week.

Moreover, they ran Arizona schemes that were so foreign to them that, again, coaches held up index cards before each play. At least this time the cards were held up long enough for them to understand.

"Here we go, let's see it," Hayes said to his players.

From the start, a new dynamic took hold. The freshmen held their own. Not all of them, of course. Troha remembers lining up at defensive end that day and being double-teamed by juniors Rufus Mayes and Dave Foley. Each stood 6-5 and weighed 250 pounds, or a few inches and 50 pounds more than Troha did. He remembers peeling himself off the ground, play after play, to a surprising sight. Stillwagon or Adams or some other freshman had made a big play. The first team offense was having trouble moving the ball.

Over on offense, running an option play late in the first quarter, Kern split the defense, juked a couple of players, and scored. There was cursing from the coaches. Later in the first half, Ron Maciejowski ran 9 yards for a second freshman touchdown.

Suddenly, it was Freshmen 12, Varsity 7. Suddenly, the coaching staff saw itself a week from the opener with a team that couldn't beat freshmen. Suddenly, it wasn't the new kids getting a furnace blast of emotion thrown at them. It was the varsity players.

"DO YOU KNOW WHO YOU'RE LOSING TO?"

"THAT'S NOT MICHIGAN OVER THERE!"

"YOU CAN'T BEAT A BUNCH OF FRESHMEN?!"

The varsity led at half, 14-12, but only because the freshmen didn't have a kicker. Hayes told reporters afterward he did some yelling at the break and "the varsity did better in the second half." And they did. They won easily, 34-12, against freshmen undergoing their first week of practice.

Still, the game didn't swing in the second half simply because Hayes did some yelling. The varsity was given a strategic assist. In a second-half huddle, assistant Larry Catuzzi showed the offense a play card for a quarterback bootleg. Kern became excited. This play went right to his strength. It's one he loved to run, and judging by what the defense was doing at that time, one he expected to go for a big gain.

As he walked to the line of scrimmage, however, Kern glanced behind him. Catuzzi had flipped over the card and was holding it up for the defense to see. The coach was telling everyone what was coming. Any element of surprise was gone, and Kern was thrown for a loss.

The defensive coaches jumped around, extolling their players. Kern walked to the huddle, wondering what the heck was going on. And that was how it went much of the second half.

"We didn't get anyone hurt," Hayes told reporters afterward. "That's the best I can say."

The coaches felt the landscape tilt that day. None dwelt on it because there was a season opening in a week. Still, it was like dawn had broken. A glimpse of tomorrow was seen. It wasn't always that obvious as the autumn wore on. Some days, the freshmen would get dragged around the field by the varsity for a few laps. But typically they held their own. Often, they did better.

Tackling the freshman runners proved especially embarrassing. Earle Bruce, the defensive backs coach, set up one-on-one tackling drills between his senior-laden group and the freshmen. One on one side. Another on the other. They competed between five yards of cones. Jack Tatum, John Brockington, Leo Hayden—the seniors couldn't bring them down. And Kern? Bruce began offering an orange drink to anyone who could just touch him.

Before the Purdue game that year, McCullough wanted to practice his goal line defense. He put the ball on the 1-yard line for the freshman offense.

"You've got four plays to score," he told them.

On the first play, a sprint-draw was called. John Brockington took the hand-off. No one touched him. Touchdown.

"That's bat shit!" McCullough screamed at the defense.

The ball was put back at the 3. The same play was called but for Larry Zelina. He scored. McCullough moved the ball back to the 6. Jack Tatum scored. The freshmen were getting into it now. Guard Phil Strickland remembers watching the scene play out, runner after runner getting into the end zone, and thinking, *These boys can't keep up with us.*

"Damn it, Tiger, you're not running the play right," McCullough said to the freshman coach, Tiger Ellison. "You're not blocking like Purdue does."

"You can't stop our Baby Bucks," Tiger said.

On the fourth play, Leo Hayden got the carry. For the fourth straight time, the freshmen scored. At the time, no one knew Brockington, Hayden, and Tatum would each become Number One NFL draft picks. They were freshmen. They shouldn't be able to do that. The coaches became infuriated at their varsity players. Once, defensive line coach Bill Mallory kept raging at the way his players couldn't tackle the freshman running backs. Finally, he ran over to the backfield.

"Give me the ball!" he said.

On the next play, Mallory, in shorts and T-shirt and in his mid-30s, took the pitchout. He ran straight into a defense that happily flattened him. He bounced up quickly.

"Give it to me again!" he said.

Same play. Same pitch. Same Mallory disappearing under a wave of defenders. By the time practice was over, Mallory's lip was bleeding and his body bruised. But at least the defense was tackling him.

It was the same at the other end of the field. Only louder. There, the first team offense, Woody's hand-run unit, went up against the freshmen who posed each week as that week's opponent. If a play didn't work, Woody yelled,

"Goddammit, do it again!" If a defensive player did something unexpected to disrupt a play, something that might not have been the next opponent's method of playing, he yelled, "You can't do that!"

He developed a particular rivalry with Stillwagon. It didn't take much for Hayes to realize Stillwagon's talent. Each time the freshman disrupted a play, Hayes went ranting at the line, yelling a string of good-natured curses at Stillwagon.

One time, preparing for Iowa, Hayes put in a blocking scheme to counter its talented nose guard. The play worked perfectly.

"Ha, Stillwagon!" Hayes yelled across the line at the pile of trampled bodies. "We just ran that right over you!"

Stillwagon, who happened to be getting a pad put on a bruised arm at the time, said, "I'm over here, Coach!"

"Why aren't you in there? We've got to run that again. Get in there!"

The upperclassmen quickly realized how different practices were that fall. When they were freshmen, the varsity players would tell them to take it easy. Just make it look good, they'd say. There was no need to get beat up in practice. That was the developed culture. Of course, sometimes they'd go too far. Once, Hayes realized nose guard Vic Stottlemyer was half-stepping against his offense, charged out on the field, and began kicking him as he lay on the ground. And kicking him. And yelling, "Don't you dog it, you sonuvabitch!"

With these freshmen, dogging it was never an issue. Practices turned intense. Dave Foley, a junior in 1967, saw something change on the varsity, too. They began to improve. What began as a 2-3 season, with cries growing louder for Woody's firing, turned around and the Buckeyes finished the year with four straight wins. The howling stopped. Foley pointed right to those practices against the freshmen.

"Wars," he called them.

Sometimes, literally. One day, Strickland hit Stottlemyer in the groin. Stottlemyer slugged him back. A couple of other players jumped in. Soon, a full-scale, eleven-on-eleven brawl erupted on the practice field, freshmen against varsity, defense against offense, one hard punch bringing another harder one.

The coaches stood there, smiling.

(3)

That December, at the annual football banquet, Tiger Ellison was the keynote speaker. This, in itself, wasn't surprising. Ellison was such a renowned speaker he went around the state delivering talks and even had written a book called *Tiger Ellison's Secrets of Persuasive Speaking for Coaches.*

But what he said was unusual.

"Freshmen, stand up," he said. "Come on, stand up."

This was near the end of the ceremony, after Hayes talked about the turnaround that season, after junior linebacker Dirk Worden was awarded the team's Most Valuable Player award, after Worden and Foley were announced as captains for the next season.

All season, Ellison had been privately telling Woody to hang in there, that the best class he had ever seen was coming. In many ways, he and Woody were the oddest of professional marriages. Ellison was the inventor of the run-and-shoot offense, author of a best-selling book on it, and coach of legendary proportions at Middletown High for thirty years. He turned out eight All-Ohio quarterbacks. His offense once scored 98 points in a game, despite Ellison applying such brakes that his third-string quarterback led the state in passing after that night.

Only now, at 56, Ellison wasn't using any of his developed expertise. He was coaching ineligible college freshmen in a three-yards-and-a-cloud-of-dust philosophy. There was a back story why, and it went to his junior year in college. A linebacker, Ellison sidestepped a freshman's block in a practice, accidentally catching the freshman with his elbow. The freshman got off the ground and threw a left uppercut into Ellison. After being separated, their coach told them to shake hands. The freshman refused. Subsequently, both were kicked out of practice, although as Ellison walked to the locker room, the freshman came running up from behind with his hand extended.

"Hi, I'm Woody Hayes," he said.

They became friends for life. In 1963, Hayes asked Ellison to become an Ohio State assistant. Ellison figured it was, in part, to open up Ohio State's attack. Hayes, however, wanted Ellison's high school connections to recruit the state's talent. In Ellison's first staff meeting that spring, Hayes asked him to go to the chalkboard and discuss the philosophy of the run and shoot. After an hour, Hayes erased the board and talked about his off-tackle play. That was all anyone heard formally about the run and shoot.

Ellison, forever optimistic in manner and somewhat professorial in tone, never lost that manner while working with Hayes. He was a calm voice with the freshmen in 1967, though not a silent one. When they were in a tight game with Pittsburgh at half, Ellison said, "Boys, I don't know what I'm going to do. I can't tell Woody that this primo class he recruited is a bunch of girls. What am I going to do?"

They won, 36-20.

Ellison became more of a sounding board for Hayes than an agent of change. But in the week after Hayes suffered one of his worst defeats, 41-6 against Purdue in Ohio Stadium, Ellison sat down in his office and suggested Hayes should revamp his offense. Initially, Hayes erupted in anger. Later, he slipped into Ellison's office. "I think we better get ourselves a few new young coaches in here in the spring and add some dimension to this offense," he said, according to a biography by Tiger's daughter, Carolyn Ellison.

That was the first hint of coming change. The second came after Ellison had the freshman players stand up at this football banquet.

"Folks, these are the lads we call the Baby Bucks," he said. "But I want you to know, men of the varsity, that next fall they will become the Super Sophomores. And, fellas, they are hot to earn your spot."

A nickname was born.

A challenge was laid.

(4)

The coaching staff wasn't alone in seeing something percolating in 1967. Robert Grossman was a freshman student taking the prescribed two quarters of Reserve Officers Training Corps classes. As he entered the room for the first day of the ROTC Map Reading Class, he saw several students joking among themselves, obviously knowing each other well.

"Who are those guys?" he asked another student.

"They're on the freshman football team," he was told.

Over that fall, Grossman overheard the likes of Rex Kern, Jan White, Bruce Jankowski, Dave Cheney, and Bruce Maciejowski discuss their heated practices, their scrimmages with the varsity, and their two lopsided games. He heard them replay a moment of Kern dropping back to pass, pulling the ball down, and running through an Indiana defense for a touchdown.

At a time when "Goodbye Woody" banners were sold on the Oval before games and dragged from airplanes during them, Grossman heard enough to imagine a different future. When he told a cousin who attended California-Berkeley that Ohio State could play in the Rose Bowl the following season, he was laughed at.

Ohio State? In the Rose Bowl?

But Grossman was swept up by the conversation in that ROTC classroom. He had grown up in Columbus and remembered a freshman class of Lucas, Havlicek, and Nowell leading the basketball team to a national title as sophomores.

"I want to be a part of this," Grossman thought to himself.

He had played trombone in the Whetstone High School band. That was his ticket, he figured. So in the summer of 1968, he tried out for the Ohio State Marching Band and was chosen. Thanks to a map-reading class, he would spend his sophomore year with a front-row seat to Ohio State history.

Change in the
air

*Q*uestion turned to concern, then doubt, and ultimately
to panic as George Chaump sat in a meeting with the coaching
staff in February of 1968. At a blackboard, Woody Hayes had
written, "ROBUST," and proceeded that morning to lecture
for three hours about his Robust T-formation's off-tackle play.
For three *more* hours, that is.

Hayes already had spent the previous day sermonizing
on every nuance of it. How tackles set up a precise twenty-four
inches from guards. What foot blockers should lead with.
Where helmets were placed.

"Mark this down," he'd say.
"Underline this," he'd say.
"Write this," he'd say.
All the assistants would, too. No one said anything. For going on two
days! Over this most vanilla of plays! These were some of Chaump's first
tactical meetings since being hired that winter out of John Harris High School
in Harrisburg, Pennsylvania, where he had been undefeated the previous
three years running a wide-open offense. Dennis Green, who went on to NFL
coaching fame, had played for him. So did Jan White.

Rufus Mayes

Hayes had visited Harrisburg to recruit Chaump's latest quarterback, Jim Jones, and ended up taking the coach to lunch. It turned into a job interview. Whether he liked it or not—and confirmed by those talks with Ellison—Hayes knew he had to upgrade the offense. So the trip to Harrisburg ended up differently than anyone foresaw. Jones signed with Southern Cal after hearing about the quarterback waiting to take over Ohio State, Rex Kern. But Hayes got a recruit that trip, after all. Chaump signed a few weeks later as Hayes's quarterback and receivers coach.

For his first two months that winter, while the existing staff finished the recruiting season, Chaump studied film from the previous year. He watched every practice, every game, every frame of film there was. And he marveled at what he saw. The freshman class had more athletic talent than the varsity. It was at the impact positions, too. Quarterbacks. Running backs. Receivers. What speed. What size. What fun toys these would be for an offensive coach, he figured.

But now, hour after hour, all he heard about was this same off-tackle play. "Robust 26" and "Robust 27," as it was called in the Ohio State playbook, depending on if it was run to the left or right. The other coaches were accustomed to this. The players, too. They practiced this play endlessly. Everything had to be precise. Hayes would show the running backs where to take their first step. In minute detail, he went over the quarterback's handoff. He ensured the splits between linemen were perfect.

"If you were one inch too close, he'd stomp on your foot," tackle Dave Foley said. "Woody being 250 pounds, you learned pretty quickly you didn't want to be stomped on."

This play was an extension of Hayes. Direct. Aggressive. No nuance at all. "Three yards and a cloud of dust," wasn't some line arbitrarily hung on Hayes's offense. It was who he was. It is how he saw himself. Punch them in the face. See if they can take it. Keep punching them, too. That's what this play did. Before moving to the secondary in 1968, Gerry Ehrsam was a reserve quarterback and would be drilled in meetings on what plays would work in different situations. Whenever Ehrsam was stuck for a play, he would answer that it looked like a good place for "26" or "27."

"You're damn right, Gerry, good job," Hayes would say.

When the fullback ran the ball, Hayes kept control of the game. He was renowned for lines like, "The only pass I like is the one in the classroom," and how, "Three things can happen when you throw the ball and two of them are bad." But when a fullback carried, the ball was in Hayes's hands. Fullbacks, therefore, were his babies. He treated them differently than other players. He recruited them by the dozen, too. Just on this team, Jim Otis, Paul Huff, James Coburn, Alan Jack, John Brockington, Leo Hayden, Mark Debevec, Ralph Holloway, and John Dombos had all been recruited as fullbacks. Hayes's philosophy was to grab as many as possible. He needed a great one in his offense, he figured, and they generally were talented enough to help elsewhere if they didn't become The One. Jack became a starting guard, Debevec an All-Big Ten defensive end, and Holloway provided depth on the offensive line.

As with everything important to Hayes, he had exacting ideas on how the fullback should run the ball. Brockington, in his first scrimmage, saw the off-tackle hole was plugged and juked outside for a nice 7-yard gain. Next play, same thing. That time, he gained 6 yards. As he kneeled down to put on a shoe that had come off, he noticed two legs straddling him. It was Hayes. Glowering down at him.

"If you ever run the football like that again, you'll never play a down at Ohio State," Hayes told him.

Anyone who carried the ball had a similar experience. Tatum, who ran fullback as a freshman, bounced an off-tackle outside and ran for a long run in a scrimmage. Hayes was livid.

"Tatum, what the hell did I tell you to do?" he screamed.

He didn't want any back bouncing out of that hole, no matter how much the play gained. Hit the hole. Punch the defense in the face. Don't be twinkle-toes. This philosophy was crucial in Hayes deciding who would be his fullback.

In his first few weeks as an assistant, Chaump didn't have this background. He just saw a lot of time being spent on this one simple play. He didn't understand it. Nor did he understand why Hayes stood at the front of class and lectured while no one else added anything.

"Is this how you handle meetings here?" Chaump asked the other assistants at lunch that second day of meetings. "Woody just talks and you listen? There's no give-and-take? No one wondering if there's another way to do something?"

As the new guy, Chaump understood that his voice was diminished. And he didn't want to upset protocol. But that afternoon, when Hayes began lecturing again about his off-tackle play, Chaump raised his hand.

"Coach, I'd just like to ask a question, if I could," he said. "Is this what we plan to do on offense this year?"

"Yeah," Hayes said, "unless you think of something better."

"Well, you gave me film to look at. The only thing I really saw that I liked was the talent we have. Starting with Rex Kern at quarterback, we . . ."

"You think Kern is better than Billy Long?" Hayes asked.

"Coach, I think Rex Kern is far ahead of Long in talent," Chaump said.

Hayes snickered. He was constitutionally opposed to playing young kids, and Long had been a two-year starter.

"I'm sorry, Coach," Chaump said. "I see a lot of talent. I don't think this tight formation is going to utilize this talent. We've got to open it up to both running and throwing the ball."

When Hayes asked for suggestions, Chaump said to put a big, speedy receiver like White out wide. Throw a quick-out pattern. Force the defense to double-team him. That would open up the running game. Also, start employing the I-formation, he said, with a wingback in the slot, instead of the old-fashioned T-formation.

"Show me," Hayes said, holding out a piece of chalk for Chaump. So Chaump went to the blackboard and began designing short-passing plays. Quick outs. Little flare patterns. Anything to take advantage of the team's size and speed.

"Okay, enough of throwing the ball," Hayes said. "What would you run?"

Chaump drew the I-formation's off-tackle play. The formation was more spread out. The tackles moved more. The . . .

"That won't work in college," said Hayes. He cited a Notre Dame defense stopping Southern Cal's I-formation years earlier to back this up.

"A lot of people do it, and a lot of people do it successfully," Chaump said.

Hayes, by now, with each give-and-take, was becoming madder. His volume was going up, and up, until at this point he finally shouted, "No high school coach is going to tell me what to do! You don't belong here! You can leave!"

"Coach, I didn't mean to . . ."

"You're gone," Hayes said.

"What?"

Hayes took a step forward and said, "*You. Are. Gone.*"

Getting fired was part of the Hayes process. Each of the assistants had been fired. Some several times. Bo Schembechler, then coaching Miami University, counted fifteen times he was fired by Hayes. But in his opening weeks, Chaump didn't know any of this. Nor did he feel support from the other assistants. He left and packed up his desk. He began walking down the hall to the door, wondering what the heck had just happened, when a voice called after him.

"Get back in here," Hayes said. "I've never fired a coach, and I'm not going to break the record on you."

Back in the room, the mood had broken a little. Something had happened. The staff had rallied, after all. Hugh Hindman, who coached the offensive tackles and tight ends, was saying how he understood Hayes better than anyone. He had played for Hayes at Miami University. He had been an assistant under him for years.

"But, quite frankly, this way hasn't worked the last couple of seasons," Hindman said. "I think this would be a perfect time to see if we can do something and change."

Earle Bruce, the offensive line coach, agreed. Hayes began to budge. Just a little. But it was like the Walls of Babylon had cracked, so crucial was this moment for what it meant and how the offense would shift this upcoming season.

"Okay," Hayes finally said, "if we're going to do this, we'd better do this right."

He wanted film of Arkansas under Frank Broyles, Oklahoma under Chuck Fairbanks, and Southern Cal under John McKay. They ran I-formations and open offenses. They'd copy from the best, Hayes said, not some high school coach.

"But inside the 20," Woody told his staff that day, "we're going to run it my way. We're going to go the Robust formation."

Thus began the daily battle between the assistants to open the spigot of this offense and tap its talent and Hayes's constitutional desire to control everything in a way he understood. The players saw what was happening. They preferred to open up the offense, too. Kern became known for changing plays in the huddle. Bruce Jankowski would run full speed in pre-game warm-ups with the thought of catching Hayes's eye and selling him on throwing the ball that day. Quiet, bordering on bashful, Jankowski then would position himself close to Hayes on the sideline and say of some defensive back, "I can beat him, Coach. Throw me the ball."

"We've got to be careful," Hayes would say. "We'll watch for it."

Many weeks, Hayes would tell the offense in practice they would throw more that week. Then they'd focus on the passing game more, often very successfully. But in the game Hayes reverted to his comfort zone of running backs and a power game. The challenge wasn't to change that. The idea was to shift it by degrees. Mike Polaski, a junior defensive back in 1968, once walked past Hayes's office at Room 142 to see Lou Holtz, the secondary coach. Hayes was looking at film and yelling for Chaump. Some opponent was running a 4-4 defensive alignment, meaning eight men were set up close to the line to stop the run.

"How the hell we gonna block that in this offense?" Hayes said.

"We're not," Chaump said.

"What the hell are you talking about?" Hayes said.

"I've seen this tape," Chaump said. "Run it three plays ahead."

The offense put a man in motion. The defense immediately switched to a more balanced 5-2 alignment.

"Coach," Chaump said, "we're not going to block it because we're going to make sure they're not going to be in that formation."

As the years turned, and their careers rolled, Chaump would leave Ohio State after eleven seasons to join John McKay at the Tampa Bay Buccaneers. He never met two coaches more different. Woody was brash; McKay smooth. Woody drove an old truck; McKay drove the newest-model luxury car. Woody had said during Chaump's interview no assistant could play golf because it took too much time and was too expensive. On Chaump's second day at Tampa Bay, McKay asked for his golf handicap. When Chaump said he didn't have one, McKay said he'd better get one because everyone on his staff played golf. Most pertinently, Woody plotted everything about his team carefully and deliberately. McKay drew up plays on the sideline during games.

Success was their only common denominator. It showed Chaump there were many ways up the mountain. It also told him that the most important job of the head coach was to get the most from his assistants and players, in the mode of his personality. Chaump felt Woody could push people hard because, deep down, they knew he cared for them. They felt his passion. It reminded Chaump of a saying: *No one cares how much you know until they know how much you care.*

That first season at Ohio State, Chaump's fight for opening the offense didn't end with his firing and re-hiring in that off-season meeting room. It would go on for all his years with Hayes. At the end of spring practice, each assistant wrote a critique of his area of responsibility. In a report dated May 7, 1968, Chaump wrote about Hayes's favorite Robust-formation, off-tackle play:

"It is my opinion that this is a real good, sound, football play. However, it is vastly overemphasized in our system, even to the point of monotony. Statistics bear out that other plays have as good a consistency and average, and I venture to say if they were given as much emphasis and practice time in game-like scrimmages or games they would be equal or superior in basis."

In pen, Hayes wrote one word in response, which he underlined for emphasis:

"BULLSHIT!"

(2)

Leo Hayden stood on the Oval after a speech class, joking with a white girl whom he knew when his girlfriend approached, full of fury. "I get so sick of white people!" she shouted.

"What?" Hayden said.

"You know they killed him, don't you?" she said.

"Killed who?" he said.

"You haven't heard Dr. King was assassinated?" she asked.

April 4, 1968. Their world buckled, as it often did that year. It was a year in which the societal template was always shifting. Robert Kennedy was assassinated and Richard Nixon was elected. The *U.S.S. Pueblo* was captured by North Korea, and the Tet Offensive was mounted by North Vietnam and the Viet Cong. Americans protested the war. Paris rioted against Charles de Gaulle. Prague rebelled against the Soviet Union. Two American sprinters raised black-gloved fists over the Mexico City Olympics. *Sports Illustrated* ran the cover story, "The Black Athlete—A Shameful Story." The Beatles looked ahead and sang, "You say you want a revolution?" and Simon and Garfunkel looked back and sang, "Where have you gone, Joe DiMaggio? A nation turns its lonely eyes to you."

On the April afternoon King was assassinated, the Ohio State campus began to bubble, just like dozens of colleges across the country. Groups of African American students began protesting. Police took up positions on the Oval. Tear gas was thrown. Names were hurled. School officials quickly suspended classes until after King's funeral.

In a meeting that afternoon, Hayes addressed the assassination and the loud reaction that threatened to split America into two camps. Sometimes it was pro-war/anti-war. This one was more simple to see, much more complex to solve. Black and white America.

"You're bigger than this," Hayes told his players. "You're a family. Every one of you counts the same as the other. It doesn't matter what class you're in, what position you play, what color your skin is. Don't let them sons of bitches out there destroy what we've built here.

"There's a lot of stuff going on out there that's not going to be a part of this team. There will not be a black-and-white thing in here. I absolutely will not have it."

Several African American players thought it was the most important speech Hayes gave in their time at Ohio State. Without it, they could not have moved forward as a team. For many of them, each day was a minefield. They felt tugged by two distinct worlds. On one side, African Americans were raising newly discovered voices that year and demanding to be heard in books like Black Panther Eldridge Cleaver's *Soul on Ice* and James Brown's hit song, "Say it loud—I'm black and I'm proud!" On the other side was their football team, which was deemed part of the machine.

These players saw sports and race colliding around them. At Penn State that November, 175 black student-athletes were allowed to announce their goals and attitudes to a sold-out Beaver Stadium. Then they marched off the field with fists held high as the crowd booed. At Indiana, ten of fourteen blacks were dismissed from the football team after boycotting two days of practice. One of those taken back sat on the bench, crying, in the final moments of the next game against Iowa. At Wisconsin, a group of black athletes boycotted the football banquet, complaining about the attitudes of an assistant coach, who was then fired.

About forty Michigan State athletes, including twenty African American football players, threatened a boycott of the school's sport programs in April of 1968. They called it off a couple of weeks later, citing evidence of progress. One measure of progress was the hiring of the school's first African American football assistant, something Hayes had done that winter with Rudy Hubbard.

As African American athletes raised their voices across campuses, Ohio State players felt pressure from the campus Black Student Union to join the national fight. A group of them met with Ohio State athletic officials regarding ways to improve relations, although as Jack Marsh observed, the meeting evolved into a discussion between the football players and Woody Hayes. The Black Student Union wanted action.

"They sent messages that we were Uncle Toms and said we should quit the team," Tim Anderson said. "They said, 'If you're really black, you won't be part of that.' We were looking at them, and most were guys that came from a family with some money. They would have ended up at Bowling Green or Ohio University.

"Most of us had no money. If we quit the team, we'd have to go home. We told them they were out of their minds if they thought we were going to give up our scholarships."

At a Black Student Union meeting that fall, Rufus Mayes entered with several African American football players. Mayes was generally quiet and easygoing. This night, however, he walked into the meeting and asked who kept suggesting the football players should quit the team and that they weren't as black as anyone in the room. The meeting's leaders said none of them had suggested that. No one else came forward.

The issues didn't fade. Nor did the larger ones that inflamed them. Three weeks after King was assassinated, seventy-five black students took over the Ohio State administration building and held two of the school's vice presidents hostage. "BLACK TEACH-IN," read a bedsheet sign hung from the building's window.

The protest was triggered by a Columbus bus driver telling four African American girls to be quiet when they began "talking about blackness," as the *Columbus Dispatch* wrote. The hostage situation ended after several hours when university officials agreed to a five-point plan to address grievances.

All this was felt inside the football team. And none of it was. Inside the huddle, there wasn't the kind of bubbling divide found in the larger world. Maybe they were insulated from it. Maybe familiarity bred understanding. Maybe, for the first time in some of their lives, some of them saw a member of the opposite race performing the same tasks and taking on the same challenges. Maybe, just maybe, football provided the one common bond needed to get along.

In 1966, when Kevin Rusnak and Mike Radtke, both white, were freshmen, they were looking where to sit for a team meal and took two open seats at a table with Ray Gillian and Dave Whitfield, two African American players. At a team reunion years later, Gillian told Rusnak how important that moment was, for it showed all of them the team could be together.

"When he said that, it made my life," Rusnak remembered.

With the ten African Americans in the sophomore class in 1968—the nine recruited plus walk-on Bruce Smith—the dynamics changed some, too. Rufus Mayes, by comparison, was the only African American in the senior class. There were five others with him as a freshman. But, one by one, they didn't come back and only Mayes remained. The junior class in 1968 consisted of two African Americans, Gillian and Whitfield. So when these sophomores became part of the varsity, they joined an upperclass of three African Americans.

Gillian, whom many white players considered the most outspoken on the team regarding racial issues, did some research on the recruiting classes through the years and saw a pattern: Big recruiting class of African Americans, then small recruiting class of them, big, then small . . . .

"Like there was a number they would allow," he said.

Bill Willis, in 1941, was the first African American to play at Ohio State. He went on in 1945 to become the first black in the National Football League in a dozen years. There were other notable players at Ohio State—Jim Parker, Jim Marshall, Matt Snell, Paul Warfield—but the school wasn't known for pushing the envelope for blacks. This wasn't just in athletics. Of the 40,000 students on campus, less than a couple of thousand were considered to be black. The total is lost somewhere in history. The registrar's office felt it necessary to tabulate the number of women and married couples in 1968, but not black students.

Still, at a time the African American athlete hadn't been allowed into some football programs in the South, Hayes—using the vernacular of the times—had been regularly stating the importance of African American players.

"Without Negro athletes, I could never have had great teams at Ohio State," he said in 1962. "They are fabulous in ability and fun to coach. Sports gave the Negro his greatest opportunity and provided the means whereby the white boy and the colored boy learned they could play and work together. We can't beat Russia with second-stringers. We need boys who can win."

Hayes was never oblivious to the changing times. Between 1968 and 1970 on the Oval, there would be protests of war, protests of race, and protests against protests. Hayes was often seen walking amidst them, listening to the speakers, and talking with students. Sometimes he would be called up to the stage, though typically for cheap entertainment value more than his message. He supported the very generation, institutions, and authorities the protesters railed against. Once, the crowd chanted as he talked, "First and ten, do it again!" Another time, he went with some African American players to a protest, soon moved on stage, and began telling everyone to go back to their dorms. He was booed, laughed at, and eventually, forced off the stage. Of all the emotions

Hayes evoked from these players over four years, sympathy was a unique one reserved for that afternoon.

"They threw him off the stage," Tim Anderson said. "Some of us players caught Woody. He looked at us and said, 'Let's get the hell out of here.'"

The African American players thought Hayes adjusted to the times as best a white man in his mid-50s could. As the old line regarding Vince Lombardi went, Hayes treated everyone equally: like dogs. But he addressed issues. He discussed topics. He purposely roomed black and white players together in hotels. He asked Hayden questions involving race, from big things ("Are there any concerns I should know about?") to little things ("Why does Jan White part his hair on the side?")

His rants on life in team meetings took up the topic, too. Before that 1968 season, he discussed the reluctance of Alabama coach Bear Bryant to recruit African American athletes and how Bryant would change soon, because he couldn't compete. As Ray Gillian listened, he wondered what possible significance that had to Ohio State's African American players. Two years later, watching Southern Cal fullback Sam "Bam" Cunningham romp over all-white Alabama in 1970, Gillian understood Hayes had been discussing the value of the African American athlete.

"It was like he was a prophet," Gillian said.

There was practical education inside the team, too. Steve Crapser, a white defensive tackle, remembers asking Jan White the differences in meaning to African Americans between the words "nigger," "Negro," and "black." The world was changing so quickly that *Sports Illustrated*, in its cover story on "black" athletes that July, freely interchanged "Negro" and "black." *Time* began 1968 by calling the world's best boxer "Cassius Clay," by summer referred to him as "Muhammad Ali, alias Cassius Clay," and by the end of the year the magazine identified him simply as "Muhammad Ali."

White explained the nuances of each word to Crapser, ultimately saying the differences in meaning rested on another word altogether.

"Respect," he said.

In the locker room, on the field, with their day-to-day interaction, the African American players felt this respect across the roster. What issues there were, they felt, arose from personalities, not race. Race almost never infected the team, they thought. Race almost always stayed in the outside world. They almost never wondered if Hayes had some bias at work.

Almost.

One coming issue threatened to split their locker room.

(3)

As always, the offensive staff sat on one side of the long table in the meeting room, the defensive staff on the other. But this morning in the spring of 1968, they weren't assembled to watch game film, lay strategy, or discuss personnel.

They had come to flip a coin.

And chart a future.

"Whattya call?" Woody Hayes asked.

"Heads," Lou McCullough answered.

One way to measure how Hayes was adjusting to tough times was with the offense he would allow in the coming season. The coin flip was a second way. For the past several years, McCullough had been on Hayes to divvy up the roster more equitably between offense and defense. Partly it was because McCullough was the defensive coordinator and wanted better players. But most of it, the coaches felt, was because Hayes hoarded talent for his offense like a child hoarded toys. The offense was his creation. It was where he put his time, what defined his coaching. He didn't just want to win against Purdue and Michigan on Saturday. He wanted to win against McCullough's defense on Tuesday, Wednesday, and Thursday.

The best way to assure this would happen was to grab the better players. That's what Hayes did, year after year. In one previous class of thirty-three, McCullough counted, Hayes handpicked twenty-four players for his offense.

"The rest is for the defense," he said.

Through the years, some of the players who couldn't get off the bench on offense would have helped on defense. Or so the defensive coaches thought. They'd mutter among themselves. And grow frustrated at their lack of depth. And daydream what would happen if they could ever get some of the talent wasting away on offense.

This wasn't just about ego. It was about winning. The defense was fine against good offenses. But against an offense with the best talent, like Purdue the previous season, the defensive coaches felt outgunned. They thought it all came back to Hayes's fundamental philosophy of keeping the best players for himself. How could Ohio State ever be a contending team if the defense wasn't given as much attention? Didn't defense win championships? These were some of the issues McCullough raised with Hayes, year after year. Finally, during the '67 season, after the recent dips in the program, Hayes relented.

"I'll tell you what we'll do," Hayes said one day. "Next year I'll take a player from this freshman class and then you'll take one. And I'll take another one and you'll take one."

"Will you remember that?" McCullough said.

"That's what we'll do," Hayes said.

"You remember it," McCullough said.

So on this March morning in 1968, as McCullough called heads, Hayes flipped a coin in the air. Everyone in the room felt their stomachs rise with it, knowing this was a new way of doing things. There were two players especially up for grabs: John Brockington and Jack Tatum. Both had the speed and talent to be stars no matter where they played. The only question was which side got them. The coin came down . . . and down . . . and . . . Hayes caught it and turned it over on his forearm.

Tails.

Hayes got the first pick.

"Rex Kern," he said.

That only made sense. Kern had starred both ways in high school. He mixed in at defensive back drills as a freshman. But everyone knew he was Woody's idea of a quarterback. He was full of the leadership gene, too.

Now it was McCullough's turn. The defensive staff had talked about this among themselves. There was some debate who to take. They also had agreed, since they'd be happy with either Brockington or Tatum, to appease Woody a little. Let him draw first blood.

"Mike Sensibaugh," McCullough said.

Like Kern, this pick didn't especially hurt the other side. Like Kern, Sensibaugh had played quarterback in high school, as well as defensive back. But Sensibaugh had made his choice clear. On the opening days of practice the previous summer, two of the freshman quarterbacks were scheduled to practice on offense and a third would rotate to defense. That's not quite how it worked out. Sensibaugh had watched Kern and Maciejowski throw those opening practices, and when it came his turn to rotate to the defense, he stayed there. He never returned to the offense. He saw how much better Kern and Maciejowski were at quarterback. On defense, he figured, he had a chance to play.

It was Hayes's turn again.

"John Brockington," he said.

Freshman coach Tiger Ellison called Brockington "Wild Horse," for the manner in which he thundered with high-pumping thighs through the line. In handing off to him, Kern had to be careful not to brush against him or he might be knocked sideways by his power. At the same time, with all his size and speed, the defensive coaches knew he could be a linebacker. Now they knew something else: blood had been drawn.

The game was on.

McCullough's turn. He was ready. In a clear and defined voice, as if announcing royalty, he said:

"JACK ... TATUM."

Hayes's face scrunched. He took a wastebasket and flung it across the room. "You sonuvabitch!" he said. "I *knew* you were going to take him!"

Mallory couldn't help chuckling inside. All the coaches knew that Tatum would be the test case, as to whether Hayes actually would follow through with his idea. Tatum was a rare athlete. Fast. Smart. Fearless. And he had only played fullback his freshman season. He possessed such magic as a runner that Sensibaugh, who would become an All-American safety, said that in his career Tatum was the only player he could never tackle.

Catuzzi had raised an independent concern: Recruiting. By now, Catuzzi had left Columbus for Williams College, where he would be the youngest head coach in college football. But whenever the idea of Tatum playing defense was raised, he expressed a concern about recruiting repercussions. Tatum had been recruited as a running back. He was All-New Jersey at that position. How could a recruiter go to some kid's home in New Jersey and not have this thrown in his face? In light of Tatum's shift to defense, wouldn't their promises mean little?

Fortunately, Tatum saved the decision. He said he was fine with the move. He preferred it, actually. It wasn't so much the jam in the offensive backfield that concerned him. It was Woody. He liked Woody, for the most part. He just didn't like how he was always telling running backs how to run, where to run, what hole to run. Nor did he like that Woody wielded such control over who would play at running back. He saw problems ahead with his running style and Hayes's running beliefs. It wasn't just the day Hayes corrected him for bouncing an off-tackle play outside. Once, returning a punt, Tatum reversed field, retreating several yards in an arc across the field, then broke a long run. He returned to the sideline laughing, enjoying his moment.

"Goddammit, that's not the way you play football here," Hayes said.

"You run straight upfield."

As Hayes walked away, *Columbus Citizen-Journal* reporter Kaye Kessler stood on the sideline and watched how Tatum would react. Tatum shrugged. "Damn, the Old Man's crazy," he said to some teammates.

Still, in years past, Hayes wouldn't have allowed such a talent to move from his offense. Now, if he didn't like it, at least he didn't block it. He let the decision stand. And so went the rest of the most important draft in Ohio State football history.

Defense, for the first time, was on an equal playing field with the offense. The defensive staff walked out of that room, exhaled, congratulated each other, and went to work deciding how to use their new talent.

(4)

That March, before the start of spring practice, the team gathered for dinner at the Jai Lai restaurant. At the table for the defensive backs, Mike Polaski found his name tag and sat down. The only other person already at the table was a short, scrawny guy with glasses. Polaski figured he was a student manager.

"Hi," the guy said, holding out his hand, "I'm Lou Holtz, your new coach."

Adding a lisp to the first impression of short and scrawny, Polaski thought to himself: *Uh-oh, we're in big trouble.*

Holtz, in turn, was wondering the same about his new job. He grew up in East Liverpool, Ohio, and, from the angle of a child's view, saw Ohio State as football Nirvana. Working for Iowa, William and Mary, Connecticut, and South Carolina in the first seven years of his apprenticeship, he never shook his early picture. Coaching defensive backs at South Carolina in 1967, he told a coaching friend he'd love to learn under Woody Hayes at Ohio State. A lunch meeting was arranged between Holtz and Esco Sarkkinen, the long-time Hayes assistant.

That led to Holtz meeting Hayes at a coaches' convention that winter and being offered an assistant's job on his 31st birthday. It was the second job Holtz had been offered at the convention. The first was from Georgia Tech and offered $13,000 plus moving expenses, a down payment on a home, a car allowance, and a Florida vacation every year.

Hayes offered $13,000. No moving expenses. No down payment. No perks. Take it or leave it. Holtz took it. But a week later he called Hayes and said he'd changed his mind. He didn't want the job. What he didn't say was he turned it down after hearing South Carolina coach Paul Dietzel warn what a crazed personality Hayes could be.

Hearing Holtz back out, Hayes seemed to confirm Dietzel's warning, cursing to the point that Holtz nearly hung up. Finally ratcheting his voice down, Hayes said, "Okay, you're not taking this job. But whatever voice told you to take it, whatever voice inside you convinced you this was the job for you, that's the voice you'll have to listen to the rest of your life. It won't go away. You'll always wonder why you didn't follow it."

Hayes had pushed the right button. Holtz reversed himself again and took the job. But when he arrived at his first staff meeting he wondered again if he had done the right thing. He was smoking a pipe, as usual, using a self-mixed blend of tobacco that players joked "smelled like it came from the bottom of a shoe."

"What are you doing smoking a pipe?" Hayes said upon entering the room. "Paul Brown wouldn't let you smoke a pipe. He says pipesmokers are soft and lazy."

"That's why you're smarter than Paul Brown," Holtz said. "You don't believe that stuff."

A few minutes later, Hayes began cursing Bill Mallory because one of the defensive linemen had skipped Hayes's 8 a.m. football class. After Hayes went on, Mallory rushed around the table at him, fists up, and the other assistants had to step between them. Sitting there, watching this, Holtz asked himself for the first of many times that season, *Lou, what have you gotten yourself into?*

On the way out of the meeting, Holtz asked Tiger Ellison if this was a normal day at the office.

"Don't worry," Ellison said, "you'll get used to it."

Holtz would come to view Hayes as a brilliant motivator and one of the most remarkable people he ever met. But he'd never get used to some of it. He'd always wonder about the tantrums Hayes threw, even as he knew many were calculated. In conversations about Hayes, he'd inject, "While I didn't agree with everything . . . "

At the Jai Lai dinner that first night, Holtz watched his defensive backs arrive. Four of them would have professional careers, three for at least five seasons. But he didn't yet know the talent at the table. Nor did these defensive backs know, as each would say, how Holtz would be the perfect teacher for all of them.

"Let me tell you why I took this job," Holtz told them. "I came to Ohio

State for one reason. I came to go to the Rose Bowl."

He said they'd beat Purdue next season.

They'd beat Michigan.

And they'd go to the Rose Bowl.

For a short, scrawny guy with a lisp, he sure did think big things. What's more, he expected his players to think them. Soon, they discovered, they actually *believed* them. Forty years later, in Polaski's playbook, those three goals were listed precisely as Holtz said them that night.

(5)

"HE FARTED IN OUR FACE!" Hayes yelled.

He stood before the team, before the first day of spring practice, talking about Purdue coach Jack Mollenkopf. And how Mollenkopf had acted during the second half of the 41-6 win against Ohio State the previous season. He didn't even stand on the sideline.

"HE SAT ON THE BENCH WITH HIS ARMS FOLDED!"

And there was his derby hat.

"IT WAS TIPPED OVER HIS EYES!"

Hayes was worked up now. He wanted his players worked up, too. Did they know Purdue's starters sat almost the entire second half? And that Leroy Keyes, the great Purdue running back, was so worn out by playing them he played golf the next day? That's what he said! *Golf!* That won't happen again!

"And if you guys don't beat Purdue, I guarantee you one goddamn thing," Hayes said. "When Mollenkopf comes out to shake my hand after the game, I'll beat him up at midfield!"

With that, he took a framed glass picture and threw it against the wall.
The players began yelling. And jumping. And woofing.

"WOOO-WOOO-WOOO!"

They ran out to practice field like a stampede on the plains. George Chaump, attending his first Ohio State practice, thought this was a speech a coach would give before a national championship game, not before the first of twenty spring practices, six months before the next meaningful kickoff.

But then it was a spring full of surprises. And decisions. Never before, never after, would these coaches have the smorgasbord of talent in one incoming class. The question was how to blend it among some talented upperclassmen. How to create the best team of it all. Who would start? Who would play where? And if you moved this guy over here, could you move that guy over there? It was a game of chess, with knights becoming bishops, bishops becoming rooks, players moved to new positions and coaches measuring the team's overall strengths against individual talents.

Take Jan White. He liked track more than football. As a high school senior, he set the Pennsylvania 110-meter hurdles record. He had only started playing football in junior high because the coach promised to teach him to run faster. He quickly discovered that was a line to get him on the field. Even as he starred in football, even as coaches beat a path to his doorstep, White had considered attending Southern Cal mainly because the warm weather and palm trees spoke to his runner's heart.

But this spring, senior Rufus Mayes was moving from tight end to offensive tackle, and the team needed a tight end. The coaches struck on White as the obvious choice. Never mind that at 6-2 and 205 pounds he didn't have the prototypical tight end's build. Never mind his speed would be lost much of the time at tight end. Never mind, too, that White said that he liked running free as a receiver more than playing inside amid bumper-car traffic.

White was their best option at tight end, and so now he was one.

"I don't know anything about blocking in the line," White said.

"We'll teach you," said Hugh Hindman, who coached tackles and tight ends.

"But I don't want to learn," White said.

Suddenly that spring, instead of lining up wide by himself, White was a measured twenty-four inches from a 250-pound Mayes or Dave Foley. Across from him, a defensive end or linebacker acted like a sledgehammer against him all year. Even when he went into a pass pattern, there were bodies bumping him. He went into survival mode, just trying to get through each day in one piece. Gone forever to White that spring were the days of running free as a receiver. And since he now was a tight end . . .

One day that spring, Bruce Jankowski looked at the lineup posted before each practice and saw that he was now a receiver. That's how the news was broken to him. Unlike White, he was pleasantly surprised. He had arrived the previous fall and discovered one hole in his halfback game for this offense: he didn't know how to block.

He didn't need to know in high school, since he was always the guy getting the ball. But as a halfback in Hayes's offense, blocking was a primary role. He had to learn. And he had to block well, if he wanted to play. And at first, that was a problem.

"I was a crappy blocker," he said.

He developed quickly enough to become a decent blocker that season. But it didn't solve the underlying issue Jankowski faced—a backfield loaded with stars. Three of the players he had competed with as a freshman—Brockington, Hayden, and Tatum—would eventually be first-round NFL draft picks. Then there was Dave Brungard, the returning starter. And Jim Otis was the returning starter at fullback, so he'd get the ball most of the time, anyhow.

Jankowski saw enough talent to figure his future wasn't at running back. Wingback, maybe. Except Larry Zelina had been put there with the previous year's starter, Ray Gillian. As a freshman, he played some split end in practice. He liked it, too. He quickly saw that he was a more natural receiver than a running back. When he saw his name listed as a receiver, he readily accepted it.

That spring, no games were won, no championships grabbed. There was no stadium applause. Yet something tangible happened in the practices. The upperclassmen, who had merely practiced against these freshmen the previous fall, realized it in the most routine of moments. Just running sprints after practice felt different, linebacker Mike Radtke sensed. He saw what speed the team now had, what gifted athletes the freshmen-turning-sophomores were. From practicing against them the previous season, the upperclassmen knew the kids were good. But it was different now. The kids were eligible to play. Radtke pushed himself harder to stay up with them. In so doing, he knew, all of the upperclassmen were being pushed.

The coaches could see it all coming together, even if there were moments that suggested otherwise. Some plays, Lou McCullough ordered his defense to blitz an offense trying to learn the nuances of George Chaump's changes. Just for fun. Just to watch Mt. Woody erupt. The code word they used for the tantrums was "megaton."

"We got him mad now," McCullough would chuckle to his defense. "Look at that megaton!"

Hayes questioned anew this newfangled offense. Its I-formation and more-open alignment took him beyond his comfort level. At 55, he wasn't sure about such dramatic change. Hadn't he been successful with the Robust T? And now he was changing a central principle of that success?

Some days it was too much for him.

"Men, we're all going to get our asses fired, listening to some damn high school coach," he'd tell his assistants.

At such moments, the other coaches talked him off the ledge and the learning resumed. For the previous two seasons, these coaches had wondered about their jobs. Now they were breathing a bit easier. How much better this team was than the ones of the previous seasons! They understood why, too. In the spring report every assistant was required to write for Hayes, Tiger Ellison summed up all the coaches' thoughts in three sentences:

"Most of our freshmen came through as expected. Our future rests with fourteen sophomores. Lose them and we start packing."

(6)

Every season, his assistants felt, Hayes selected one of them as the personal vessel for his irascibility. It was typically a young assistant or someone in a new position. This unofficial appointment meant that the particular coach could never do anything right. By April, after a spring scrimmage when Hayes introduced his assistants to the parents of the players, Hayes's choice for the new season became obvious.

One by one, he called up each assistant, giving his name and title. Here was Lou McCullough, the defensive coordinator. Here was Esco Sarkkinen, the defensive ends coach.

Then Hayes began, "Here's our guards and centers coach . . . "

And he stopped. Extended seconds crawled by. It looked as if Hayes couldn't remember the coach's name.

"Earle Bruce," Anne Hayes whispered from the front row. "Earle Bruce!"

Bruce was stunned. Hayes's memory was renowned. It was one of his more amazing traits. He remembered dates, places, full speeches verbatim, such as Winston Churchill's "we will fight them anywhere" speech to the British people. And names? He never forgot them. Ever. Everyone had a story as testament. Bruce's story was that, while dating his future wife, he introduced her to Hayes one day in passing. Six months later, they saw each other again.

"Hi, Jean," Hayes said.

She got this look on her face. She was speechless. Later, Earle asked if she was okay.

"He remembered my name," Jean said.

"He remembers *everybody's* name," Earle said. "That's just Woody."

"No one remembers my name," Jean said.

And yet on this spring afternoon, in front of players and parents, Hayes couldn't remember Earle Bruce's name. Or wasn't saying it. Or something. Bruce didn't know what had just happened. He knew only that it didn't signify anything good.

By then Bruce was in his third year under Hayes, after winning his way through several Ohio high schools. Mansfield. Salem. Sandusky. Massillon. Bruce made them all champions. In 1966, he was 35 and decided if he ever wanted to coach in college he'd better do it.

"I can't afford you," Hayes told him.

Bruce was making $15,000 at Massillon High School, where his teams had gone undefeated in 1964 and 1965. Hayes offered $11,000, the same salary Bo Schembechler offered Bruce a month earlier at Miami University. Hayes promised to try for $11,500, though when the first paycheck came it was at $11,000. It was a feeling Bruce never forgot. When he became head coach, he would leave a little wiggle room in the agreed price so an assistant's first paycheck reflected a salary of $500 or $1,000 more.

But Bruce didn't base his decision on money. It was love. From the moment he arrived as a freshman running back in 1950, he fell in a big way for Ohio State. The next season, Hayes's first year as coach, Bruce blew out his knee and saw his world crumble. At that time, injured players typically lost their scholarships. They couldn't help anymore, right? So why should they be paid like it?

Bruce began hitchhiking home to Maryland. Hayes heard about it and sent assistant Harry Strobel to find him. When Strobel came back alone, a call was made to Bruce's Maryland home with a message that awaited his arrival: *Return to school. Help coach the team. Get your education. That part of the equation doesn't change just because you got hurt.*

"A deal's a deal," Hayes told Bruce.

For years, Bruce saw this side of Hayes. When Bruce needed a car to get to his first job interview in northern Ohio, Hayes lent him his car. When he needed help getting his first head coaching job, Hayes got on the phone with the school officials. Whenever Bruce needed some advice as a young coach, Hayes was there for him.

But working as an assistant to Hayes, he discovered, was a different animal. They all found that out. And switching from the defensive secondary to the offensive line, as Bruce did in the spring of 1968, multiplied the Hayes Factor dramatically. Hayes ran the offense, which meant every meeting, every practice, every little decision. Bruce soon found he could do nothing right.

One practice, he was watching a play develop, studying his guards and center open a nice hole in the defense. But Bruce thought fullback Jim Otis read the hole wrong. Bruce walked over to Otis and began pointing out where he should have run. Immediately, Hayes was on Bruce, hat pulled down to his eyes, voice on low boil.

"Get over there and coach the defense!" he said. "I'll coach the offense!"

That moment, Bruce discovered the First Commandment of being an offensive assistant: *Thou shalt not talk to Woody's fullback.* Quickly, Bruce concentrated only on his guards and centers. They were an unlikely group in some respects. There were many starters who were upperclassmen on a sophomore-laden team. Each of them was undersized, too.

The starting center, John Muhlbach, whom Bruce had coached at Massillon, weighed around 190 pounds. None of the four guards in the rotation weighed more than 215 pounds. But Bruce found they compensated for this by using picture-perfect technique, unexpected quickness, and—to his added delight—by simply working hard.

"One-hundred-percenters," he called them.

This group, he thought, almost could make being in Woody's doghouse acceptable. Almost. During one practice, Hayes called down from one end of the field to the other end for Bruce to send him a center to snap for the quarterbacks. Bruce was in the middle of a drill and didn't hear. Hayes called again. Bruce still didn't hear. Hayes took off in an all-out, leg-lifting, arm-chugging sprint down the field toward Bruce. Practice stopped. Heads turned.

"GODDAMMIT, YOU DON'T WANT ME TO HAVE A CENTER!" he yelled at Bruce.

Mallory watched it all and shook his head, smiling to himself. *Poor Earle. But better him than me*, as all the other assistants said.

There were also the other little jobs Bruce had: locker room music and Friday night movies. How'd he get those? He didn't know. Everything went fine with the movies until the 1969 season when he showed *Easy Rider* with Dennis Hopper and Peter Fonda playing hippies who sell drugs and motorcycle across the country.

Hayes went ballistic. Pot smoking? Sex scenes? On the eve of a game? Ohio State nipped Minnesota 34-7 the next day, but Hayes blamed the movie for the score being *that* close. Bruce was fired from movie duty. Rudy Hubbard was put in charge of movies ever after.

Fine with Bruce. Sometimes, though, being Woody's whipping boy was more than he could take. He was returning to Massillon to open a pizza store, he'd tell George Chaump. Or he'd say: "I'm going to the top of the building, get a bucket of cement, and when the Old Man walks by, drop it on him."

It all brought to mind Anne Hayes's line when asked if she ever had considered divorcing Woody.

"Divorce, no," she said. "Murder, yes."

Bruce could understand such thinking.

"I was looking for a new job from the first day that year," he said.

As much as Hayes had done for him, as much as Bruce appreciated his mentor, working beside him could be a pain. He'd survive, he told himself. Maybe he believed that, too. Compounding matters was the promise he had made to himself not to bring work home with him. He wanted home time to be for his wife and young girls. Not that he could expect much sympathy there anyhow. Once, he told Jean how Woody had become so angry he threw a movie projector into the wall.

"You lie," she said.

"No, really, it stuck right in the wall," he said.

"I've met Woody," she said. "He wouldn't do that."

Add it all up and there became an uncomfortable tightness in Bruce's chest. He went to the team doctor, Bob Murphy.

"Join the club," Murphy said. "You've got what every assistant who works for Woody gets."

Stress. Anxiety. Inner anger. Call it what you will. And the more coaches kept their emotions in, Murphy told him, the worse it became. Every coach had to figure how to work it out on his own, the doctor said. He suggested one remedy: Go home at night, take a Valium, sit in a hot bathtub, and curse at Woody in private. Don't be shy. Get it all out. Behind that closed door, tell him what you really think.

As 1968 went on, Bruce began to take the doctor's medicine more and more.

"Who's daddy talking to?" his young daughters would ask from outside the door.

(7)

One morning near the end of his freshman year, Rex Kern woke up and realized he couldn't get out of bed.

Worse: he could barely move at all.

As Kern had moved from basketball season to spring football, he was nagged by what seemed like a hamstring problem. It had flared up in basketball. It hampered him in football. He had to miss some practice, and during the spring game, taped the hamstring heavily so he could play.

But now, as doctors investigated this latest issue, the diagnosis wasn't a hamstring issue anymore.

It was his back.

Nor was it something he could tape up and play on. He had a ruptured disc that needed surgery. His athletic career was in jeopardy. So was his college education.

At the time, many players didn't return to big time sports after major back surgery. And it was an unwritten rule in college sports that the scholarship was tied to playing. The team physician, Jud Wilson, said everything would be fine, that they'd just go in and clip off the offending piece in his back. Kern trusted him. His faith told him whatever happened was for the best. But for a 19-year-old whose life had revolved around sports, and whose game revolved around speed and passing and being hit, this was serious business.

Kern had never been seriously hurt before, much less undergone surgery. What added to the strangeness was he didn't even know how this injury had occurred. As best he could guess, he had injured his back while high jumping in a physical education class. As he twisted his body one day, he felt a twinge in the back. But it hadn't even kept him from playing basketball that day or football that spring.

After surgery on June 19, 1968, Kern was resting in his hospital bed when Hayes asked to talk to his parents out in the hall. When they returned, they informed their son what Hayes had said: no matter whether he played another down of football, his scholarship would be honored, as would Hayes's recruiting pledge to make sure a degree was earned. It was Earle Bruce's story from 1951 all over again. For a family preparing for the worst-case scenarios, this lightened the concern considerably.

The Kerns were a quintessential midwestern story. Trenton ran a two-chair barbershop in Lancaster. As a youth, Rex swept the floors. He once tried to cut a friend's hair, and the comical result suggested he'd find a career elsewhere.

Rex means "king" in Latin, so people imagined greatness had been forecast for Kern from the start. Of course, his parents joked that in naming their son the only Rex either of them knew was a dog on his mother's side.

Trenton played baseball growing up, but his wife supplied the athletic genes. Jean Ritchie was all-everything in Amanda, a star in softball, basketball, track, seemingly whatever sports she tried. Trenton would tell their sons that if their mom and her sister weren't saddled with the daily chores of the family farm they could have competed in the Olympics.

Sports came naturally to Rex, too. He stood out at every level in any sport. At 5, he began playing baseball, and, perhaps since it was his first sport, his first goal was to make the major leagues. At Lancaster High, he was a three-year starter at third base, hit .460 as a senior, and led the school to the state semifinals. The Kansas City Athletics drafted Kern that summer. Later, as people marveled that he played football and basketball at Ohio State, George Hill, who was Kern's high school basketball coach and later an Ohio University assistant, said in 1969, "As good as he is in football and basketball, the boy could be a major league baseball player."

Basketball quickly became his favorite sport as a kid, which wasn't surprising. Woody Hayes said no one ever made a tackle with a smile on his face. But basketball players smiled. It was a fun game to play. Even in winter, Kern slept with his clothes on so he could wake up and immediately play basketball with his older brother, Keith, before school started. As with many teammates, the championship Ohio State basketball teams of the early 1960s inspired him. On the Lancaster courts, he would often be Mel Nowell, John Havlicek, or Larry Siegfried.

"I could never be Jerry Lucas," he said. "I could never throw up the little 'Johnson & Johnson soft baby hook.'" That was the expression TV announcer Jimmy Crum coined for the shot. It showed just how closely Kern followed the games.

He was a three-year starter at Lancaster High, averaged 23 points as a senior, and left with the school's scoring record. He also jumped center despite being only 6 feet, and typically he guarded the opponent's biggest man. By the time he was a junior, it was the college basketball coaches who began to come around. Ohio State coach Fred Taylor reached out to Kern a full year before Woody Hayes made contact.

Football, meanwhile, was all sandlots and backyards for Kern until seventh grade. One day, watching a Pop Warner team practice, he began throwing passes on the sidelines with a friend. He was immediately asked to play quarterback. Unlike the other two sports, football appealed to his unbounded aggressiveness. As the starting safety, he led the team in tackles his junior and senior years. By then, his quarterback talents were obvious, and he was blessed with sound coaching, which accelerated his progress in the coming years. The quarterback option he became renowned for at Ohio State, for example, wasn't learned in college. He was taught its intricacies at Lancaster High.

At 6-0 and 175 pounds, Kern didn't cut an imposing figure. He did have one physical gift that contributed to his reputation as a magician with the ball: the size of his hands. George Chaump measured them. They were 8½ inches from the tip of his finger to the start of his wrist. The stretched span from his thumb to his index finger was 9½ inches. Decades later, when Chaump was asked to write a chapter on "Perfecting Quarterback Fakes" in a coaching book, he would offer Kern's hands as an example of how size does matter.

Still, from normal size to boyish looks, the first impression of Kern didn't translate into a superstar. When tackle Dave Cheney met him at the annual Ohio All-Star Game in August of 1967, he observed Kern closely in practices. He had read all about Kern's talent, and they were part of Ohio State's incoming freshman class. But Cheney detected nothing special in Kern's play.

"Then we got in the game and you saw it right away," Cheney said. "We didn't practice a lot together, as you can imagine, and Rex was a master of the broken play. That's when I first noticed how good he was. If something broke down, Rex would take off. You could just see he was a different talent."

Kern's athletic gifts were matched by an aura he projected. He carried himself in a way teammates admired. The first word most of them used to describe Kern was: leader. The second word: Tough. One description backed up the other in the athlete's world, and he expected those attributes of himself, too.

His leadership was an invisible force, like gravity, something tangible that all players felt, black or white, young or old, star or reserve. He had a gift, Bruce Jankowski observed, to match the moment with not just the proper thing to say, but the proper tone to say it in. In the huddle, he could be serious and tell Foley, "Duke, we need this block," or Jankowski, "'Ski, you've got to beat him. You got to get open." But after a good play in games with the most tension he could also smile and say, "Hey, got that one, didn't we? Let's keep it going."

"He made everyone feel part of the team," Jankowski said. "And he made you feel good about yourself, made you feel like an instrumental part, no matter what your role was."

If Kern's in-game manner was serious, the full scope of his personality stretched far beyond that. He had all the red-haired look and mischievous nature of Huck Finn. In this regard, he wasn't the stuffy star on the marquee. He was just one of the boys. With teammates he threw water balloons at passersby from high up in their dorm room. He'd tickle a piece of grass against Hayes's neck in a practice, and they silently chuckled when Hayes slapped at it like a mosquito. He had one of the team-best impersonations of Hayes, too.

"Do a Woody," teammates would ask him. If he felt the moment was right, he'd jut his jaw and rock on his heels and bust into a "Mmm-hmmm, sons of bitches, mmm-hmm."

Hayes would sometimes catch Kern in the act. But if he cared, he didn't show it. He, too, was caught under Kern's spell. Teammates quickly picked up on it. Jim Stillwagon would break into a Woody imitation around Kern and tease, "Aw, my boy, Rex. This is my son. You can't hurt my son."

On the 1968 team's picture day, Hayes looked at Sensibaugh wearing jersey Number 3. "That's not your high school number," Hayes said. "Don't you want to wear your number from high school? What was it anyway?"

"Number 10," Sensibaugh said.

Kern's number.

"Oh," Hayes said, walking away.

If Kern's personality and leadership skills were tangible, his toughness gave him credibility. What later became evident before thousands on the football field was seen in the privacy of a basketball practice Kern's first winter in Columbus. Since freshmen weren't eligible, he was relegated to helping the varsity. Being a newcomer, he was tested. One practice, Kern saw a lane to the basket and went in strong for a layup. As he went up with the ball, he was nearly decapitated by a beef sandwich consisting of Bill Hosket, a 6-8, 225-pound senior who would be an Olympian and NBA star, and Dave Sorensen, a 6-8, 220-pound sophomore who also would have an NBA career.

Kern's nose was broken. His lip was bleeding. Trainer Ernie Biggs took one look and told Taylor to sub in another player. But as Taylor motioned to do so, Kern went back on the court and took the ball. He ran the same play. He made the same move. This time, when he went up for the layup against Hosket and Sorensen, he made sure to score.

Even that freshman basketball season, the tug of football was always there. Hayes called him to the side one day before basketball practice began.

"Rex, come with me, I need you to help me recruit," Hayes said.

Kern said he couldn't. He had to practice. There was a game the next night. Hayes insisted. "Have you talked to Coach Taylor?" Kern asked.

Hayes stomped off. Ten minutes later, he returned and said it was fine for Kern to come with him. They drove a few hours through a wicked snowstorm to Avon Lake to watch Dick Wakefield play a basketball game. The storm was so bad Hayes had actually sent Wakefield a telegram saying he wouldn't be attending the game as he had promised. But there Hayes was, driving 60 mph in awful conditions. "All of a sudden we hydroplane, do a complete 360, and come out heading in the same direction," Kern said. "I'm scared to death. Woody stopped talking for ten minutes."

They made the game and Wakefield became a star receiver at Ohio State. But the result for Kern, other than being told by football coaches never to ride in a car when Hayes was driving, was the next night's basketball starting lineup. He wasn't in it. He sat the bench. All the other players were put in the game. Finally, an assistant told Kern, "We're under orders not to play you tonight." They thought he skipped practice the day before. Hayes hadn't asked anyone for permission to take him.

One of Kern's disappointments at Ohio State would be that he never had a real chance to play basketball. He started on the freshman team. But the football season ran so long and his body was so damaged in 1968 that he would never have the time to be the Nowell or the Havlicek of his youth. Football quickly became his public identity. By that sophomore season's end, a sign would be placed at the city limits of Lancaster: *Welcome to Kernville.*

But as he sat at home the summer before that season, waiting for his back to heal, wondering what his athletic future was, such a possibility seemed far away. He did very little for nearly six weeks. The question of his back was always there, but he didn't dwell on it. His optimism carried him through, as did his faith. For the first several weeks after surgery, his most significant exercise didn't involve any running or jumping or stretching at all.

It consisted of bowing his head in prayer.

(8)

12 July 1968

Dear Woody,

Hope you remember me from Vung Tau. Remember the Lt. from the Pacific.
The drunk one when you were with Lt. Bogden. I never did see you again. Hope
your tour and stay here was relaxing and comfortable. I am sure, if all the other
GIs are like myself, that you inspired a lot of boys. It really did my heart good
to see a football coach . . . that really takes an interest in the American cause and
the men that are fighting for it. . . .

> *Sincerely yours,*
> *Bounty Hunter 21*
> *David C. Burch*

For twenty-one days in June, Hayes went on his third goodwill trip to
Vietnam. He bent over a hospital bed to ask a soldier who hadn't drank or eaten
in thirteen days, "You've had it pretty rough, haven't you, son?" He talked
with an African American sergeant who tried to rescue a white soldier only to
need rescuing by a few white soldiers himself. He went by helicopter or military
convoy with Bill Hess, his former assistant and current Ohio University coach,
to places like Pleiku and Da Nang to show Big Ten highlight films. He answered
questions in Saigon from a transportation company: about the first quality he
looks for in a player ("personal character"), the team to beat this upcoming Big
Ten season ("Purdue"), and if Southeastern Conference teams could play with
Big Ten schools ("I have my doubts they could stand up against consistently
bigger teams through a full season").

In a complex era of civic unrest and changing mores, Hayes's beliefs were
simple, declarative. He believed in the Vietnam War. He trusted the American
government. He was a football coach, military lover, and hero-worshipper.
He saw his heroes again on this trip. Some were the boys he met fighting for
America. Others were the men who led them. He talked with them in a jargon
they both understood.

"What rules do you live by?" he asked General Lewis Walt, whom Hayes
admired for passing up a Chicago Bears offer to join the Marines.

"He who would be first among you must be the servant of all," Walt said.

"What is the essence of leadership?" Hayes asked General Creighton W. Abrams.

"A man must know what he can do, and he must be himself," Abrams said.

His office wall in St. John Arena had autographed pictures of these Vietnam generals. "To Woody," the one from General William Westmoreland was inscribed, "Thanks much for your support." Over the coming months, he often injected into any conversation his thoughts on these generals or the Vietnam situation, deploring the "acceleration of lawlessness" that Communist governments encouraged, as he once told reporters.

"If we don't start living by our laws, there won't be any laws," he said. "We respect rules in football. We have to live within the rules. Maybe we don't like them. When we don't, we try to have them changed."

Hayes lived the mixed metaphor of football and war. The Battle of Britain was "the greatest goal line stand ever," he said. General William Tecumseh Sherman's march through the South in the Civil War showed coaches that a "successful offensive team must maintain the initiative over the defense."

To Hayes, there was no difference in the tactics generals used in war and those he used in football. When writers asked how he used safety Jack Tatum, Hayes would say, "Remember what General Von Schlieffen said, 'Keep your flank strong.'" When asked about overcoming a more experienced team, he'd say, "There's no substitute for experience and you can't do anything about it when you don't have it. But as General Patton said, 'Never take counsel of your fears.'"

Once, after a game, Hayes drew a diagram on the blackboard for reporters and vowed his team would never get caught repeating Hitler's blunder at Stalingrad.

"I'll be damned if I'll ever let anybody pin us down on the goal line," he said. "If they want to dig in there to stop Jim Otis, fine! Go ahead and stop Otis. Then, by God, we'll fake the ball to Otis and take it away from him. Kern will throw the pass. Or he'll run wide on the option."

He then quoted Sun-Tzu, who wrote in *The Art of War*: "The worst policy is to besiege walled cities."

"Yes," Hayes said, "or to attack a man in his foxhole. A defender in his foxhole is damn near impregnable. You can't block him until you coax him out."

In his 1957 book, *Football at Ohio State*, the chapter on scouting was introduced by a segment called "The Margin of Victory: Midway." He wrote of that World War II battle: "Here is an excellent example of an underdog team achieving victory while operating under a plan of action that was ingeniously conceived, accurately evaluated, and intrepidly carried out."

Once, when a reporter tired of this, it wasn't for the politically incorrect mixing of war and football. Tom Pastorius, who wrote for the *Columbus Citizen-Journal*, threw up his arms and stomped away as Hayes talked of Patton. "Aw, Woody, you weren't even there," he said. "You were in the Pacific. I was *there.*"

Pastorius had fought in the Battle of the Bulge. "Tom, Tom," Woody went chasing down after him, as Kaye Kessler watched. "You were there? Tell me about it."

Hayes collected Patton stories like kids did baseball cards. After all, he called his Ohio State offense "Red One," which was the name of Patton's army that romped across Europe in World War II. The essential audible calls of his offense —"Patton 1" and "Patton 2"—were the fundamental plays of fullback over left tackle and over right tackle (the passing series was named after Air Force General Curtis LeMay, an Ohio State alum).

That summer in Vietnam, Abrams told Hayes a story of Patton's leadership. After an especially trying stretch, the general called his officers to a farmhouse not to discuss strategy but simply to express his appreciation. Hayes's study of history was such that he knew Abrams drove the first of Patton's tanks into Bastogne during the Battle of the Bulge.

"Is it true that General Patton once said he had only one peer as a tank commander, and that was a man named Abrams?" he asked the American general in front of his troops.

"Some newspaper man wrote it that way, but he never said it to me," Abrams said.

For three weeks, Hayes didn't stop working, speaking several times each day, visiting twelve of the twenty-two U.S. hospitals in Vietnam, always wearing army fatigues and a block "O" cap. He carried a small notebook with him that he kept in his shirt pocket. While talking with a soldier he'd ask his name, then, "Where are you from, son?" He'd jot it down, as well as a phone number and details about the soldier. Upon returning to Columbus in early July, he called or wrote the parents of more than a hundred soldiers he had met.

He called Jeff Hall's parents in Zanesville. He phoned the Cambonis of Grove City to say he met their son in Nah Trang. He called a mother in Akron with news of her son. "If you were here right now, I'd give you a big hug!" she

73

said. He drove to the home of Paul Ballard in Grandview and showed his mother photos of her son.

Lucille Peterson, who had moved from Zanesville to Hollywood, Florida, received this letter:

Dear Mrs. Peterson:

I returned from Vietnam last night. During my visit,
I ran into your son, Larry. As you probably know he is stationed at a radar site
on top of the mountain, Bung-Tau.

At the time I saw him, which was about two weeks ago, he had 94 days
left, so by this time it should be down to 80 days. He seems in excellent spirits
and of course is looking forward to getting home. I am sure you are very proud
of your son for the job he is doing in Vietnam.

My reason for visiting Vietnam is merely to say 'thanks' to the many fine
young men who are there. Young men just like your son, Larry. Also your son,
Jim, who has been there for three years.

Sincerely,
Woody Hayes, head football coach, Ohio State University

Hayes regretted one thing about his trip: he was close to the front for only about a day and a half.

"Next year, I hope we can get up there and do more," he said.

Already, he was plotting his return trip. He told the troops if Ohio State won the Big Ten and played in the Rose Bowl he'd return with the game film.

(9)

That summer, Bill Mallory wanted to check up on his defensive linemen, but he didn't trust his 1960 Volkswagen bug to survive the rounds. So he got Hayes to approve the use of a university car, pulled out a map, and one by one, visited his players.

He drove a few hours north to Oberlin to see Jack Marsh one day, then an hour south to Chillicothe another day to see Vic Stottlemyer and John Sobolewski. Brad Nielsen was in Columbus and Jim Stillwagon was an easy drive to Mount Vernon. Paul Schmidlin was in Perrysburg.

The longest trip was to Donora, Pennsylvania, where Bill Urbanik lived.

Mallory broke up the five-hour drive by visiting an aunt in West Virginia.

To each player, Mallory took a piece of equipment he had designed and the equipment staff had constructed. It was a pad for the linemen to practice their forearm shiver technique, which was the motion to gain leverage against blockers. It was built so it could be nailed to a tree. It spoke more about Mallory's search for a winning edge, his players figured, than any tangible benefit to their games.

Mallory was always searching, always pushing, always in their corner, the players felt. At 33 that summer, his secret dream was to become head coach at his alma mater, Miami (Ohio) University, and in 1968 he couldn't have known that was just a year away.

He understood what it meant being on Hayes's football tree, though. Hayes disciples were popping up everywhere. At Miami, Mallory had played for Ara Parseghian, who began his career there as Hayes's freshman coach and in 1968 was coaching Notre Dame. Mallory had been an assistant at Bowling Green under Doyt Perry, who also was on Hayes's Miami staff. When Mallory moved to Yale, the coach was Carmen Cozza, who also played for Hayes. Having been with Parseghian, Perry, and Cozza, Mallory figured Hayes had plenty of references to hire him.

He wasn't going to pass up the chance to work with Hayes, even though the job carried the identical $12,000 salary he was making at Yale. Moving expenses weren't included, either. He and his wife, Ellie, drove a U-Haul truck to New Haven, Connecticut, loaded their belongings, and drove back in one day just to keep down the price of the truck rental.

"You still awake?" Bill would ask, driving the return leg.

"Yeah, you still awake?" Ellie would say back. They were so tired by the end they dropped the washing machine, denting it, while unloading it at their Columbus home.

Mallory loved the life, though. His defensive linemen were small even for the times. None weighed more than Paul Schmidlin's 220 pounds. Nor were they particularly gifted athletes, with the sizeable exception of Stillwagon, whom Mallory ranked as the best lineman he ever coached. The group's overall talents consisted of a measured quickness, which was important. Even more important, Mallory thought, is that they were what he called "program players." Hardworking. Disciplined. Great attitudes.

That's how Mallory saw himself. And those attributes, he told them, is what would win games.

Mallory enjoyed working with his players, and the feeling was mutual. "Maddog," the players nicknamed him, for the manner in which he jumped around and actually foamed at the mouth when he became excited. If he wanted to impress a technique on a player, he wouldn't just describe it or walk the player through it. In shorts and T-shirt, he'd get down in a stance in front of an offensive lineman.

"Fire out and hit me hard," he'd tell the offensive lineman, because he wanted to show the technique at full speed. The lineman did exactly that. Mallory often left the drills with a bloody nose or lip.

"Man, Maddog, he's something," the players whispered to each other.

Besides the defensive line, Mallory was in charge of the movie projectors and the weather. Well, not the weather itself. That was Hayes's department. It became part of Hayes's legend how, one day, during a driving thunderstorm with lightning, he told everyone in the locker room to get ready and buckle up for practice.

Don't worry, he said. He'd stop the weather. The players were laughing at this idea when, suddenly, the rain stopped. And the wind died.

For nearly ninety minutes under dark skies, they practiced. Finally Hayes said, "Okay, that's it. I can't hold it back." They ran into the locker room just as it began to hail.

"Hey, Coach, do you walk on water?" Phil Strickland asked.

"Not recently," Hayes said.

Mallory simply had to read the daily weather report in the 8 a.m. staff meeting. Either he, or more often Ellie, called to Port Columbus just before the meeting. Sometimes Mallory looked out the window on his drive into the office and made up some report.

He was a football coach, after all, not Ted Baxter.

Folded into this duty was assuring that, when needed, the field was properly covered. Hayes was obsessed about field condition. In 1966, this led to the entire coaching staff meeting at 3 a.m. during a downpour to pull the tarp on the Ohio Stadium field. Lou McCullough, awakened from his bed, was in his pajamas. Larry Catuzzi was wearing a ruined cashmere sweater.

"Welcome to the big time!" Hugh Hindman said to Mallory.

That was part of working for Woody, Mallory figured. But these summer trips were an extension of what kind of coach he was, of Maddog at work. Every assistant monitored his players in his own manner. Holtz, for instance, had his defensive backs sign a contract before they left for the summer, listing the time in which they'd run the mile upon their return to school. That, he felt, guaranteed they would work to meet that goal.

On his visits, Mallory would help a player nail the new pad to a tree in his backyard, then put him through a workout there, honing the player's technique. They'd then go to a local track. Mallory would have the player run 20-yard warm-ups, followed by a couple of 40-yard sprints. He'd then time a 440-yard dash, and finally a mile run, to gauge the player's shape.

To most of the linemen, this wasn't a favorite part of summer. To one, especially, running was like factory work. Urbanik hated it. But he knew the first day back at practice they would be timed in a mile run. Each position had a different time requirement. If a player didn't make it, he would have to report the next day at 7 a.m. He'd have to keep reporting at that time, until the mile was properly run.

On that first day of practice, after a summer of visiting and phone calls, Mallory was sure all his players would make the mile except Urbanik. That's why, roughly halfway in, Maddog began running with Urbanik. And not just running with him. Yelling beside him. Cursing at him. Anything to move him across the finish line in time.

As he crossed the line, Urbanik fell to the ground, heaving like a horse.

"Did I make it?" he said.

"You made it," the timekeeper said.

Urbanik looked at Mallory in exhaustion and relief. "Shake my hand," he said.

Happily, Maddog did.

Of dreams, daring, and
dying

*P*icture Day. September, 1968. The seniors took the first row. The juniors got the second row. It was the normal pecking order to photographed permanence that every team followed, and so the underclassmen were sent to the remaining rows. As everyone moved into position on the small bleacher on the field, Hayes went before the team with an announcement.

"Jim Conroy, come down here," he said.

Conroy, a walk-on lineman, wondered what this was about. As a freshman, he had been meat for the varsity. Now a sophomore, he had returned in great shape, running the required mile earlier that morning in five minutes, 23.5 seconds, the fastest of any lineman. His athletic genes didn't make him destined for a spot in the lineup or even, he figured, to be called before the team like now. *What was happening?*

"Anyone who has conditioned themselves as well as you have, and reported in such condition, deserves to be put on scholarship," Hayes said.

He then gave Conroy a tie clasp with a block "O" on it. Hayes shook his hand. Conroy, decades later a successful lawyer, considered the moment one of his life's highlights, right down to Jim Roman jokingly asking afterward if he ran track in high school.

Six players in that sophomore class were walk-ons, survivors of what began the previous year as more than a hundred students trying out. After two weeks of workouts, dozens were cut. After an imposed minimum ACT test

John Brockington, leading Leo Hayden

score, thirty-three remained. Of those, six were now left. Another walk-on, Bruce Smith, had his moment of moments the previous spring. After making a tackle one day in practice, he was getting up when Hayes came charging in, patting him on the shoulder, and grabbing his hand to shake.

"You just got a battlefield promotion!" he shouted at Smith. "You just earned a scholarship!"

A third walk-on, standing in the fifth row for the team picture, was a player whose unheralded presence contained a powerful story never known by many of his teammates. Rick Hausman grew up in the Columbus suburb of Hilliard, an All-District pitcher on the high school baseball team and a star linebacker on the football team.

Like most youth around Columbus, Ohio State was a focal point of sports interest. Hausman went to Buckeye football games with a school friend, who was a son of the team doctor. So when he decided to go to Ohio State, he also decided to walk on the football team to test his talent, and he hoped, show he could play at the school he always had followed.

In many ways, he was happy practicing with his hometown team, enjoying the locker room camaraderie, even having his family come down on the Friday night before home games to eat hamburgers on picnic tables under the stadium with the other players' families.

At some point during that '68 season, however, he felt pulled in another direction. Maybe he tired of school. Maybe, since his father fought in World War II, he thought he should serve a country embattled in another fight. Several players had friends who had enlisted in the military, served in Vietnam, and come back with a seemingly more mature attitude and focused habits.

Hausman joined the army sometime during that 1968 season, and by the time the team was preparing for the Rose Bowl, he had been shipped to boot camp. On March 17, 1969, he arrived in Vietnam. In early May, his younger sister, Ann, was having dinner with her boyfriend at The Explorers restaurant when they saw Hayes eating across the room. They went up to him, talked about her brother's plight, and got Hayes's autograph.

A few weeks later, on May 27, Private First Class Henry Richard Hausman died in a battle in Phuoc Long, South Vietnam.

A scene that played out thousands of times across America involved Ohio State football for the only time. Most players never knew of their fallen teammate. The word trickled out to a couple of walk-ons at the time, but only as a whisper months later. Hayes, however, went to the family's home immediately when the word came and expressed his sympathy to Hausman's parents. He visited the funeral home in downtown Hilliard for the service.

Decades later in Washington, Jim Conroy searched the Vietnam Wall and found his fellow walk-on's name—Panel 23W, Line 1. Just to remember. Just to consider two paths taken.

Ann Hausman married her boyfriend from that time, Greg Lisk. For years, the 1968 Ohio State team photo has hung in a hallway of their home. There is Rick, Number 96, in the fifth row between Ed Lapuh and Jack Marsh.

Ann and Greg named their son Henry Richard Hausman. Now grown, the son and his wife were expecting a child in the fall of 2008. If it was a boy, he, too, would be named Henry Richard Hausman.

(2)

Day by day, little by little, as July turned to August and August inched toward September, Rex Kern's back began to feel better. The day he walked without any pain was a milestone. Then he was able to do some light stretching. In early August, he jogged a mile. These small landmarks represented significant gains as he tried to regain a foothold into his athletic life. Hayes sent down a leg curl machine, but Kern was unable to use it much. He didn't do any of the work his teammates were doing to prepare themselves for the season—no conditioning, no strength exercises, no throwing the football to get his arm in shape.

Over the coming season, Kern came to wear the badge of the injury-prone. Back, jaw, head, shoulder—he was a litany of broken body parts. And maybe he did have a physical nature more fragile than others. But if so, it was compounded by another problem: Due to the back surgery, his entire preparation for the season consisted of about a week of serious physical conditioning. When summer practice began, his weight had dropped about ten pounds to 167. His strength wasn't back, either. The back injury, he figured in later years, had a residual effect on the rest of his body in the season.

One bonus for Kern was that Ohio State had one of the more progressive training and medical staffs in the country. On the advice of the school's dean of dentistry, who traveled with the team, they began making and wearing mouthpieces in 1966, long before it was fashionable. When linemen's necks became sore from blocking, trainer Ernie Biggs and equipment manager Phil

Bennett invented from Resilite the horse-collar pad. When Dirk Worden's helmet kept tilting forward, bloodying the bridge of his nose, they invented the four-snap chinstrap to better hold it in place. Individual pads were formfitted out of fiberglass onto the bruised arms and legs of players.

Mike Bordner, in his third season as a trainer in 1968, considered Biggs "an *Encyclopedia Britannica* of getting people well." Kern would test that knowledge in the coming season. Heat was used before workouts. Ice was put on his back after practice. Whirlpools. Ultrasound. Diathermy to send healing electro-currents. Kern wiggled into an orthopedic corset to provide back support. He also wore a brace with two metal rods that ran down his spine.

As much as he willed it out of his head, Kern couldn't help but think of his back's status when in late August he was pronounced ready to practice with the team. One early practice consisted of a controlled scrimmage. First-team offense vs. first-team defense. Or, better yet, Hayes vs. McCullough. They were already at it.

Kern was given a yellow jersey, which meant he was off-limits to the defense. They could approach him. They could tap him with their hand, signifying they had tackled him. They just weren't allowed to hit him.

Everything proceeded fine until the offense faced a fourth-and-1 play. Woody, being Woody, called an option play involving Kern. He knew the defense couldn't tackle Kern, so who better to carry the ball for the demanding yard than the one player the defense couldn't tackle?

On the other side of the line, coaches were firing up the defense.

"C'mon, this is where games are won!" McCullough said.

"Who's gonna make the play?" Mallory said.

Kern took the ball down the line and saw the running back he could pitch the ball to was covered. He had to keep it. He turned inside with the ball and —WHAM! He was leveled from behind by Jim Stillwagon. It was the first time Kern had been hit since surgery. And it wasn't any tackle. It was a direct hit from the guy who would be voted college football's best lineman.

Kern stayed on the ground, mostly in fear, taking an inventory of his body parts. The practice field went quiet. Then Mt. Woody erupted.

"YOU SONUVABITCH, YOU'RE DONE!" Hayes shouted, running up to Stillwagon, smacking him in the helmet and shoulder pads. "YOU'RE FINISHED! YOU DON'T HAVE A SCHOLARSHIP ANYMORE!"

He motioned to a security officer, who had been attending practices ever since concern about Michigan spying had arisen several years earlier.

"OFFICER, GET THIS SONUVABITCH OUTTA HERE!" he said. "I DON'T WANT TO SEE HIM AGAIN!"

As Kern lay on the ground, hearing the swirl above him, the officer walked onto the field, took Stillwagon by the arm, and escorted him to the locker room. Once there, Stillwagon immediately began packing up his gear. The truth was, he wasn't especially happy at Ohio State. He had tired of being overworked as a freshman with no game-day payoff. The coaches were relentless. Now this.

Mallory, the defensive line coach, came into the locker room while Stillwagon was in the shower. He was actually foaming in the corners of his mouth, which happened when he was worked up.

"You did the right thing, Jim," Mallory said. "Don't worry, you did the right thing."

Stillwagon wasn't in a mood to be calmed. "Coach, I love you, you're a good man, but I don't need the rest of this," he said. "It wasn't a cheap shot. I didn't mean to hit him like that. It was just football."

Mallory continued trying to defuse the situation, but Stillwagon wasn't having it. He said he was packing up and transferring to West Virginia. He had thought about this before. Now, he figured, that might be the best thing. At this point, Stillwagon turned around and there stood Hayes.

"You did the right thing, Jim," he said.

"No, Coach, you took my scholarship," Stillwagon said. "This is not what I want."

"No, you did the right thing," Hayes said.

"I'm gonna leave, Coach."

"You don't want to do that," Hayes said.

"I think I do."

"Okay, go ahead and quit," Hayes said. "But what's your mom and dad going to say?"

Stillwagon went silent. His parents especially enjoyed having their son play right down the road. They had been in a car accident visiting him at the Virginia military school. Stillwagon had no response for this. Hayes knew the names of Stillwagon's parents, as he did every player's parents. These were easy ones to remember, though. Stillwagon's parents had virtually the same names as Hayes and his wife.

"What's Woody and Anna going to say?" Hayes asked.

This sucked the anger right out of Stillwagon. He got dressed, went back to his dorm room, and as the steam subsided, knew he wasn't going anywhere.

Meanwhile, on the practice field, Kern stood up. Again, he checked his back. He felt fine. Actually, he felt better than fine. He had just taken the first hit since surgery—a hit as big as any he could receive in a game. And he had gotten up and walked away. The fear of what might happen to his back was gone now. He was going to be okay. Confidence returned to his game.

"A wonderful christening shot," Kern called it.

Opening kickoff was three weeks away.

(3)

The sophomores may have been the emerging story, but the anchors of the team were a small group of seniors who were tough as walnuts, smart as textbooks, and hadn't fallen to injury, academics, losing, disenchantment, or some other predatory miscreant that ransacked their class.

One of the lost members, Jerry Tabacca, got a phone call from Earle Bruce just that summer saying that since he had played on the baseball team that previous spring, Woody was dropping his football scholarship.

"But he promised I could play baseball when he recruited me," he said.

Click.

Thirty-two players had entered as freshmen in 1965.

Sixteen survived to this senior season.

Five were starters.

Three of them—center John Muhlbach and tackles Rufus Mayes and Dave Foley—provided the foundation to the offensive line. Muhlbach, at 5-10 and 190 pounds, had a quiet toughness that somehow compensated for his lack of size. "Deacon," he was called, because he was a lay minister in the Episcopalian Church.

Mayes and Foley, meanwhile, were supreme talents. Each would become first-round NFL draft picks after this season. "The Twin Towers," they were being called by their senior year, because the tackles were bookend boulders to Ohio State's power-ball philosophy.

Just as they played on the opposite sides of the line, Mayes and Foley were the left and right of personalities, too. Mayes was friendly, outgoing, and rarely without a smile or a lighthearted comment. "A one-in-a-million man," said Jim Oppermann, who had a locker beside Mayes and played behind him. Each Thursday during the football season, Mayes's good-luck routine was to buy a new pair of boxer briefs to wear to the stadium on game day.

"Ruf," everyone called him, including the Ohio Stadium crowd in short-yardage situations. They knew what play was coming, who it often would come behind, and inevitably a chant circulated through the air:

"RUF! RUF! RUUUUF!"

The previous two seasons, Mayes played tight end. But there was one piece missing in Mayes's tight-end inventory: he had granite hands. Players jokingly counted his drops in practices. Hayes grew so frustrated he ordered Mayes to carry a football with him around campus every day to improve his feel for it. Good idea. Didn't help. In the eighteen games he started at tight end as a sophomore and junior, Mayes caught only 13 passes.

For Mayes's senior year, with tackle Dick Himes off to the Green Bay Packers, he moved to his natural position—tackle. It was like putting a round peg back in its proper round hole. His game wasn't physical force, as might have been expected. He moved with such fluidity for a big man, always having the proper balance and position on his opponent, that the rest of the linemen marveled.

Foley's game, by comparison, was as subtle as a punch in the face. By the tip-top standards he would be measured by in the NFL, he wasn't a great athlete. But what he lacked in foot speed or balance, he made up for in pure power and sense of purpose. He had an intense personality to match, too.

One of the perks of being an Ohio State player was watching movies for free at the State Theater on High Street. Foley loved John Wayne movies. *In Harm's Way. Cast A Giant Shadow. The War Wagon. El Dorado. The Green Beret.* They all came out during his college days, and he couldn't see them enough. His teammates picked up on this, as well as the rugged swagger he carried like Wayne.

"Duke," he became forever after, named for the actor.

While Muhlbach came from a powerhouse Massillon program, Mayes came out of Toledo with his pick of colleges and Foley was such a Cincinnati talent that Dick Butkus showed him around Illinois. And the final two senior starters arrived at Ohio State by happenstance. Even in a state where everyone from big time businessmen to the governor of Ohio aids your recruiting, they showed luck could be just as important.

And in the case of Dirk Worden and Mark Stier, Ohio State got all kinds of lucky. The pair were a coach's dream—smart, dependable, fundamentally strong kids who made up in will what they lacked in size. And tough? Worden, teammate Bill Hackett thought, was the toughest guy per pound on the team.

He looked the part, too. His helmet would ride down to the bridge of his nose, cutting it, and adding a gladiator's trickle of blood to his appearance.

Worden and Stier started at linebacker for three years and traded off as the team's Most Valuable Players in 1967 and 1968. But neither was recruited. At least not in the normal sense.

Worden was recruited so lightly as a senior in Lorain, Ohio, that he went to a West Virginia prep school for an extra year of high school in hopes of growing beyond his 5-11 and 175 pounds. His older brother, Jim, had been a late bloomer and shot to 6-2 and 225 pounds. Jim went from tiny Wittenberg College to playing for the Saskatchewan Roughriders of the Canadian Football League by the time Dirk was in high school. Their father, also named Jim, had played for the old Cleveland Rams of the National Football League.

So Dirk came from the family tree of football. And, to some extent, his year in West Virginia worked. He grew an inch and put on fifteen pounds. Still, no big-name school recruited him. None even called, actually. He always secretly hoped to attend Ohio State. As an 8-year-old, he sat in front of the family's little black-and-white TV, screaming for Ohio State, which was playing in the 1954 Rose Bowl. That day, he told his parents he wanted to be a Buckeye. He never lost the dream, either.

But now, after his fifth year of high school, he figured the dream had sailed. He was looking at Kent State or maybe Virginia. That's when fate, destiny, luck—whatever it's called—knocked on the door. Ohio State began recruiting a running back at his former Lorain Clearview High. One of the coaches there said Ohio State should look at this kid no one seemed to want. Films were sent to Hayes, who was impressed. Worden was invited to Columbus, and once there, offered a scholarship.

Stier was a similar afterthought. On the night of his high school football banquet in Louisville, Ohio, he was considering attending the Naval Academy. That night, Hayes came to the school to speak, mainly because he had been recruiting Stier's teammate, Bob Gladieux, who was deciding to attend Notre Dame instead. So the banquet took on the appearance of a salvage job for Hayes. Waste a trip? Not him. And in watching the film of Gladieux play for Louisville High, he noticed Stier. This undersized linebacker ran down ball carriers. He gave offenses fits. He did the sort of detail work that convinced Hayes to take a chance on his decent speed and average size.

Especially since Hayes had one final scholarship in his pocket. "You sure I'm good enough to do this?" Stier asked Hayes.

There was just enough doubt in Stier's mind to ask. He understood he wasn't Hayes's first choice for it. Or maybe even his fifth. But there was an equal amount of fuel in Stier for merely asking the question, too. Outwardly, he shrugged at his chances, saying he could just do his best. Inwardly, he was primed.

I'll show them, he said to himself.

As a sophomore in 1966, Stier couldn't believe he was starting for a football power like Ohio State. He figured the juniors and seniors would be that much better. He soon discovered the flaw in his thinking that was discovered by all the survivors of that class: Ohio State *wasn't* a power.

Okay, we're not fast and we're not big, he said to himself that year, analyzing the team. *How are we going to win?*

It played out that way, too. The losing record. The "fire Woody" sentiment. More than anyone else on the edge of the 1968 season, these seniors understood the change in talent and attitude. As a reminder, they just had to look across the practice field. In 1966, *their* sophomore class was being hailed as the future.

Now just half of them were left.

(4)

As the season approached, the starting battles took care of themselves in every case but one: fullback. Woody's signature position. A daily debate raged: Jim Otis or John Brockington. Otis was the junior incumbent, Brockington the hot sophomore. Otis was a prototypical fullback, thick and strong; Brockington was a new-age running back with an uncommon blend of size and speed. Otis was a star; Brockington, many felt, already stood out on a team of stars.

Otis was white.

Brockington was black.

And, while no one on the team publicly talked about this last point, it was discussed privately in the locker room, especially among the African American players. And it wore heavily on Rudy Hubbard, the new and lone black assistant who worked with the running backs.

Hubbard felt sympathetic to Brockington in a manner no one else could. He had finished playing for Hayes the previous year and thought he should have had a larger role than being primarily a blocking back. Did race contribute to that? He couldn't say. But he thought about it. He wondered if it did. His frustration bubbled to the surface after his senior season, after he had gotten the ball and starred against Michigan in a win that—some assistants thought—saved their jobs.

After the season, Hayes drove a few hours for an appreciation dinner thrown for Hubbard in his hometown of Hubbard, Ohio. The coach spoke first to the crowd and praised Hubbard in the manner expected at these types of affairs. Hard worker. Great character.

"And he's earning his degree, which is more important than any football he played," Hayes said.

Hubbard spoke next in a style never heard at such events. He questioned if Ohio State was the right school for him. He wondered why Hayes hadn't played him more. He said the coach handled him wrong. And he talked in such a loud and unrestrained manner that he remembered leaving that night thinking, *I'm guessing I'm done with Woody Hayes for the rest of my life.*

Two weeks later, Hayes called Hubbard. That was the first surprise. But what came out of that conversation was shocking. Hayes offered him an assistant coaching job. That told Hubbard something he never knew about Hayes, something profound that made Hubbard view his coach from a completely different angle. Hayes, he realized, was loyal to the guys who played for him no matter what they did or said. It was a one-way street. They were forever on his team.

Also, Hubbard suspected, since black assistants were becoming important commodities in college football, Hayes was reaching out in some manner to embrace the changing world. Just the year before, four black players didn't return to the team.

One of them, Glenn Hodge, was an especially significant loss. He had been practicing as a starter at both receiver and defensive back that spring of 1967. But a series of incidents left him uncomfortable with the program. He had quit once before, at which point Hayes called him into his office and asked why he hadn't talked about his concerns. This second time, there was no going back.

"I don't know what you guys did to him, but he says he's not coming back and that's that," Hodge's mother told Hayes when the coach called a second time.

Hodge, who returned to Ohio State to study and became a General Motors executive, thought if he could have talked more with Hayes that would have helped. But what was lacking from his two years of Ohio State football was someone in his corner, some coach he could talk with, some trusted voice to encourage or lecture or just give him some trustworthy counsel.

It was too late for Hodge, but starting in 1968, Hubbard would fill that role. With the largest African American class in Ohio State history now sophomores, it was a significant move. Hubbard would confront full-fledged racism in various forms at Ohio State. Decades later, he still had a letter from St. Petersburg, Florida, that threatened what would happen if he took that assistant's job in 1968. Once he was running outside his apartment building in Columbus when a security guard pulled a gun on him. Another time, on a recruiting trip in southern Ohio, he was told there was no vacancy at a hotel. At the next one, he was told the same thing. And the next. Finally, he had to sleep in a black-owned hotel far below the standards of an Ohio State coach.

When he told Hayes, the coach was livid. That mattered to Hubbard. As did the fact that Hubbard never heard—in any meeting or side conversation—any hint of prejudice from Hayes.

So when it came to Otis or Brockington, Hubbard didn't think Hayes infused race into the equation. Hubbard thought Brockington was the better player. No, he *knew* it. He wanted to support him, too, in a manner in which no one supported him as a player.

But Hayes, he figured, saw Otis as the perfect fullback for his 3-yards-and-a-cloud-of-dust philosophy. Otis was a star in his own right, too. He had won the starting job as a sophomore. He would go on to have a nine-year NFL career.

But if Otis was good, Brockington was rare. He didn't just have moves. He had power. And style. At almost every practice, his size and speed created some moment where everyone looked at each other and said, "Wow."

"It wouldn't surprise me a bit if he beats out the other two fullbacks," Hayes told reporters during spring practices, referring to Otis and Paul Huff.

"The guy runs with more desire than any back we've got," Hayes said in the first week of summer practice. "When he sees an opening, he really goes."

A *Columbus Citizen-Journal* story after a September 13 scrimmage struck on the inside debate surrounding each player. "John Brockington continued to impress with his patented broken field running," the story read. "He scored on a 3-yard plunge and turned in a half-dozen sparkling runs of the 15-25 yard variety." Otis, the story said, "punched over for two scores inside the five to give him four touchdowns for the fall practice."

On the final scrimmage before the opener, Brockington scored three straight touchdowns on a 70-yard run, a 3-yard run, and a broken fourth-and-11 play where Kern shoveled the ball to him. "It was another of many eye-popping performances from this New York newcomer," the story read.

Ultimately, the issue was this: did you want the newcomer sparkle of Brockington or the fundamental soundness of Otis? The question would grow louder the following season, Brockington felt, when he considered transferring to Syracuse. But even in 1968, players debated among themselves who should start. Affecting the locker room swirl, fairly or not, was how Jim's father had been Hayes's college roommate at Denison. Otis was seen as Woody's boy. That was one strike against him in the locker room culture.

But what gave the issue traction was that Hayes would solicit the defensive players as to who was better. Bill Hackett, a linebacker, told Hayes they were both strong runners, but Otis couldn't block. This was a shared idea. In 1969, third-string quarterback Kevin Rusnak felt Rex Kern and Ron Maciejowski were both injured in a game because Otis threw "lookout" blocks, as if shouting to his quarterback, "Look out!" Rusnak stepped in the huddle and said to him, "You've got two guys hurt. Don't give me one of those goddamn lookout blocks."

"Everyone said Otis was the best runner we had at getting the 3 or 4 yards on a third down," Maciejowski said. "Maybe that was true. But with Brockington you wouldn't *have* third-and-4. He'd gain 5 or 6 or 7 yards a carry."

By 1969, it became an all-out debate, sifting into each practice and staff meeting until Hayes had enough.

"Let's vote on it," he told his assistants.

It was Brockington 8, Otis 1. But this was democracy, Woody style.

"It's 1-8 against you sons of bitches," he told his staff.

When Otis was named the starter that year, the African American players held a meeting. Voices raised. Anger simmered. Plans were hatched. They talked of approaching Hayes with their questions. They talked of walking out on a practice. They talked of leaving the program altogether. They'd leave it in support of Brockington, if it came right down to it. Across the country, African American players were raising their voices in the self-discovery of the times. Would this be the issue that demanded a stand be taken by Ohio State's players?

That's when Brockington interrupted.

"There's no sense putting your scholarships on the line," he said. "I'll work through it."

Sitting in that dorm that night, Jack Marsh remembers sighing in relief.

He wasn't alone. Upset as they were, unfair as they thought this move was, they, like Marsh, didn't want to lose their scholarships.

Privately, the assistants counseled Brockington. Hubbard told him to focus on the work.

"John, keep your chin up," George Chaump said to him. "Your day will come."

It would, too. But, as this issue worked out in 1969, Brockington wasn't the only one whose nerves were frazzled. Hubbard became so stressed he lost a patch of hair.

In 1968, the issue became easier to deal with. Brockington just wanted to get on the field, not to be featured. He was named the starter at wingback. Otis was kept at fullback. Everyone happily moved on.

For now.

(5)

There was a cost for having so much young talent. It was not, as Hayes often said in speeches, "You lose a game for every sophomore you start." The cost was measured in dreams dying. Many of the upperclassmen expecting to start, and maybe star in the 1968 season, suddenly found themselves buried by the sophomores.

Ray Gillian was a starting wingback for much of the 1967 season. Suddenly, he was third string. Kevin Rusnak, who had made a start at quarterback in 1967, was relegated to split end. Paul Huff had been the UPI Midwest Back of the Week the previous November for gaining 120 yards and scoring two touchdowns against Michigan State in his first start. Now he was third string. By the following season, he would be a guard.

Perhaps no one felt the slap of this changing world harder than Bill Long. He had been the starting quarterback much of the previous two seasons. Now, after playing baseball in the spring, he returned in August to start his senior year and discovered how much the ground beneath him had shifted. He was listed as the Number Two quarterback behind Kern, just part of the change. He also learned Chaump's new offense with the "Rip" and "Liz" formations was up and running —up and passing, actually. What fun it was. What a change for a quarterback to learn overnight, too.

"Okay, I'll just work my way back up," Long told himself.

Long grew up in West Milton, a small town in southeastern Ohio, which was right off the paintbrush of Norman Rockwell. Its main street was called Main Street. Its town square was actually square. West Milton had a love of country, small-town values, and sports, and no family was bigger in that last category than the Longs. Bill's father, Bob, had played quarterback at Otterbein College outside of Columbus. He then became a successful high school coach in West Milton. Bill grew up on the school sidelines, one eye on when he could play in high school and the other on Ohio State. He saw his first game at Ohio Stadium when he was 7, watching Hopalong Cassady run for the Buckeyes. As a teenager, his heart broke when Ohio State's basketball team lost to Cincinnati for the championship game. Always, Columbus was Mecca.

In high school, the Longs moved to Dayton, and Bill was quarterback in the Ohio All-Star game and an All-Ohio shortstop. Stardom beckoned. So did Hayes. At halftime of an Ohio State basketball game, Hayes ushered Long up to his St. John Arena office. Long figured this would be where they talked football philosophy. Instead, Hayes pulled a copy of *Word Power Made Easy* off the shelf and grilled Long on vocabulary for ninety minutes.

What's this word mean? Can you use this in a sentence? How do you define this? By the end of the session, when Hayes closed the book and flatly asked if he was coming to Ohio State, Long's head was spinning. He wanted to visit other schools. "I'm 95 percent sure I want to come here," he told Hayes, "but I'd like to wait a little bit."

Later that night, while eating dinner with Long and his parents at the Jai Lai, Hayes called over Dayton sports writer Ritter Collett. "Bill has something to tell you," Hayes said.

Long, cornered, blurted out, "I'm going to commit to Ohio State."

It was Woody at his finest, closing the deal. As a sophomore, eligible for his first game, Long was told in the pre-game locker room that he would be the starting quarterback. He completed 12 of 14 passes in an easy win against Texas Christian. He started every game of the 1966 season, and as disappointing as the losing record was, threw for 1,180 yards, the second most in Ohio State history.

That first off-season, he planned to play baseball for Ohio State, as he had been promised. Hayes, as expected, lobbied him to play spring football. One day, Hayes called him into his office. Long walked across campus preparing his argument for baseball. The baseball team had a spring trip to California, after all. But when Long arrived at Hayes's office, his father and athletic director Dick Larkins were there, too. Long felt blindsided.

"They were talking about the athletic department's revenue losses, and how important it was for me to play football in the spring," Long said. "I gave in. I said, 'Okay.'"

He did play baseball over the summer, though, and returned for August football practices with a bad hamstring. Hayes was furious. He played Long sparingly the first four games. Finally, with the team 2-2, Long was reinserted as starter. The team went 4-1 the rest of the way and Hayes said, "We were not a football team until we got Bill back in there."

Was it all Long? Probably not. He completed 43 percent of his passes with two touchdowns and four interceptions. He did, however, win the games. Isn't that how you judge quarterbacks?

Long felt vindicated. And he played baseball again. He knew about the Super Sophomores. But he was the starting quarterback.

"Woody never sat down with me and said, 'Your job is on the line,'" he said.

Maybe that would have changed his decision to play baseball. Or maybe Hayes had become convinced, as Chaump already was, that Kern was that much better. Maybe the first clue was when Hayes never questioned Long playing baseball that spring. Maybe, Hayes figured, it made for an easier transition to Kern and Maciejowski.

All Long knew was that when he returned to practice that summer, like several upperclassmen, he was out of a job.

(6)

A few weeks before the season opener, the coaching staff realized they had speed, talent, attitude, discipline—everything that could make a special season. Except one thing. One very obvious, potentially very troublesome thing.

They had no kicker.

Kickers weren't actually recruited. On a team of about a hundred players, the idea was someone could kick a football. This went back to Lou "the Toe" Groza at Ohio State. Woody Hayes always found someone who could kick. But this team couldn't find anyone who stood out as a kicker. The coaches began frantically searching. Players were worked with. Coaching friends were called to see if they knew of someone who might know someone who could kick.

One day, through his Miami University connections, Bill Mallory struck gold. Miami's freshman kicker the previous year, a guy who booted a field goal 48 yards in a game, a guy who owned the high school record with a 55-yard field goal, was no longer at Miami. He had quit the team, and he was planning to attend Ohio State as a regular student.

Immediately, Mallory called Dick Merryman in the Ohio River town of Hannibal and explained the situation.

Would he like to kick for Ohio State?

"Well, I guess," Merryman said.

The truth was, Merryman hadn't so much as touched a football in well over a year. He had been a star running back and quarterback in high school, who also happened to have a mighty leg. It was the leg that got him the scholarship to Miami. But he had tired of the regimen under Bo Schembechler at Miami. He switched to Ohio State mainly because his girlfriend was there. And now, encouraged by family and needed by a big time team, Merryman walked into the football facility two weeks before the opener and introduced himself. He was given two bags of balls and pointed to a field.

"Go warm up," he was told.

A week later, in the final scrimmage of the season, Merryman was trotted out on the final play in a 30-0 game. He kicked a 33-yard field goal. The final score was 30-3. Ohio State had its kicker. At least for now.

"He can thump the ball," Hayes told reporters.

Years later, Merryman would say of that day: "I could have missed that field goal, and it would've been over with then. No one would have thought anything about it. Instead, it went on, and I have to think about what happened."

(7)

On a Sunday in late August, Ray Gillian had eaten dinner with his longtime girlfriend, Charell Harrison, at Kuenning's Midtown Restaurant. The players and a guest could eat there for free on Sundays since the college dining hall was closed. Gillian, a junior wingback, and Charell were Sunday regulars.

Nothing about this meal was regular, though. Over dinner, Gillian suggested they get married before the season started. The two had dated since high school in Uniontown, Pennsylvania, and had planned to be married the following May.

But Gillian's roommate, David Whitfield, had gotten married a few days earlier. That triggered the thought in Gillian: *Why wait?*

"Let's do it now, too," he said that dinner.

"But we had plans for next spring," Charell said.

"Yeah, but so what?" he said.

Mr. Romance, he wasn't. But he received points for spontaneity. Eventually, they set a new wedding date. September 22—Sunday before the opener. Less than a month away. That didn't matter to Gillian. But then he wasn't fazed by much, not even by his future father-in-law saying they had been expecting a May wedding and didn't have funds for one so immediate.

"That's okay," Gillian said, "I'll pay for it."

He got a $200 loan from athletic director Dick Larkins and went to tell Woody about his marriage plans, which could have been a problem. The coach wasn't always approving of such news. He didn't like his players waking up every morning next to "soft bodies," as he would say.

There were plenty of soft bodies waking up next to players, though, as marriage was a growing business on this team. Jim Roman. John Muhlbach. John Brockington. Whitfield. They were all married. Muhlbach, who also got married that summer, didn't just inform Woody. He asked for the coach's permission, as if Hayes controlled that decision like he did the off-tackle blocking assignment. Hayes leaned back in his chair for a second after Muhlbach asked if it was okay and looked over the desk, as if contemplating the idea.

"Well, goddammit, John, I think you can handle that," he said. "I know Bobbi. She's a good girl."

Muhlbach exhaled. He wasn't sure what he'd have done if Hayes held out his blessing.

Gillian simply told Woody he was getting married. The coach sounded happy about it anyway. So after the final Saturday scrimmage the week before the opener, Ray and his brother drove over to Uniontown. Charell, who was attending Bliss College in Columbus, was already there, finishing preparations.

That next day, in a simple ceremony in their hometown church, they were married. By the time the reception began, Rufus Mayes, Tim Anderson, Leo Hayden, Jan White, and Whitfield arrived from Columbus. After a few hours of eating and congratulating and laughing, everyone got back in their cars and drove back to school.

Ray and Charell's honeymoon consisted of a Monday off.

By then, the opener was six days away.

Birth of a
season

arti Radtke, an Ohio State senior, dropped her husband, Mike, off at Ohio Stadium on the Friday afternoon before the opener and kissed him goodbye. Mike would follow the weekly football routine from there: Practice. Shower. Check in at team hotel. Eat team dinner at Ohio State golf course. Watch team movie. Eat snack of hot chocolate, apple, and cookies that Hayes thought conducive to a good night's sleep. Go to bed. Wake up ready to play.

Marti, meanwhile, had a more unique day planned.

She was going to the hospital to deliver a baby.

Her water had broken before she dropped Mike off at the stadium. Not that she told him about it. He wouldn't learn until a student manager approached Radtke at the team hotel that night.

"Coach wants to see you," he told Radtke.

Radtke was scheduled to start at defensive end the next day and immediately thought the worst. Well, the worst that his world contained at the time. Had he lost his starting job? Had he done something wrong?

Radtke knocked on Hayes's hotel room door. Hayes answered it wearing a white dress shirt, tie, boxer shorts, and high dark socks. No pants. Radtke pretended not to notice. Hayes had been drawing plays on a blackboard in his room, though now, as his player entered, the coach broke the big news.

"Your wife is fucking everything up," he said.

Mike Sensibaugh

"Pardon me, Coach?" Radtke said.

"Your wife is in labor," Hayes said.

Radtke was stunned. "Can I go see her?" he asked.

"Goddammit, you're starting tomorrow, right?" Hayes said.

Radtke promised that if one of the managers could take him, he'd be back at the hotel by 9:30 p.m. Reluctantly, Hayes agreed. So Radtke was driven to Riverside Hospital, hustled to his wife's room, and immediately saw two "X" marks in black pen on her stomach. This was in the days before ultrasound, before firm due dates, before a more modern science would take some of the surprise out of the delivery room.

"What're the two Xs for?" he asked.

"The nurse is predicting I'm having twins," she said.

Mike was 19. Marti was 20. And they were having twins? They sat and talked and waited and wondered and planned and held hands and *Uh-oh, what time was it already?* Mike didn't feel comfortable leaving his wife. But he had promised he would be back to the team hotel at the anointed hour. Their doctor and Marti's sister promised to stay with her until the baby was delivered. Or the *babies*.

Radtke's family was hundreds of miles away in Wayne, New Jersey. A few years earlier, Hayes had visited their two-bedroom apartment and spent two hours talking to his mother. She didn't follow sports much. And Mike's dad was the firm head of the household. But Woody was following his recruiting master plan, and it worked again. As the door closed behind Hayes that evening, Radtke's mother turned to Mike and said, "It's over. You're done making trips. You're going to Ohio State."

That's how he became one of Larry Catuzzi's first out-of-state signings. And how the following year he met Marti on her birthday at the North Heidelberg campus bar. He was a freshman. She was a sophomore. They married in March of his sophomore year. Now, as a starting junior linebacker, he was about to become a father. Maybe twice over.

Upon arriving back at the hotel, Radtke wanted Hayes to know he had returned on time. Again, he knocked on Hayes's door. Again, Hayes brought him into the room. Again, he had been drawing up plays on the chalkboard.

And yet again, the coach had monovision.

"Now, I want to say one goddamn thing," Hayes said. "Women have babies every day of the year, and we only play SMU once this year."

He let that sink in a second.

"I want you to make sure your priorities are straight," he said.

Radtke looked at him. *Was this guy for real?* Some people might think his priorities already were a bit warped, given the fact that he was here and his wife was about to give birth. Radtke went back to his room that night and slept. Or tried to, anyhow.

He finally drifted off, wondering how Marti was doing. He woke up wondering the same. There was a general rule on game days that players didn't speak much and wore their game face. So Radtke, game face on, sidled over to a student manager and mumbled, "Did my wife have the baby yet?"

"I don't know," the manager said.

"I know you don't, but can you call the hospital for me?" he asked.

The news came back that, no, Marti hadn't yet delivered the baby. Or babies. As the players got their ankles taped at 8 a.m. in the hotel, there was no news. There was still none when they arrived at the stadium. Right up until kick-off, he had someone calling the hospital to find out if he was officially a father. The word kept coming back that he wasn't yet.

Then the ball went into the air. Southern Methodist's circus game came flying. And, well, dad was busy for a while.

(2)

A couple of hours before kickoff, Lou Holtz walked by his defensive backs in the locker room.

"They got off the bus throwing the ball," he said.

Holtz smiled as he said this. That was the relaxed mood he wanted to project. He pulled it off, too. Outwardly, Holtz was the picture of confidence and loose assuredness. Inwardly he was petrified. He hadn't been more nervous for a game in his young coaching life. It was his first game at Ohio State, and, as he wrote in his critique at the end of spring practice, "The defensive backfield has good talent but is woefully lacking in experience."

Sophomores Jack Tatum, Mike Sensibaugh, and Tim Anderson were starting their first game. And what a game they drew. Southern Methodist put up such passing numbers it made people dizzy. In an era when 20 passes was considered a wide-open offense, Southern Methodist led the NCAA with 33 passes a game in 1967. It threw 48 passes and scored 37 points in beating Auburn the week before this Ohio State game. Holtz went with Esco Sarkkinen, the regular advance scout, to watch the Auburn game. He came back saying the only way to prepare for receiver Jerry "The Jet" Levias was to "find a rabbit that could catch a football."

On Friday, Holtz put a mimeographed news report on the player lockers:

BEWARE

IT HAS BEEN REPORTED THAT THERE WILL BE
A "BOMB" SCARE!

"There have been reports from the various news media that SMU is expected to unleash many bombs in OSU Stadium on September 28. This uncalled-for attack of aggression upon the young OSU secondary . . . "

This was Holtz's personality, as they would realize that season. He often injected a smile into his message. He had two magic tricks—one with cards and another with a newspaper he'd rip up and reassemble—that he used to lighten the moods. But if the smile didn't get across the message, an iron fist was waiting. When Tim Anderson was two minutes late to one of the secondary's first meetings under Holtz, he said, "Son, if you're late to another meeting, I'll have your scholarship taken away."

Message sent. Message received. No one was late for another meeting.

What won the players over to Holtz's side were neither tricks nor discipline. It was his thinking. His ingenuity. Sensibaugh played eight years in the NFL and felt there was no transition from the system Holtz introduced to him. For juniors Ted Provost and Mike Polaski, who were versed in the previous years' system, it was like stepping from a black-and-white world to a colorized one. The playbook was thick. The schemes were complicated. There were double zones. There was man-to-man coverage on the corners with two-deep zones for the safeties. Sometimes players switched assignments to confuse the offense. Down, distance, opponent's tendencies—Holtz expected his players to understand all of it.

This wasn't like coaching running backs who needed little help, Holtz thought. Coaching the secondary was an involved process. It was doubly so with such a young group.

"Gentlemen," Holtz said to his players that summer, "we take film of what we do around here. I'm going to teach you the techniques to play. If you go out and do the techniques, you'll play. If you don't do them as I teach, we have someone to take your place."

In that first game, Sensibaugh had one interception and nearly two. But instead of lining up 12 yards from the line of scrimmage as Holtz demanded, Sensibaugh kept playing deeper and deeper as Southern Methodist kept throwing the ball. "I'd like to give you a grade, son, but I can't find you in the film," Holtz told him the next day.

Sensibaugh didn't start the second game against Oregon.

Against Oregon, Anderson became the lesson. Holtz clicked the film back and forth to show Anderson, so excited before plays that he was practically dancing as the ball was snapped. Holtz expected players to take a shuffle step when the ball was snapped, then freeze. If it was a running play, you planted off your back foot and moved forward. If a pass, you moved off the back foot into position.

"Timmy, did I teach you that?" Holtz asked in the film session after the second game.

Anderson went to the bench.

So went Holtz's class in Secondary 101 early that season. But on the edge of this first test against Southern Methodist, he wasn't sure just what kind of team he had. Talented? Sure. Seasoned? No way. And so as the kickoff went up, he said a little prayer, the way he always did, "Please, Lord, let's just make it through this."

(3)

Across the years, whenever Elvis Presley was asked when his star was launched, he inevitably pointed to a few nights on *The Ed Sullivan Show* when for the first time America watched the shaking and shimmying in his hips and understood what the noise was about. Or at least as much as the TV camera showed. That's when all the advance talk turned into a national phenomenon. That was The Moment he was discovered.

For Rex Kern, it came late in the second quarter of this first game. But this wasn't just his Elvis moment alone. This was something more. On any great sports team, there are plays that define players and plays that define games, plays that define reputations, and plays that define championships.

This play did something more.

It defined a full Ohio State era.

It was The Moment that told everyone—players, coaches, fans, opponents, media—that something different was afoot, something better, something fun even.

And it said all of this through the player who led them.

Kern stood on the field late in the second quarter, a bit frustrated even though Ohio State led, 20-6. Kern and Otis had scored on short runs. Dave Brungard had a dazzling, 41-yard run, eluding tacklers down the sideline.

Kern sensed something wrong, though, as this series seemed to flicker out late in the first half. He felt the offense was just missing. The plays weren't clicking. A missed block here. A split second of mistiming there. And now, facing fourth-and-10 at Southern Methodist's 41-yard line, as Hayes sent punter Mike Sensibaugh onto the field again, Kern, the first-year starter playing his first game, did something no one had ever done to Hayes before or ever would again.

He waved Sensibaugh back to the sideline.

He told the control freak of a coach that he was taking control.

Elvis stood in the spotlight with the cameras pointed at him. Immediately, everyone understood what was happening. The crowd buzzed. The Southern Methodist defense pointed. In the Ohio State huddle, John Muhlbach said to himself, "Boy, I don't know if he knows what he's doing."

Sensibaugh ran back to the Ohio State sideline, which, as everyone translated this event, felt as if an electric current were running down it. Hayes's arms were waving, his voice lost in the crowd's buzz. "He was going berserk," Sensibaugh said.

Bill Long, the backup quarterback, looked over at Jim Roman and said, "I'll be in next series."

Larry Zelina turned to the other reserve quarterback, Ron Maciejowski. "Oh, this is going to be interesting," Zelina said.

George Chaump loved what he saw. "Good, Rex, good," he said to himself. It didn't matter to Chaump whether this fourth-and-10 situation was the right moment for Kern to assert himself. The coach had seen in practice that Kern had the physical talent to be a great quarterback. This play showed something equally important.

"That he had guts," Chaump said. "I saw a quality there, the ingredient, the mental thing you need to be great."

But in the moment, with the clock ticking, with the punter waved off, Jim Otis said with clarity what anyone who knew Hayes thought: "Rex is nuts."

Looking back through the prism of age, Kern realized several components came together in his decision. It didn't matter that he had only a few seconds to make the decision. A perfect storm of events led to, as he said, "that God-given point and time."

He could even break the events down, like a scientific study:

(a)

Hayes had sat Kern down before the game. "Rex, there's going to be times on the field that you'll see what the coaches or I can't," he said. "You've got to go with your instinct at those times. You've got to make the decision for what will or won't work."

"That was like giving me the keys to the church," Kern said. "Woody was saying, 'Hey, I've got confidence in you, and you should have confidence in yourself.' At least that's how I read it."

(b)

During one practice, as the offense was implementing Chaump's playbook, Woody got upset in the huddle. Something snapped. He had a megaton about how players were taking instruction.

"By God, you think you can run the team, *run* the team!" he said to Kern.

He stomped out of the huddle. There was a tower beside the field, the kind Bear Bryant made famous at Alabama, sitting in it while watching practice. Hayes never climbed the tower. But as players watched that day, Hayes walked off the field and up the tower steps.

"Okay, guys, it's our turn now," Kern said in the huddle. "We'd better make things happen."

They did, too. With Kern calling the plays, with players motivated, the offense took the ball down the field and quickly scored. Then it scored again. Kern noticed after this second touchdown that Hayes wasn't in the tower anymore. He was standing on the sideline.

As the offense took a third possession down the field, Hayes walked halfway out on the field. A couple of plays later, he was coming in the huddle, scooting Kern out of the way, saying, "Okay, let's try this . . ."

But from that practice, Kern realized he could run this offense successfully without Hayes watching over him every play. He had grasped the elements of it, and just as important, the players had accepted his leadership.

(c)

Earlier in that Southern Methodist game, Hayes had punted on a third down. It was deep in Ohio State territory, and it could only be explained as a veteran coach not wanting his young offense to make a mistake that might sink the day.

The decision frosted many of the offensive players. Kern, especially, tucked it in his mind. It seemed to say the coach didn't have faith in him.

(d)

Kern felt the offense needed a jump-start. On the other side, Southern Methodist's Hickson was putting on a show, passing like no one ever had in college football, running in an offense that seemed light years ahead of what Ohio State's punt-on-third-down team was doing.

But Kern knew what this offense was capable of doing. He had the distinct feeling if they could just get one play to work in a big way they'd be fine. As quarterback, he felt it was his job to find that play.

(e)

After he looked to the sideline to see Hayes wave in the punt team, he turned to his teammates in the huddle and didn't see anyone moving to the sideline. He felt the opposite. He saw players who wanted to stay on the field. Maybe this was a case of seeing what he wanted, considering what players were saying to each other in the huddle. But no matter.

"I looked into their eyes, into their hearts," Kern said, "and they seemed to be saying—this is only a read on my part—'Rex, don't let him send in the punter. Call a play and let's get out of here.'"

So he called a play.

"Robust Fullback Delay," he said in the huddle.

What a fifteen seconds it had been: Sensibaugh running on and off the field; Hayes staring in surprise, screaming something no one caught; Long and Maciejowski thinking they might profit; Chaump loving the bravado of it; Otis thinking Kern was nuts; this low buzz rising from Ohio Stadium.

Then Kern came to the line of scrimmage.

And found he had called, as he said, "The worst possible play you could come up with."

Robust Fullback Delay lined up the backfield in that sepia-toned T-formation. Kern would fake a run into the line. Otis would pretend to block the defensive end and slip over the middle in the space between two linebackers. Kern would throw to him for the first down.

Simple.

At least it was on the blackboard.

On the 41-yard line that day, the play didn't resemble anything like the blackboard. Otis indeed slid over the middle. But he was covered by two linebackers. There went Kern's only receiver.

That wasn't the only problem. The left side of Southern Methodist's defensive line was crashing in on him, first the middle guard, then the end a couple of steps behind. The play hadn't just broken down. It was breaking apart and threatening to take Kern's career with it.

Kern began scrambling to his right, away from the linemen, looking for an answer, knowing he had to find one. After all, he was the one who got them in this mess.

A defensive back came up at the perfect speed and angle. As he went in for the tackle, Kern jumped in the air, causing his body to spin upon contact. He did a full 360-degree pirouette, putting his hand on the ground to keep from falling. He landed on his feet at the 45-yard line. And he started running again.

He caught a block from tackle Chuck Hutchinson. And he ran past the 40-yard line.

He moved against the sideline and over the 35.

At the 33, he somehow dodged a linebacker, somehow stutter-stepped to make him grab air, somehow kept going.

He was inside the 30 now, and it was as if all the oxygen had been vacuumed out of the stadium. No one was breathing. Everyone was mesmerized.

At the 28, Kern was hit again. This time, he was ridden out of bounds at the 26-yard line. But the danger had passed, replaced by a feeling that never would. Kern had run for 16 yards, run for a first down and straight into the hearts of Ohio State fans forever. A love affair began right then. He gave them a moment to press like a rose petal in the pages of their football memories. Everyone understood it immediately.

A noise blew out of Ohio Stadium that is only heard on its best days, a noise of joy and surprise and success and welcome. Maybe it said, most of all, *Welcome, kid.*

As Kern ran off the field for a quick rest, the noise grew to full volume. Long turned back to Roman and said, "I'm gonna have the best seat in the house on the sideline this year."

Zelina looked at Maciejowski. "It's going to be a long three years, Mace," he said. (Later in the game, Brockington caught a pass and went 65 yards. "At least I'll have company," Maciejowski said to Zelina.)

Two plays later, Kern threw a 26-yard touchdown pass to halfback Dave Brungard. That put Ohio State up 26-7 with 35 seconds before halftime. And that was it.

The first game was won.

The new era had begun.

(4)

Afterward, all the coaches were relieved. None more so than Holtz. He still didn't quite know how to digest the afternoon. Ohio State won, 35-14, but Southern Methodist quarterback Chuck Hixson had completed 37 of an NCAA-record 69 passes for 417 yards.

His arm became so tired that Coach Hayden Fry brought in a reliever to throw seven more passes. Seventy-six was a number for trombones or patriotic independence. But passes? In one game?

Tatum and Anderson had never been so tired in their lives as after that game. And while the defense had five interceptions—two by linebacker Mark Stier—Holtz could see how the defense was pushed around. The interceptions, good as they were, had stopped Southern Methodist drives at the Ohio State 9, 15, 18, 2, and 10-yard lines.

After the players were gone, after the locker room had emptied, as Holtz sat at his locker and tried to translate whether it was a good day or simply a lucky one, he felt a hand on his shoulder. He turned.

"Good game," Hayes said.

That was what he needed to hear. The next week, he would be "fired" when Hayes thought he hadn't disciplined a player hard enough in practice. But for six months, ever since he had arrived from South Carolina, Holtz had been searching for some confirmation of his work. Now, at a time he was second-guessing himself, Hayes delivered it. Maybe that was the point, Holtz thought later.

He wasn't alone feeling good that night. Brungard, a junior, had spent the spring and summer hearing about the sophomore running backs. It's all anyone talked about. Brockington had a big game before spraining his ankle.

But who provided the punch in the game? Was it any sophomore? Brungard scored three touchdowns. He showed a full repertoire of talent, too. He had 14 carries for 101 yards. He caught three passes, including two for touchdowns. He left that locker room sensing this was a great team on which he would play a significant role.

It would never feel this good again for him.

(5)

Mike Radtke ran off the field after the game still looking for news. At halftime, he again had a manager call the hospital. Nothing yet, he was told. Later, as he pieced everything together, someone said that just as the game ended there was an announcement over the stadium public address system regarding Radtke's fatherhood. But Radtke didn't hear it. He only knew as he entered the locker room that someone shouted to him, "MARTI HAD TWINS!"

"She *did*? Twins? When?" Radtke said.

"Just now! Congratulations!"

The delivery came at 4:30, or right about the time the game was ending. So his daughter, Laura, and son, Michael Douglas (later renamed Douglas Michael), had good timing right from the start.

Teammates congratulated Radtke. Hayes, the victory evidently proving his player's priorities were straight, awarded him a game ball. Radtke rushed out of the locker room and hitchhiked the short distance to Riverside Hospital. After the story of the twins made the news, fifteen baby gifts arrived at the hospital from anonymous fans. Their phone kept ringing. And, of course, sleep would be hard to come by for, oh, the next couple of years.

But that night, in the afterglow of new fatherhood, Radtke looked through the hospital window at his two babies. It might seem intimidating to be a 19-year-old father of two. Especially one who was only a junior in college. And who was playing football. And who had a newlywed wife still going to college.

But the primary point was that he was 19.

"I was too young to know anything," Radtke said years later.

Newborn twins? Merely another day in the life.

Hayes barking at him? *That* was scary.

A capital
question

$\mathcal{A}$s the price of gas rose to thirty-four cents a gallon
in America and the House Committee on Un-American Activities
opened hearings on anti-war demonstrations in Washington, some
truly alarming news landed on the morning doorstep in Columbus.

The front page of the *Citizen-Journal* carried the headline:

"Football Attendance Dropping At OSU".

Talk about hitting you where you live. Columbus billed itself as "The
College Football Capital of the Nation," and until recently, there was no room
for doubt. It had led the country in attendance for the past decade. The school
president once said, maybe only half-seriously, "We want to have a university
of which the football team can be proud." There was even historical proof to
back up football's municipal impact: in 1940, a year in which Ohio State went
4-4 and was pounded by Michigan, 40-0, the city's very future wobbled as bonds
of the Columbus Railway Power and Light Company were suspended on the
New York Stock Exchange.

As far back as 1914, Columbus was zany for football. In a game against
Penn State, a fan jumped onto the field, doused a blue-and-white-wrapped goal
post with kerosene and set fire to it. Hey, in Pamplona they chase bulls.

In the mid-1960s, Albert Schwartz, an Ohio State sociology student,
researched the impact of Buckeye football. He polled 2,000 random Columbus
residents of various ages, races, and social status. Eighty-five percent said they
had attended at least one game. Seventy percent said apathy to Ohio State

Rex Kern vs. Oregon

football was "downright unpatriotic." Fifty percent said it was their primary conversation piece.

Schwartz concluded that the person who was apathetic to Ohio State football went against "normative social pressures" and was "in the category of a freak."

Yet here was a newspaper headline in which ticket director George Staten said about 2,400 fewer season tickets had been sold in 1968 than in the previous season. The attendance averaged only 76,700 fans a game in 1967, too. It was all part of a steadily downward swirl at Ohio State games from a peak of 83,391 fans back in 1964 when, if it mattered—and no doubt it did—Ohio State was last ranked in the polls at season's end.

That signified a drop of 6,700 fans. At $6 a ticket. At up to six home games a year.

Or nearly $250,000 less a year.

Plus the half-million dollars less that boosters were giving.

At a time when the athletic budget was $5 million.

"We'll still be Number One in the nation in attendance," Staten said.

But for the first time that idea teetered. Ohio State attendance had dipped below 80,000 fans a game in 1967 for the first time in fourteen years. What with the losing year in 1966 and the only passable year in 1967, it signified to *Sports Illustrated* the "passing of a frenzied football era at Ohio State."

The start of 1968 reflected that. Southern Methodist drew 73,855 fans in the season opener. And now, in the second game, Oregon brought just 70,191 fans. Sure, they weren't marquee games. But it was still Ohio State football. It was still the only show in town. It was still the biggest football show in the land. Or was it?

Who knew anymore?

All of this played into the public pressure on Hayes. Over the previous six years, his record was 35-18-1. Good, not great. Noteworthy, not legendary. If the plane toting the "Goodbye, Woody" banner had been grounded by four straight wins to end the 1967 season, the sentiment still percolated just below the surface. George Chaump was approached by another assistant after he took the job that winter, wondering what he was doing, that there was a good chance they'd all be fired this upcoming year.

If Hayes felt this, he didn't show it. He seemed callused to such pressures in his eighteenth season in Columbus. He had been criticized and saluted, castigated and admired, told he couldn't coach in 1951, and voted the nation's best coach in 1954. The outside world, by now, didn't matter much to him. Maybe it never had.

He wasn't the people's choice when he took the job in 1951. That was Paul Brown, the pro coach who had briefly directed Ohio State in the 1940s. Nor was Hayes the school's first choice. That was Don Faurot, the Missouri coach who took the job and then two days later gave it back.

The Ohio State job sat open seventy days before it was offered to Hayes. No one was quite sure what kind of a job it was at the time. The school had ground through six coaches in the previous twelve seasons. It had become known as the "Graveyard of Coaches."

"Columbus's stress on winning" was what Wes Fesler gave as the reason he quit under fire after the 1950 season and went to Minnesota. That stress hovered in the air like humidity. When Francis Schmidt coached at Ohio State in the 1930s, he drove into a gas station one day to get his oil changed. He sat in the car as it was hoisted in the air, drawing plays on index cards he always carried.

After a few minutes, Schmidt struck on something exciting. *Ah-ha! Look at that!* Lost in his world of X's and O's, he opened the car door, stepped out, and fell eight feet to the ground.

Hayes told his staff a story of how to handle pressure. After his first struggling season, he overheard a neighbor saying how he'd be run out of town by the next year. Right then, he set the alarm on his wristwatch to wake him an hour earlier. That was how he handled pressure. He worked. Then he worked harder.

He survived that early crisis. He bought enough insurance in winning the 1954 Rose Bowl that he asked for a show of hands at a Cleveland alumni gathering. "How many of you were here last year?" he asked.

He also had enough of a developed portfolio to survive that losing season of '66. "We're Still Here!" the front of the Hayes family Christmas card said that year.

It was tough becoming a sports legend.

It was tougher still living up to it.

(2)

Early Saturday morning, in Hayes's hotel room at the Olentangy Inn, the quarterbacks met with him for their weekly pre-game drill.

"Okay, Rex, Oregon just kicked off," Hayes said to Kern. "Ball on the 32. What do you call?"

"Rip 14, Coach," Kern said.

"Gain of three," Hayes said. "What's the next play?"

"Coach, if I come up and see the defense backs off Jankowski, I'll go Green 98 right away."

"Okay, Green 98 picks up six yards. Third down and 1. You're at the 41."

"Robust 26, Coach."

"That gets you three yards. First down . . . "

Down the hypothetical field, they went every Saturday morning. Hayes reviewed different scenarios with sophomores Kern and Ron Maciejowski and senior Bill Long. Kern, as the starter, might as well be seated in a wooden chair with a bare light bulb swinging above him. Hayes would have him list series, envision possibilities, think of plays they could run at that specific defense all day.

And each week, in the middle of this interrogation, Hayes would stand up.

"Mmm-hmmm, just a minute," he'd say.

Here came the bathroom break, the players knew. As Hayes entered the bathroom and closed the door, the quarterbacks looked at each other, already stifling laughter. They knew what was coming next. Always, it was an explosion from behind that closed door. Always, it would send the quarterbacks rolling on the floor, laughing a laugh that increased inside them as they tried to keep it silent.

"Shhh . . . "

"Don't lau . . . "

"Stop, stop.'

Sophomoric humor, maybe.

Then again, who better to have it?

(3)

In the ten-day calendar of Ohio State football, there were games—the Rose Bowl, for instance—to build goals around. There were games such as Purdue and Michigan in 1968 to build seasons around. There were Big Ten games to circle. And then there were the other games, the trivial ones, the out-of-conference ones.

"Exhibitions," Hayes called them.

And no game was treated more like an exhibition in the 1968 season than this upcoming one against Oregon. Some of that was because Ohio State had beaten Oregon the previous season, 30-0. The larger part was that the next game came against Number One Purdue. Ohio State's offense prepared most of that week for the Purdue defense. It barely watched Oregon on film at all.

Not that Purdue would get any glimpse of what was coming against it. Hayes wasn't just holding his cards to his vest against Oregon. He was putting them inside the vest and sealing it. But Ohio State had prepared for Oregon. Well, a little.

After Oregon's first three plays went nowhere, Mike Polaski was ready for his fifteen seconds of fame. He had practiced days for this and had the bruises on his forearms to prove it. It began at Monday's practice, when Lou Holtz called him over.

"Ski, you're going to block a punt this week," Holtz said.

Holtz talked as if this were the most natural thing in the world, as if he were saying Polaski was going to pick up milk at the store or mail a letter at the post office. Holtz truly believed it, too. And he imparted that belief to his players. That was part of his gift.

But block a punt? When's the last time that had been planned at Ohio State? Besides, Polaski's job was to return punts. How was he going to *block* one?

"You're not going to return punts this week," Holtz said. "We've found a flaw in their punt blocking. You're going to be the guy to attack it."

This was interesting, Polaski thought. No one before had worked on such details of special teams. There was no special teams coach, per se. It was a kind of a free-for-all of coaching. And planning. And, later on, in another play, this game again would prove how.

But here was Holtz not saying he could, might, or even had a good chance to block a punt. He was flat-out saying he would. Polaski watched the tape and saw why. The Oregon end on the punt team simply released to the outside. He was so focused on getting down the field to tackle the punt returner that he left an open lane to the punter. All you had to do was be quick enough to get there.

Holtz figured Polaski was. As the week went on, Polaski did, too.

"I'm not just going to block it," he said later in the week. "I'll score a touchdown with it."

"Just block the damn thing," Holtz said.

Polaski, a junior, was a Columbus native, a Brookhaven kid who nearly slipped through the cracks in the Ohio State recruiting. He was destined for Florida State or a Mid-American Conference school when Hugh Hindman came to scout a couple of players from a rival high school. Instead, Hindman recruited Polaski.

Now here he was, lining up at right end, looking down the line for the long punt snap, ready to launch himself like a rocket in . . . *three . . . two . . . one . . .* and it wasn't even difficult.

Polaski nailed the punt right on his arm bruises. The ball shot high in the air ahead of him, hanging in the sky like the Goodyear blimp. Polaski became an All-American shortstop at Ohio State, so dropping an easy pop-up like this wasn't even a concern. Well, almost.

Don't drop it . . . don't drop it, he thought to himself as he waited for the ball to come down.

He didn't drop it. He caught it at the Oregon 12-yard line. He had nothing but sweet memories between him and the end zone. He took the ball as he crossed the goal line and flung it high into the stands. It was 7-0, and it was pretty much over. The defense gave up six first downs all day.

The issue was the offense. It gained 421 yards, which was more than in any game the previous season. But the Buckeye quarterbacks also had four interceptions, and Kern was knocked out of the game with a wicked helmet-on-jaw hit in the second quarter. The jaw was X-rayed, and Kern was told it wasn't broken. But he ate liquid food through a straw for the next week. To protect the jaw the rest of the year, his helmet was changed from the two-bar facemask that quarterbacks used for a lineman's grid.

Decades later, while getting some dental work done, a dentist would ask Kern, "So when did you break your jaw?" It took him awhile to remember the hit in the Oregon game.

After the hit on Kern, all Hayes wanted was to get out of the day alive. But Leo Hayden fumbled, then kicked the ball 10 yards, like some comedy skit. That put him on the bench for a while. Then Bill Long threw an interception on his first pass.

And then a second one on his second pass.

"Maciejowski, I want you in there," Hayes said.

So on the field, in the third quarter, Maciejowski did what he would become renowned for doing across his Ohio State career. He wrote the finish. "Super-Sub," he would come to be known, though that wasn't on his mind as he ran on the field. Getting the science experiment in his stomach to stop was.

Nervous? You could say that. This was his first time in an Ohio State game. And you could multiply those nerves when Maciejowski came to the line for his first play in a 14-6 game. He saw how Oregon's cornerback was playing off receiver Bruce Jankowski.

That called for an automatic "Jet" pattern. Jankowski breaks to the outside. Maciejowski throws. If the cornerback comes up and makes the tackle, they make a few yards. And if he misses? You get the 55-yard touchdown that it became, Maciejowski-to-Jankowski, which Hayes crowed was the longest in school history.

"Pole-to-Pole," he said.

That touchdown effectively ended the game at 21-6, but the year's special teams fire drill continued. After the interceptions, Long was so far in the doghouse that Hayes didn't even want him on the field to hold for the extra point. He told Maciejowski to do it. That would've been no problem, except Maciejowski had never held for an extra point in his life.

"What do I call to get everyone ready and the ball snapped?" Maciejowski asked the kicker, Dick Merryman, who was just finishing his third week with the team.

So began Maciejowski's jack-of-all-special-teams seasons. Against Iowa, when the Buckeyes knew an on-side kick was coming, he was thrown on the front line of the kickoff return team. He had never practiced for that. Against Wisconsin, center John Muhlbach got hurt. Jim Roman, the back-up center, was by then the kicker. The third center, Tom Backhus, hadn't made the trip because of injury.

"Goddammit, can any of you guys snap the ball?" Hayes called out after a touchdown.

"Coach, I'll try," Maciejowski said.

How hard could it be? Earle Bruce told him to make sure and keep his head down. Someone ran out with a 70-something jersey for him to put on so he'd pass as a lineman. Not that it wasn't pretty obvious who he was. He started at quarterback that game!

The middle guard smiled as Maciejowski settled over the ball.

"Heh-heh, Number 18," he said.

As he snapped the ball, he remembered Bruce's advice. He kept his head down. Which was a good thing. After he released the ball he heard a strange sound overhead.

SWISSSSSSSSHHH!!

The middle guard's arm flew over him like a broadsword.

(4)

After the game, Hayes already was thinking about Purdue. He was concerned. Kern was hurting. Long had thrown two interceptions. Even Maciejowski, after his touchdown, threw one. That would be a long week for George Chaump. Hayes talked about how he always hoped he never had a great passer.

"When you get fancy, you get beat," he said.

"You may score some spectacular victories passing, but can you win the championship?" he asked.

Woody knew he had to answer that question. He had already laid the blueprint to surprise Purdue. But reinventing himself at 55 wasn't easy. Sometimes he wondered. Sometimes he doubted.

And, always, those around him took aspirin.

Keep cool, *baby*

*T*hat buzz.

"Do you hear it?" they asked each other.

They could even feel it. Riding through the window as their ankles were taped. Coming through the walls as their pads went on. Flooding the locker room with energy just before noon as they got ready for Purdue. None of them had experienced anything like it.

Several players climbed to the second floor of the locker room and looked through windows to see its origin. And there it was. Nearly two hours before the game, Ohio Stadium was full. The horseshoe was alive. It was electric. It was the buzz of the big time.

After two games of questions about tickets and fans and if Ohio State was losing its shine as the football capital, most of the 84,834 fans were already waiting for the kickoff. It was the largest crowd in Ohio Stadium history. Seeing the full stadium, the players' nerves stood at attention. They inhaled its energy.

"Wow, do you see that?"

"Man, it's loud out there!"

"This is so cool!"

Bill Pollitt, while getting his ankles taped, felt his body tingling from the noise outside. And he didn't even start!

For the past year, everything in their football lives pointed to this one afternoon. Michigan was always the big game. But Purdue put the yardstick

General Lewis Walt at Purdue game

to a year's work. That 41-6 loss in 1967 provided the motivational fuel the program had run on.

At an alumni golf outing that summer in Warren, Hayes had the staff meet at 6 a.m. and go over Purdue film. During a coaches' night out to watch a Grandview Inn performer, Hugh Hindman leaned over to the newcomer, Lou Holtz. "You won't be having such a good time when you play Purdue," Hindman said.

Holtz said they'd beat Purdue. Beat 'em? They'd shut 'em out! They'd even return an interception for a touchdown!

"Wanna bet?" Hindman said.

"One hundred dollars," Holtz said.

They shook. They smiled. The next day they rolled up their sleeves and went back to work. Every play Purdue's offense ran in the ten games from the previous season was charted and analyzed. The top fifteen plays were identified. They were spliced together on a film, which was distributed to the defensive staff. Their summer was spent solving these plays.

And on offense?

Well, give Hayes a year and he would come up with something. Some twist. Some surprise. He always did. In 1964, for example, his year-long demon was Illinois. Linebacker Dick Butkus said he relished playing Ohio State because it ran directly at him and "There's always as much hittin' as you want in that one." Hayes put in a series of misdirection plays just for Butkus, and Ohio State won, 26-0.

By this point in 1968, Hayes felt his team had come a long way since the last Purdue game. There were the sophomores. There was the I-formation offense. There were the coaching changes, the tough personnel decisions, and all those countless hours spent on the Purdue Project, from Hayes saying he would fight Purdue coach Jack Mollenkopf if they lost, to coaches dropping jerseys of Mike Phipps and Leroy Keyes outside the locker room door. They wiped their feet on them. Or spat. Or jumped up and down. One assistant even urinated on them.

Still, they all knew there was only one way to prove they had actually taken a step forward in the past year.

It wasn't by beating up the opposing coach or peeing on a jersey.

They'd have to whup the team that whupped them.

Purdue entered Ohio Stadium that morning wearing Number One pins on their jackets, signifying their national ranking. Its offense averaged 41 points in the first three games, including 37 in an easy win against Notre Dame.

It returned Mike Phipps, the Big Ten's top passer, and Leroy Keyes, the conference Player of the Year in 1967. It strutted. It boasted. It was good and everyone knew it.

This was the dragon Ohio State would have to slay.

"Dee-ah Lawd," Lou McCullough said in his Southern pitch as players knelt and held hands in the pre-game prayer. "Puh-leeze let us duh-stroy our en-nuh-me. Ah-men."

"AMEN!"

(2)

The buzz in the stadium built, and built, right to the moment Purdue teed up the ball and . . .

"A-a-a-a-A-A-A-AHHHH!" the crowd roared.

. . . kicked to Ohio State's Jack Tatum, who returned it to the 23-yard line. The Ohio State offense ran on the field. Right into position. And immediately ran a play as the Purdue defense tried to set up. Jim Otis gained 5 yards over right tackle.

Ohio State didn't huddle up again. It lined up again as the referee put the ball down. *Boom!* Dave Brungard went wide to the left for a gain of 12.

Again, no huddle.

Again, it was Otis, over left tackle, for a 1-yard gain this time.

The Purdue defense knew what was happening by now but couldn't match the tempo. Its players were pointing and shifting as the ball was being snapped. They weren't the only ones surprised. Ohio Stadium looked like the answer to a one-liner: *How do you silence the largest crowd in Ohio State history?*

You have Woody Hayes run a no-huddle offense.

You might as easily have a cave man read French.

The crowd needed a translator. What was this? Better yet, *who* was it? And where did Woody Hayes go with his back-to-basics offense?

John Brockington took a pitchout and ran for 6 yards to the Ohio State 47-yard line. Still no huddle. Still none needed. Brockington got the ball again and went around left end. He broke tackles. He hit the accelerator. It was surprising. It was exhilarating.

It was now Ohio State's ball at the Purdue 31.

"TIME-OUT, TIME-OUT!" Mollenkopf called from the Purdue sideline.

Less than two minutes into the game, Ohio State had sprinted downfield against the nation's Number One defense. This is exactly what Hayes spent months planning. Earlier that fall, he took Ohio State's offensive coaches and quarterbacks to an Upper Arlington High School game. Hayes watched this offense regularly, since the games were less than a mile from his home on Cardiff Avenue. But this time he brought everyone along to show them something. It wasn't just the good football played there. It was the revolutionary offense.

Upper Arlington coach Marv Moorehead was in the midst of his fourth undefeated season in five years. His offense would average 52 points a game in 1968. But what struck Rex Kern, Bill Long, and Ron Maciejowski as they sat in the stands with their coaches wasn't just the display of points. It was the speed at which they came.

"Do they even huddle up?"

"Just long enough to call a play."

"Look, the defense can't keep up."

Moorehead had played briefly under Hayes at Miami University in the late-1940s before an injury ended his football career. He became a student coach under Hayes. That started an acquaintanceship that continued into Moorehead's Upper Arlington days. Hayes even tried to hire Moorehead to his Ohio State staff at one point.

Instead, Moorehead stayed at the high school where in the early 1960s he began the hurry-up offense. He was trying to speed up the tempo at practice one day by having the offense sprint to the huddle, then sprint to the line. That's when the concept hit him. He tried it in a game. He tweaked it to speed up even more. Soon, his offenses had the goal of running a play every eleven seconds.

Hayes wasn't considered an offensive innovator, but he recognized a usable idea when he saw one. And he told his players he wanted to run an offense faster than Moorehead's a-play-every-eleven-seconds concept. It was like a competition to him, Maciejowski thought.

The no-huddle offense had been introduced in the 1950s by Oklahoma's Bud Wilkinson, who called it the "Go-Go" offense. But it never caught on, even for Wilkinson, who dropped it and returned to a more conventional attack.

As Hayes watched Moorehead's offense whisk up and down the Upper Arlington field, he connected some strategic dots. The first was a line he quoted from Ralph Waldo Emerson: "Every excess causes a defect; every defect an excess." To Hayes, that said a team's strength could be turned against it. Purdue's excess was its size up front. By one view, it was intimidating. Purdue's tackles weighed more than 275 pounds. Not giant by the measure of later eras. But Ohio State had no defensive lineman heavier than Paul Schmidlin's 225 pounds. No offensive lineman, even the "Twin Towers" of tackles Dave Foley and Rufus Mayes, came within twenty-five pounds of Purdue's tackles.

Big was one way to say it. Hayes thought they were fat. That's where Emerson's excess came into play. After this game, on a locker room blackboard, reporters saw a capital-lettered message, which had found its way into stories from small-town Ohio newspapers all the way to *Sports Illustrated*: "KEEP COOL, BABY, AND RUN THOSE FAT TACKLES TO DEATH."

The words were actually written by Horatius Greene, a junior walk-on who had delivered a pre-game talk to fellow reserves in the "All You Others" locker room. (Greene walked around the following week scared he would get in trouble with Hayes, although nothing of consequence happened.)

No matter who wrote it, the chalkboard message dripped of the truth. Running those fat tackles was the offensive game plan. And the best way was with this no-huddle offense whose idea was triggered while watching Upper Arlington's attack. The question was how.

Initially, Hayes's idea was to tape to players' pants a sheet of paper with a series of plays written on it. A number would be called, they'd look at their pants. Simple, right? George Chaump typed up the plays, mimeographed, and cut them to size with a pair of scissors. Then, before practice, the paper was taped to the players' pants.

It rained that day.

"That was the end of *that* idea," Chaump said.

They ultimately decided the players could memorize two short series of plays. Kern was given the task of calling the proper play, through code at the line of scrimmage. So sometime before playing Purdue, the Ohio State offense began practicing plays at warp speed.

And running extra sprints after practice.

And doing it even faster the next day.

Hayes wanted everything to be perfect for this opening series against Purdue. He knew that no one would expect old, staid Mr. Three-Yards-And-a-Cloud-of-Dust to do something like this. He talked about it to his players in terms of the Germans using their "blitzkrieg" offense in World War II. "Then the Germans sent in the army to finish the job," he'd said.

His players didn't care about that. They just thought the no-huddle was fun.

They saw it was working, too. Even after Purdue took a time out to regroup, Kern ran for 21 yards on a third-and-8 play. Ohio State found itself 8 yards from a touchdown.

"Come on, let's keep it going," Kern said.

But Purdue played like Purdue from there, defending a pass to White on third down from the 4-yard line. And now things really got roller-coaster exciting: Ohio State would try a field goal. It would be Dick Merryman's first field-goal attempt of the year—his first in nearly two years, actually, going back to his freshman season at Miami.

In the opening two games, Merryman had made six of eight extra points. He still felt rusty. He didn't feel at ease yet in the big stadium. And now, as this small-town kid ran onto the field before the biggest Ohio State crowd ever, he felt like most newcomers would in that position.

"I was numb," he said.

He kicked the ball as might be expected.

"I shanked it," he said.

So the surprise start worked like they'd hoped, knocked Purdue back . . . and got them nowhere. That was the start of the big day for Ohio State. On its second drive, Ohio State again ran a no-huddle and again moved right down the field. And again stalled. This time, the drive went 41 yards to Purdue's 22-yard line. Merryman was left on the bench. Jim Oppermann was called to try the 30-yard field goal.

It fell short and off to the right.

Oh-for-two.

Then, with 26 seconds left before half, Merryman got the call again. Ohio State, out of the no-huddle by now, had driven the ball 81 yards to the Purdue 7-yard line. It was a possession pretty enough to be framed, with 41 yards rushing and Kern throwing to five different receivers for the other 40 yards. And now, as Kern held, Merryman kicked and . . .

"I hit it perfect," Merryman said. "It would've been good, no doubt in my mind."

It was blocked.

"So all anyone saw was that I'd missed another one," he said.

The kicking game was becoming an ulcer. It wasn't done, either. After Ohio State's first drive and first missed field goal, Purdue's offense ran on the field. Now was the time for Ohio State's defense to swing its sledgehammer of strategy. Ever since he was hired, Holtz knew this game was his judgment day.

Southern Methodist was a quirky first quiz that made him nervous. Purdue was why he was brought here.

He was the one who took the brunt of those fifteen key Purdue plays on film. He was the one charged with rewiring the secondary. He was the one challenged to solve the problem of quarterback Mike Phipps, who tore up the defense the previous year, completing ten straight passes in the first half for 142 yards and two touchdowns.

That day, Mollenkopf was so giddy with his 35-0 halftime lead that he pulled his assistants aside before addressing the team.

"Is this a dream?" he asked them.

Now Holtz stood on the sideline as Phipps jogged onto the field for the first time. Phipps had the same talented working parts in his offense as the year before. The main one was Keyes, who, along with Southern California's O.J. Simpson, was a prime Heisman Trophy candidate. Keyes had the great team, flashy numbers, and high-wattage personality for stardom.

He had been photographed so often, he said, "It's getting so I hear the cameras whirring when there aren't any cameras there."

He had been interviewed so much, he said, "I can ask all the questions now."

And he was so good, he said over the summer, "I don't think anyone can cover me one-on-one."

Oh, baby.

Game on.

Because in watching film and weighing the personalities, Holtz decided Jack Tatum *could* cover him. He was sure of it. First, Lou McCullough signed off, then Hayes. Not that Hayes talked that way to the reporters when they asked that week how he'd use Tatum.

"Remember what General von Schlieffen said," Hayes answered. "'Keep your flank strong.'"

Who? What?

Reporters looked at each other.

Hayes also called Keyes "the best football player in the country," whom "no man can cover one-on-one."

As Mark Twain might have said, there are lies, damn lies, and football coaches talking on the edge of big games. How Holtz proposed to use Tatum was simple: If Keyes was in the backfield, Tatum stood opposite him. If Keyes went wide as a receiver, Tatum went with him. If Keyes got a drink of water, Tatum held the cup.

When Hayes broke this strategy to Tatum, Tatum himself wasn't entirely convinced. He hadn't played defense as a freshman at all. Now, as a sophomore with two starts, he was expected to shut down a leading Heisman candidate?

"I didn't think it possible," he said.

The simple truth is that Tatum was unsure of his talent at this early point. It had not yet been fully measured, and he saw shortcomings where no one else did. He mentioned Hayes's quote in the paper about no one being capable of playing Keyes man-to-man.

Hayes smiled and said he hoped Keyes read that.

"Trust me," Hayes said.

(3)

Jack Tatum was a mystery to most of the players inside the team, especially the white ones. Most of this stemmed from his reserved nature. He preferred to sit back and observe. He rarely joined the banter at practice or in the locker room. In the unusual instance in which Tatum did say something, his teammates looked at him and joked, "Does Jack talk?"

Even his roommate, Phil Strickland, who considered Tatum a great friend, catalogued him as someone who preferred to be quiet. If he strung two sentences together, Strickland said, that was a monologue. Tatum understood how his quiet ways were seen, and years later, would have fun with it. When a microphone was passed around at the team's ten-year reunion, he raised his hand and asked for it. Many players were surprised.

"Woody asked me to speak, and I know why," he began. "It's so all the white players would hear me say something."

In the fall of 1966, Jim Oppermann, an Ohio farm boy, visited Ohio State on the same recruiting weekend as Tatum. Oppermann introduced himself and asked who Tatum was, then a second time because Tatum had answered so softly. Then he asked what Tatum did, meaning what position he played.

"I run a gang," Tatum answered.

That was true. The New Jersey high schools were noted for gangs, often composed of the school's athletes. Kevin Rusnak belonged to one at Tatum's nearby white school rival, Garfield High. There would be fights under bridges, fights over turf, fights just to have fights.

That was part of Tatum's street package. His hometown of Passaic, New

Jersey, was divided into three parts: uptown, downtown, and To-town, where he lived, a place "on the other side of the second set of tracks," as he put it.

To-town sometimes came to Columbus. As a freshman, Tatum was involved in a fight of legendary proportions with Strickland. It started one afternoon in their dorm room because Tatum was napping on Strickland's bed. They began tossing each other around their room. When they realized someone might get seriously hurt, they decided to take the fight outside. They went downstairs to the parking lot, then resumed punching each other. By the time Jim Jones, the team's academic advisor, arrived to break it up, both were battered and Tatum was in need of stitches. Jones said he'd better take Tatum to the hospital.

"You're not taking him," Strickland said. "I'm taking him."

That's how their friendship was forged. But Tatum wasn't especially happy at Ohio State as a freshman. It wasn't football Tatum was having a problem adjusting to in college. It was the Midwest. It was so different from New Jersey. And there were so few African Americans on campus. At the end of Christmas break, he didn't return for the start of classes and the coaches became concerned. Was he coming back? Was he upset about something? Can anyone even find him to ask?

He kicked around the idea of transferring to Syracuse, but his parents had pushed Ohio State and he trusted their judgment. When he finally returned from Christmas break a few days late, the coaches treated several African American players to a meal out, as if in an attempt to reach out to him. Or maybe to celebrate his return.

As time went on, the coaches often sought out fellow defensive back Tim Anderson to try and get a read on Tatum's thoughts. Anderson, in turn, asked Tatum and relayed his answers. Tatum was the one player on the team whom the others felt was treated differently. It was like he had a set of rules all to himself. Teammates watched him never finish the required six-minute mile on the first day of practice. Nothing was said. He often ran a couple of half-speed sprints after practice, then took a knee. In good part, Tatum said, it was because of ankle problems that would bother him throughout his career. Anderson also remembers coaches knocking on their dorm door to accompany Tatum to classes and guarantee his academic standing.

Everyone recognized Tatum's great talent. It was as if he moved with a force field all his own. Teammates saw that he was the first player with the ability to run right through a tackle. Not simply collide with a ball carrier. But have such power and balance that the hardest contact didn't seem to affect him. To protect

Tatum's teammates, his high school coach wouldn't allow him to tackle hard in practice. As a high school sophomore, he knocked out two of them on the first day of practice.

Holtz first understood the fear Tatum put in others during a practice exercise called the Triple-Butt Drill. One tackler and one ball carrier would move down a line, colliding with each other three times, like rams on a mountainside. The idea was to work on tackling technique while building speed until the third butt became an all-out tackle.

"Players would be counting back in the other line to see if they had to go up against Jack," Holtz said. "Then you'd see them quietly shuffle a spot up or back if they were."

On one such collision, Mike Dale's contact popped out of his eye. Several times Tatum knocked out players in practice. Those were the kind of stories that fueled his legend. But what made him so rare was the athleticism that came with such power. On one punt, Tatum was sprinting downfield as the punt returner caught it and made a couple of moves. "Jack made these slight adjustments but never broke stride, like he was some heat-seeking missile," Ron Maciejowski said. "Jack hit him right in the chest, the guy fumbles. I went, 'Holy crap.'"

Years later, Ralph Holloway would listen with some amusement to media and fan definitions of leadership in sports. He had his own definition. It was the look on Tatum's face when his specialty blitz, "Fire Game," was called. It was as if, without saying anything, Tatum's very demeanor told everyone in the defensive huddle something special was about to happen.

Any namby-pamby could snap off a few good lines to the media about leadership and sound the better for it. But when a day had to be staked out and a play made, who wanted his number called in the huddle? And then went out and delivered?

By the end of the practice week for Purdue, all of Tatum's concerns about Keyes were gone. He had seen enough film, had talked enough strategy with the coaches, to agree with his assignment. It made sense to him.

"You see how simple it's going to be?" Hayes asked.

(4)

This game became Tatum's coming-out party to America. Before it, he was unknown and a star ever after. He broke up five passes, helped hold Keyes to a career-low 19 yards rushing, sacked Phipps twice, and hurried him two other times. Watching the game film a few days later, Mike Sensibaugh was struck by how Tatum covered Keyes so closely it looked like they were "hooked together with a couple of steel poles. You didn't know who was running the pattern, Tatum or Keyes."

Purdue couldn't figure out where Tatum would line up next, either. What was he, a cornerback? A lineman? He was used everywhere. The Associated Press named him its defensive back of the week. The United Press International named him its lineman of the week.

Yet at halftime, Ohio State felt in control every way except the one that mattered. The game was still scoreless. And when they walked into the locker room, they had a surprise. Hayes had planned even this part of the game far in advance. Standing there was General Lewis Walt, the head of the Marines, who a year earlier had commanded 73,000 marines in Vietnam.

"Teamwork, boys, that's what will win this," Walt said. "Let me tell what teamwork means where I work. You sacrifice yourself so the group survives. I've seen marines your age, guys in the same shape as you, take a bullet so a medic or a radio operator can do his job. Your sacrifice isn't that, but . . ."

Tears rolled down the cheeks of Bob Smith, a reserve end. His good high school friend had been killed in Vietnam two weeks earlier. Walt's speech steeled him. He looked at his teammates, many of whom had tears of energy, too. And the others? They just wanted to get back to playing ball.

The defense picked right up on Phipps and Keyes. It was again Lou Holtz's turn to move some chess pieces. He had inserted a special coverage for this game called "Robber," which he had been holding in reserve. He called it on the third play of the second half.

Purdue put two receivers wide to the left. Tatum lined up 5 yards off the inside receiver, Bob Dillingham. Ted Provost lined 10 yards off the outside one, Keyes.

But as the ball was snapped, the defenders switched receivers. This had the desired effect. Quarterback Mike Phipps, seeing Provost move off Keyes, didn't catch what was happening and figured his receiver was open. He threw a cross-field pass toward him.

Tatum, rushing over, reaching out, deflected the ball to the ground. He was a half-step too late from intercepting it and running untouched for a score.

"O-O-O-O-ooohhhhh," the crowd moaned.

Inside the "Robber" coverage were options for Provost and Tatum to call on the field. They called one before the next play. Purdue came out with Dillingham and Keyes lined up the same way. Tatum and Provost were across from them in the same way, too.

Phipps knew what would happen next, right? Hadn't he just seen it a few seconds earlier? So the Purdue receivers had a game of their own, criss-crossing to take advantage of what they felt would be Ohio State defenders switching on them.

Check, Purdue said.

Only Provost and Tatum didn't switch this time.

Checkmate, Ohio State answered.

Phipps saw Tatum just standing there as Dillingham broke free to the outside. He threw across the field to him. Provost swooped in with the half-step Tatum didn't have a play earlier.

It's coming right at you, Provost thought, *you'd better not . . . .*

He caught the ball at the 35 and had an open lane to the end zone and into Ohio State history.

Provost was a farm boy from Navarre, Ohio, and in his own way he was as quiet as Tatum. But when he crossed the goal line, he took the ball and heaved it high into the stands, just as Holtz had told his defensive backs they could if they ever scored a touchdown.

Players piled on him. Cheerleaders stood in the end zone and bowed up and down as if he were a sultan. All the film work, all the late-night sessions, all the off-season decisions—right down to the hiring of Holtz—were coming through for Hayes.

And just when they got this edge, just when they looked in control of the game, just when they could exhale a second . . . the extra point missed. Merryman pushed it.

So here was the kicking inventory: A missed field goal on the opening drive. A missed field goal on the second drive. A blocked field goal just before half. And now a missed extra point. All in the biggest afternoon for Ohio State in years.

Hayes couldn't worry about emotion or sentiment.

When Jim Roman approached him, Hayes said, "You've got the next kick. Goddammit, don't miss it."

That was it for Merryman's Ohio State career. Later that game, Hayes called for him on the sideline and considered sending him in. But not to kick. Merryman had showed off his high school quarterbacking skills in practice. Hayes told Merryman to run the fake field goal play they had practiced. But just as Hayes began to push Merryman onto the field, he evidently thought better of it. He pulled his kicker back hard to the sideline, then punched him in the stomach to underline his thinking.

The kicker who had come out of nowhere a few weeks earlier now would disappear back there. He practiced the rest of the season with the team. He finally got his leg in shape and thought he could contribute. He mustered enough courage one day in practice and approached Hayes about getting another chance.

"You're not ready," Hayes told him.

After that missed extra point against Purdue, Merryman never went onto the field again. It couldn't have played out worse, as far as he was concerned. He didn't ask for this chance. He wasn't ready for this stage. But he suddenly found himself on it, then just as suddenly off it, and he had to deal with the emotional fallout of failing.

"It's been a part of my life for many years," he said, four decades later. "I don't discuss it. To me, I'm more ashamed of it than anything. It's depressing sometimes."

Even the best season had its victims.

Even the simplest of kicks was now risky for Ohio State, too.

Because kicking off after that touchdown, Oppermann made the kind of memory that would be accompanied through time by a laugh track. As he ran up to kick, his plant foot stepped into a small hole just before the ball. That caused his kicking foot to strike the ground a foot behind the ball. The result was a stumbling, bumbling, tripping kick where the ball . . .

DOINK!

. . . bounced off Oppermann's helmet. It ricocheted 10 yards ahead toward the Purdue front wall. A mad scramble was on. In the ensuing pileup, Oppermann knew what was at stake. He reached through a Purdue lineman's legs and got an arm on the ball.

"Give me that goddamn ball!" Oppermann yelled. "I ain't going to the sideline without it."

He was trying to add his second arm when the referee stepped in.

"BOOOOO!" he heard the crowd noise from under the pile.

Purdue's ball.

Eventually, he did go to the sideline without it. And there was Hayes, who erupted. In the game film that week, Hayes replayed the kick over and over, as if repeating it would bring some understanding to its inherent freakiness. The other coaches and players snickered. Winning allows you to do that.

But it happened so quickly on the field, and so strangely, people thought an onside kick had been called. Again they asked: Who stole Woody? When did he become such a gambler? First, the no-huddle offense. Now this?

The defense wasn't done. It was Jim Stillwagon this time. He already had a sack and a handful of tackles before Purdue abandoned running up the middle on him. Now he dropped into coverage. And now Phipps was throwing. And now . . .

"BINGO!"

Stillwagon had intercepted it. Ohio State was in business again on Purdue's 26. It was all going Ohio State's way now. Well, almost all. On second down after that interception, Kern rolled out and went down hard on his shoulder. He got up slowly, holding it. He had to come out, and Hayes had another decision in a season full of ones like this.

Which button to push? The senior, Long, who had the experience but also was intercepted twice last week? Or the sophomore, Maciejowski, who threw the game-cementing touchdown pass last week?

Hayes went with the experience. He called for Long. The crowd saw him coming onto the field and, remembering the week before, began booing.

Hearing this up in the press box, Earle Bruce's eyes watered. Can't they welcome him? Don't they know what he's going through? Instead, the noise grew. And Long's reception in the huddle wasn't any warmer. This was a team sweating and tiring and now close to a victory that was a year in coming. It could sense that. Guard Brian Donovan stepped into Long's face.

"Don't throw a fucking interception," he said.

Geez, Long thought, *can't anyone be happy I'm here?*

Hayes didn't break him in easy. Long's first play was 99 Hitch. The idea was for tight end Jan White to pretend for a couple of beats that he was blocking. When the linebackers dropped into coverage, White would move into the created space and get the pass. It wasn't a great call this close to the goal line, Long thought. The linebackers wouldn't be dropping far enough into coverage to give White enough room.

That was the problem, too. From the 14-yard line, Long dropped back 8 yards and waited for the play to develop. He pumped the ball once and saw the linebacker waiting for White. There went that idea. But as he scanned the field to find another receiver, he saw something else. A gap in the defense. A gap? It was the Grand Canyon.

All this season, Long had wanted some moment, some play, something, to show what he could do. He had forced it in the Oregon game. Now, in the biggest game, the one that would springboard Ohio State into the rest of their season, he found one coming to him. He tucked the ball under his arm and started up the middle. *Twenty. Fifteen. Ten . . .*

Up ahead, he saw a defensive back in the end zone. If he came out, Long figured, he might stop him.

Five . . .

The defensive back, for some reason, wasn't coming out.

Touchdown!

He got tackled in the end zone. No matter. He jumped into the arms of White. Jim Otis and Dave Foley joined the celebration. Long, who just a few seconds earlier was booed, now felt the noise come down on him like confetti. Bruce watered up again in the press box.

It was 12-0 now, and Roman wasn't going to be stopped from his Hayes-anointed mission. He ran onto the field to kick the extra point—"hauled ass," actually, as he said.

The snap was good. The hold was good. The kick was . . . good!

Never had extra points caused such excitement. Roman slapped some palms, shot up a fist, and ran to the sideline. There, Woody looked at him out of the corner of his eye and shook his head. Roman was told Hindman was on the pressbox phone.

"You know damn well we should've gone for two!" Hindman said.

"Hugo, the Old Man said it was my turn," Roman said.

Even when they made an extra point this year, it seemed to be all wrong.

But the kicking didn't matter. Couldn't matter. Not this day, the way the defense was playing. Keyes was ineffective. Phipps was pulled in the fourth quarter, dizzy, from all the times he'd been hit.

In the Ohio State locker room afterward, Hayes kissed Provost on the cheek. In the Purdue locker room, Mollenkopf took a look at the stat sheet, which showed Ohio State had outgained his team 411 yards to 186. He had come to Columbus with what he called the greatest Purdue team he ever had. Or ever would. Two years later, he would die of cancer.

"We were out-coached," Mollenkopf said. "I take my hat off to Woody. He got me."

(5)

Leaving the stadium that day after attending his first Ohio State game,
Ed Linser couldn't have been more excited.

He was 39 and so pumped he had awakened at 5 a.m. Walking across the
Oval and seeing bedsheets hanging from dorm windows with painted expressions
such as "GO BUCKS" and "KEYES SUCKS," it felt like Christmas morning.
Near his seat on a folding chair in the closed end of the horseshoe, he got goose
pimples when the marching band thundered into the stadium. And over the next
few hours he cheered so loudly he lost his voice for three days.

Some fans arranged a day around Ohio State football. Some arranged a
weekend. Out of this single, delirious afternoon, Linser had the kind of epiphany
that made friends consider his sanity.

He rearranged his family's life.

As Linser and his wife, Shirley, boarded their flight back home to New York
City that Sunday, he leaned close and in that hoarse voice whispered, "That's it.
We're going to sell the house and move to Columbus."

Linser had become an Ohio State fan in the navy, by proxy. In Norfolk,
Virginia, in 1948, he met Bill Wade aboard the aircraft carrier *U.S.S. Coral Sea.*
They fueled airplanes together. Linser was a baseball fan from the Bronx. Wade
was from Chauncey, Ohio, and such a Buckeye fan that it was contagious. Linser
began to follow the team, too. When they sat in the barracks and listened to
Ohio State's win against California in the 1949 Rose Bowl, Linser was hooked.

After they left the navy on the same day that year, the 21-year-old Linser
visited Wade in Columbus. Soon, he met Shirley. They married and moved back
to New York the following year. By 1968, they had four children, a comfortable
home, and the security of his machine shop job.

But Linser never quit following Ohio State, scouring the New York papers
for scraps of information, and relying on his nephew or brother-in-law for the
meaty news. On the Sunday before the Purdue game, excited by the season's
possibilities, Linser called his nephew, Eddie Cantrell, and asked if tickets could
be found for the game.

"If you can get tickets, we'll fly out," Linser said.

On Thursday, Cantrell said he had bought two field tickets. "They're shitty
seats," he warned. Linser didn't care. He just wanted to travel to Mecca. And
watching that game, enjoying the energy in the stadium, feeding off that 13-0

upset, he decided to move to Columbus. He wanted to recapture that feeling every possible Saturday afternoon.

Shirley didn't believe they were moving until a few months later when the van drove away from their home with the furniture. The family then got in their beat-up station wagon. On the drive to Ohio, they had two flat tires. They got into an accident and had to tie the headlights together to keep them functional. They drove into Columbus in April of 1969, "looking like something from *The Grapes of Wrath*," Linser said.

From 1969 through 2000, he didn't miss a single Ohio State home game. He joined the Quarterback Club, which met each week to discuss the team. From a chance meeting at the 1978 Sugar Bowl in New Orleans, he became such good friends with a freshman linebacker named Leon Ellison that, years later, he was invited to Ellison's 40th surprise birthday party outside Washington, D.C.

In 1982, a contest was held for Ohio State's best fans. The top four were brought into the WOSU-TV studio to tell their story. Viewers voted on them. Linser won in a landslide, got a write-up by columnist Brian White of the student newspaper, *The Lantern*, and was introduced during that season's Purdue game.

In 2000, leg issues began to bother Linser to the point he couldn't walk well enough to make the trek to games. He bought a big-screen TV and began watching them instead. Four decades later, on the west side of Columbus, he and Shirley lived in the same house they bought in 1969.

On the front porch, cut into the cement, a block "O" is painted in scarlet and gray. On the living room wall, the ticket stub from the 1968 Purdue game is framed.

(6)

Limping out of the locker room that day, Dirk Worden's knee was taped, his ligaments torn, his heart broken. If Merryman represented one way for a good day to go wrong, Worden represented the more conventional manner. And he hadn't seen merely a few weeks of work go kaput.

He saw his life's dream end.

In the second quarter, in man-to-man pass coverage, Worden planted his leg to drive. The leg gave out. The knee popped. He could feel it, hear it, sense right then that something awful had happened. He went into the locker room and got the knee taped. He tried to play on it in the second half, but it was no use.

Worden had gone the year at a West Virginia prep school in hopes of finding a place to play college football. He had survived the losing season of 1966 as a sophomore. He led the team with 130 tackles, and as a junior, been named its Most Valuable Player. He had seen the talent coming together this senior year and hoped to join his brother playing in the Canadian Football League. Now he had to deal with a knee that was shot, a dream that was gone.

The parade moved on.

He could only wave from the side of the road.

As the locker room emptied that evening, as most players went off to a party, as High Street began to crackle with thousands of celebrating fans, Hayes turned to his assistants.

"Let's meet at 7," he said.

There was a surprised silence. Then an expectation that he was joking. Only no smile or words of amusement followed.

"You mean 7 tonight?" someone asked.

"No, 7 next Wednesday," he said. "Of course, 7 tonight."

That evening, while Columbus celebrated the upset of the college football season and its biggest win in years, the coaching staff sat in its St. John Arena offices going over game film.

Victory *special*

$\mathcal{H}$ayes allowed one public official into his inner circle
—the one who now stood before him on the Ohio Statehouse steps
as the nation ramped up to the 1968 presidential election.

Richard M. Nixon began attacking his Democratic opponent,
Hubert Humphrey, just as he had done earlier that October day
in Cincinnati, Middletown, Dayton, Springfield, and London.
In the afternoon, he would continue on to Marion, Lima, Deshler,
and Toledo as part of a 247-mile, nine-city train ride in the closing
weeks of his "Victory Special" campaign.

Nixon had made this same trip in the 1960 election, dismissing Senator
John Kennedy for suggesting American prestige had "dipped to an all-time
low." Now Humphrey was the target.

"The issue is clear. Vote Humphrey for more taxes. Vote Nixon to have
more to spend yourself," he told the Statehouse crowd. "It's Nixon with money
in your pocket or Humphrey with his hand in your pocket."

He turned and pointed toward Hayes on the dais behind him.

"Ohio State plays rock 'em, sock 'em football, and that's what we're
going to play!" Nixon shouted.

The crowd applauded. Hayes stood and cheered. This was his guy, his
candidate, his friend, another one of his heroes. They met at a 1957 reception
after then-vice president Nixon watched Ohio State beat Iowa for the Big Ten

King Rex

title. Nixon wanted to talk football that day. Hayes wanted to talk foreign policy.

"You know Woody," Nixon said in delivering Hayes's eulogy three decades later. "We talked about foreign policy."

They were a Made-in-America match, the sports fan who soon would become president of the United States and the political fan leading a national football powerhouse.

"Texas A&M would have had one more applicant for coach if Bob White hadn't got that last touchdown for Ohio State to beat Iowa," Nixon joked in 1957 as he awarded Hayes the "Coach of the Year" trophy in Philadelphia.

During the 1960 campaign, Hayes was asked to meet Democratic vice presidential candidate Lyndon Johnson at a campus rally. He declined, suggesting a man in his position should stay out of the political fray. A few weeks later, though, he appeared with Nixon. After Nixon lost the election, Hayes said the politician had learned "what a political liability I am."

So it went through the rest of their lives. A meeting here. A comment there. A kindred spirit in a parallel life. Upon becoming president, Nixon called Hayes and asked him to lead the Peace Corps. Hayes declined. In 1970, Nixon appeared unannounced with Hayes among war demonstrators on the Oval.

"Is that really him?" a student asked.

"What's he here for?" another wondered.

"We don't care about Ohio State football!" someone shouted from the crowd. "Just stop the war!"

During the 1973 season, Nixon telephoned Hayes in the locker room after a big win. Hayes put the president on hold while he addressed his team. Before the 1976 Rose Bowl, Nixon told Hayes his team would need 24 points to beat UCLA, sending him two dozen roses to underscore the point. (Hayes handed the roses to patients at a hospital visit that night. One of those patients suggested Hayes look at a kid in his hometown of Ironton, Ohio. Hayes did, and the recruit, Kenny Fritz, later became an All-American guard.)

Donald E. Tidrich, a University of Texas professor, once related in a letter to Rex Kern: "I remember Coach Hayes describing the day in his Ohio State office after his friend President Nixon had resigned. He said he was feeling as low as he had in his life when the phone rang and it was President Gerald Ford, a Michigan man, asking how the coach was holding up. Coach Hayes said it made all the difference to him in this time of personal and national sadness."

Hayes flew to San Clemente, California, after Watergate and visited Nixon in seclusion. Later, in 1981, Nixon emerged from self-imposed exile to speak publicly for the first time at a GOP fund-raiser in Columbus. There were 150 demonstrators chanting and picketing outside the event. Inside, Hayes introduced Nixon to his fellow bedrock Republicans. "The football takes some funny bounces sometimes," said the deposed coach, who by then had suffered his own public humiliation.

On this day in 1968, on the steps of the Statehouse, all that history—Watergate, the Clemson punch—had yet to be made. Nixon was less than a month from being elected president.

"We will not let the American flag become a doormat for anyone at home or abroad!" he said.

Nixon called Hayes up to the stage with him. He grasped the coach's hand, thrust their arms together into the air, and yelled, "WE'RE NUMBER ONE!"

(2)

Actually, Ohio State was Number Two at the time, coming off the adrenaline-draining Purdue win, facing a winless Northwestern team, full of young players and . . .

The expected happened.

They let down.

They became human.

But they didn't start that way. On their first possession, Jan White went over the middle, caught a Kern pass, and braced for the big hit that always came when he caught a pass in practice. No big hit came. No hit at all. He was alone. He couldn't believe it. Then the sophomore with the tight end's body and the sprinter's heart took off doing what he loved most. He ran down the field. He felt the freedom of speed. And he was still alone.

But in the several seconds it took to complete that 72-yard touchdown, White was sprinting not out of joy or success or some lifelong dream of scoring in this manner.

It was fear.

He was scared of getting caught from behind. Scared of getting hurt. And his legs listened to what his mind was saying. This would become the model for his football career: fear pushing him faster. He wasn't alone in his trepidation. He just embraced it.

And, speaking of fear, the extra-point unit came on the field. Roman's turn again, and he missed the kick. Roman missed four of five kicks that afternoon. Hayes became so desperate he called for Larry Zelina, the wingback, to throw one conversion to Bill Long, the quarterback. At least that worked.

"It's silly," Hayes said of the kicking game. "It's all in their minds."

It was in everyone's minds by now. Zelina, who would be tried later on extra-point kicks and kickoffs, was one of five kickers used by Ohio State in the 1968 season.

So the Buckeyes trailed Northwestern after the first quarter, 7-6, led at half, 21-14, and clung to the lead, 27-21, after three quarters. The Wildcats were sniffing the possibilities. The Ohio Stadium crowd—exactly the same attendance as the record Purdue game—was growing restless for good reason.

The Ohio State defense, unmovable all season, wasn't flexing its muscle. The offense was hitting and missing. When he wasn't in the game, Kern sat on the bench with an ice bag to his head. He had been leveled in the first half and had to leave the game briefly. His back. His jaw. Now ice to his head. The kid was hurting. Nevertheless, he ran for 121 yards and passed for 170 more. Running and passing and urging his teammates on—"Let's keep it going," he said—Kern led the Buckeye offense down the field early in the fourth quarter. Jim Otis finished off the drive with a 6-yard, off-tackle touchdown.

Then they did it again. Hayden scored from 3 yards out this time. Finally, up 39-21, Kern could sit down on the bench for good. Maciejowski came in and did what he always seemed to do.

"Hey, Ed, you see it?" he called out to Ed Bender at receiver after surveying the Northwestern defense.

Bender nodded. "Yeah!"

The defensive back was on Bender's left shoulder as he made a cut to the right on a post pattern, no one was in the middle of the field, and just as Bender turned back for the ball—*plop!*—it was right there from Maciejowski. Touchdown. Bender jumped in the air. He got the ball. He had everyone sign it, rightfully figuring this would be the only touchdown of his career.

White. Kern. Jankowski. Otis. Hayden. Bender. They all scored against Northwestern. This offense, so unlike Ohio State in past years, was starting to score every way. With anyone.

In his post-game press conference, Hayes said the Buckeye offense was "explosive at times."

"When's the last time we had 45 points?" he asked.

"In 1962," someone replied.

Hayes had something else on his mind: the hit that knocked Kern out of the game. He called it "disgusting" and said it was an "obvious" attempt by Northwestern to hurt his quarterback.

"There are too many coaches who think the best way to stop the option is to put the quarterback out of business," he said. "I'm not referring to a single situation. I've seen it in game films not involving our team and I'm fed up with it. It's not right for a kid like Rex Kern to take the punishment he's taken in every game. This thing is getting out of hand."

"This has happened too damned often," he added. "Rex is lucky his jaw hasn't been broken. One of these days it'll be shattered."

Hayes was getting worked up now. His jaw jutted, his voice rose.

"THIS IS FOOTBALL! WE'RE NOT RUNNING A BUTCHER SHOP!"

"What do you think should happen?" a reporter asked.

"The officials should take charge!" he said. "A player who deliberately hits a passer after he has released the ball should be kicked out of the game. If it happens again, the coach should be kicked out of the game."

Maybe he believed all this. Maybe he was talking off the top of his head. Certainly he was trying to protect Kern in the only way he could without putting on a helmet and shoulder pads himself.

That evening, Hayes shipped the game film to Big Ten Commissioner Bill Reed. By Sunday morning, Northwestern coach Alex Agase was on the phone with Hayes. It was bad enough that Northwestern was 0-5. Now Agase was running a butcher shop? Intentionally hurting opponents?

"What the hell are you talking about?" he asked Hayes.

Hayes said it came down to the play on which Kern was hurt. Agase said a penalty wasn't even called on that play. Hayes said one should have been. Agase told him to watch the play again. Words were coming faster. Tempers were flaring.

"You owe us an apology!" Agase said.

"You'll get nothing!" Hayes said.

"One play!" Agase said. "Have you seen film of your defense?"

Hayes said, no, he hadn't. By Tuesday, when Agase addressed reporters at the weekly Big Ten news conference, he was armed with a prepared statement.

"I am amazed at a football coach who would stand in criticism of another defensive team who hasn't even seen his own defensive team's performance on film, particularly when his team was called for piling on," Agase read. "His recommendation was that the player be suspended and the coach be suspended for a week by this type of violation.

"By his own recommendation, maybe *he* should take a week off."

Hayes didn't budge. Kern, he pointed out, had been hurt for the fourth consecutive game. "That doesn't just happen!" he told reporters.

The story was kept alive by Reed being in Mexico City for the Summer Olympics. The can of film sat on his desk, and he wouldn't return for another week. So all the while, there was a back-and-forth, he said-he said jousting match between Hayes and Agase. The media loved it. Woody was being Woody.

"We haven't heard from Hayes in three or four years, and he hasn't had good teams in that time," commented the commissioner after returning from the

Games and viewing the film. "He reminds me of what Winston Churchill said about Field Marshal Montgomery: 'He's indomitable in defeat and insufferable in victory.'"

Ouch. Using history on Hayes. It was a page right out of Woody's own playbook.

(3)

Ohio State football is a grand tradition. There's the marching band's "Script Ohio" and its dotting of the "i." There's the "Block O" formed by the crowd with cards. The victory bell. The Senior Tackle. Brutus Buckeye.

There's also the "Captain's Breakfast." It's a members-only affair, and the only members, as the name suggests, are captains of Ohio State football teams. It started in 1934 on the Sunday following the Homecoming game. Walter Jeffrey, a Columbus businessman, invited twenty former captains to the Scioto Country Club to honor them, as well as the captains of the current Buckeye team. Each received a mug inscribed with his name and year.

Dave Foley remembers his first Breakfast. It was held at the Holiday Inn across from the stadium. He entered the banquet room that Sunday morning with his fellow captain, Dirk Worden, and Coach Hayes. The three stood in the buffet line, sat down at assigned seats, made some chitchat with some of the folks at their breakfast table, then left the room. For Foley and Worden, it was just another chore, not a special event. Waking up early. Dressing up for breakfast. Knowing the rest of their day was budgeted for schoolwork and game films.

Years later, Foley would recall what one of the former captains told him that morning: "This will be more meaningful to you in coming years," he said.

It was true. Foley would come to love the annual affair, which Ohio State coach Jim Tressel moved to the pre-game breakfast on Saturday mornings. He enjoyed being in the company of his brethren. Former Buckeye Dick Schafrath, the 1958 captain, who like Foley went on to become an NFL tackle. The 1964 captain Jim Davidson, whose son, Jeff, also became a captain. Davidson's co-captain, Tom Kiehfuss, whom Foley grew up watching play at Purcell High School in Cincinnati. "Getting to know all these men has added to the Ohio State experience," he said.

Now, Dave Foley tells the current captains exactly what he was told: *This day will become more meaningful as you grow older.* The seniors nod, act thankful, shake his hand, and quickly move on in their busy day.

Just as he did in 1968.

Lessons *learned*

*T*he economics professor struggled to help the Ohio State tackle answer one question, just one, and thus stay eligible for the upcoming Illinois game.

"Name one means of transportation," the professor said.

The tackle sat silent, thinking.

"You may choose among steam, horse-drawn or electrically propelled vehicles," the professor said.

Still, the tackle said nothing.

He had the "look of a man who is being led into a trap," wrote Columbus native and humorist James Thurber in his short story, "University Days." Thurber's fictional professor, exasperated, began saying, "Choo-choo-choo."

The tackle, Bolenciecwcz, merely sat there.

"How did you come to college this year, Mr. Bolenciecwcz?" the professor said. "Chuffa, chuffa, chuffa, chuffa . . ."

"M'father sent me," Bolenciecwcz said. "I git a 'lowance."

Students began imitating train whistles. Others acted like locomotives.

"What did you ride here on?" Thurber's professor asked.

"Train," Bolenciewcz said, thus assuring he could play against Illinois that Saturday.

The real 1968 Buckeyes arrived in Champaign, Illinois, early Friday morning and as if taking his cue from Thurber, Hayes asked the players

Jan White blocks for Bill Long

what they normally did this time of day on Ohio State's campus. He immediately answered the question for them.

"You go to classes," he said.

He told them to attend a class at Illinois. Any class. Players inched away from him, fearing exactly what happened next. Hayes grabbed a handful of those closest to him, Jim Stillwagon and Rex Kern included. They were going to class with him.

They walked into an auditorium where a molecular biology class was in midsession. Students immediately turned and stared. The professor asked if he could help them.

"We're from another Big Ten university," Hayes told the professor. "Would you mind if we sit in on your lecture?"

"Aren't you Woody Hayes?" the professor said.

"Yes, I am," Hayes said.

"My name's Woody, too," the professor said.

With that, Hayes waved, sat down with his players in the upper rows of the lecture hall, took out a pen and pad and began taking notes.

Sometimes to their dismay, his players discovered that Hayes was serious about them getting an education at Ohio State; it wasn't just some recruiting line he used on their parents. Every road trip included an exercise to stretch their minds. At Wisconsin, the Buckeyes took a tour of the state capitol, where they were briefed on the building's four different types of architecture. In San Francisco one year, they toured Chinatown. On another trip, to Iowa, they visited Herbert Hoover's gravesite in the president's hometown of West Branch. A voice from the back of the team kept interrupting the young tour guide.

"No, no, no," the voice said.

"Uh, I don't think so."

Then: "Well, not exactly."

It was Hayes. Finally, he walked to the front of the group and said to the guide, "Son, you sit here. I'm going to talk about Herbert Hoover."

The lecture lasted half an hour, during which Hayes spoke to his players about self-reliance and about the self-made man who grew up in a two-room cottage and became the thirty-first president of the United States. And, he noted, Hoover was a Republican.

Jim Jones was there and heard every word. Jones was a graduate student in 1966 when a colleague asked if he wanted to interview with Woody Hayes about a job. Six weeks later, he told his wife he had the job.

"That's great," she said. "What's your title?"

"I'm the Brain Coach," he said.

"Oh. And what are you going to make?"

"I'll be damned if I know," Jones said. "I was too intimidated to ask."

His salary was $6,500. Like any football assistant, he had a desk, and he sat in on all staff meetings. In later years, his position carried the inflated title, "Academic Advisor." Jones ran nightly study tables for freshmen; anyone under a 2.25 grade point average had to attend. He sent questionnaires to professors, monitoring players' attendance and performance in their classes. And, as with every assistant Hayes ever had, there were times his boss infuriated him.

"Jim, this is Coach," Hayes said in one of his middle-of-the-night calls.

"Coach who?" Jones answered in a fog.

"Goddammit, this is Woody. Now listen up . . . "

It was Jones's responsibility to keep the players' grades in line. But every assistant was expected to know where his position players stood in their classes. By 1968, Earle Bruce kept an index card listing each offensive lineman and how he fared in each of his classes, so when Hayes walked into his office and randomly asked, "Earle, how's Backhus doing in algebra?" Bruce had an answer.

New assistants weren't ready for this line of questioning. When Hayes asked Chaump how Larry Zelina was doing in English, Chaump fumbled his words.

"Zelina . . . Zelina . . . Larry Zelina?" he said.

In a response that became a catchphrase among his assistants, Hayes thundered, "No, Bobo Zelina! For God's sake, we only have one Zelina!"

Hayes showed up in the dorm rooms of players whose grades had suffered the previous quarter. When Dave Foley brought home over the academic break a pile of work from his engineering classes, he told his mother he was changing majors. Hayes called him as soon as he returned to school.

"What's this about you transferring out of engineering?" he asked.

Foley finally agreed to stay with the program, just to get Hayes off the subject.

Hayes was the son of an educator, and he always wrote his title as "Head Football Coach and Professor of Physical Education." He often ate lunch at the Bachelor's Table in the Faculty Club, where professors seated themselves indiscriminately at the long table and discussed the issues of the day. Hayes joined in the free-for-all. He also taught a class on football theory, popular not just among football players but also high school coaches across Columbus. It started at 8 a.m., and by 7:59 the class door was locked. Invariably, tardy players could be seen sprinting across campus. And invariably, someone knocked on the locked door.

"That student didn't want to come to class today," Hayes said.

One of his favorite lessons was vocabulary. He used the *Word Power Made Easy* book that each player received as a freshman. Any moment could become a vocabulary lesson. Hayes would write a word on the chalkboard in team meetings—"lascivious," Dick Kuhn remembers—and if the player couldn't provide the definition when called upon at the next meeting, the penalty was ten pushups.

Once, during a post-practice shower, Hayes said out loud, "This shower is innervating!" He looked at Bruce Smith. "Do you know what that word means?" he asked. Smith said he didn't. "It means 'energizing,'" Hayes said. "Yep, this shower is innervating."

The day before a game, Stillwagon was clowning around in the shower when Hayes, fully clothed, approached him and said, "Goddammit, don't you know too much levity will beat you every time?"

Stillwagon went silent. "Okay," he said.

After Hayes left, Stillwagon asked his teammates to explain the nature of his offense. "What the fuck does 'levity' mean?" he said.

Every August, Hayes gave the same speech on the importance of education. "How many players are in this room?" he asked. "One-hundred-and-twelve?"

He wrote the number 112 on the chalkboard.

"And I suppose you all want to play in the NFL. How many NFL teams are there?" he said.

He wrote 27 on the board.

"And how many players are on every NFL team?"

He wrote 44 on the board.

"Okay, let's do the math," he said, doing it himself to calculate their slim odds of making the NFL. "That's why you're here for an education."

Hayes regularly asked players if they wanted tutors in specific subjects. Not just to pass a class, but to move a B grade to an A. He thought anyone with a graduate degree should be able to tutor any player in any subject. The coach, himself, showed up occasionally at the study tables and reviewed the subject matter in the players' history and English classes.

"Do you like to read for pleasure?" he once asked Jones in a coaches' meeting.

"Yes, I do, Coach," Jones replied.

Hayes slid a psychology book across the table.

"Read this damn book from cover to cover," he said. "We have a quarterback who could be damn good. He needs to pass this class."

Kern, the first member of his family to attend college, had no reference for studying at this level. Hayes formulated a game plan before his quarterback's Friday psychology exam. He would tutor him in a two-hour session on Monday. Tiger Ellison would do the same Tuesday, then Esco Sarkkinen on Wednesday, and Jones on Thursday.

"Woody said, 'Be in my office at eight o'clock Monday,'" Kern recalled. "So I get in there and the first paragraph of the chapter we're going over mentions Oedipus Rex. All of a sudden, he leans back in his chair and says, 'By god, we had a player once who had that Oedipus Rex complex.' And he goes on and on about that. He does two hours on that paragraph, looks at his watch, and says, 'Now, that was a great session, wasn't it?' I've got a three-inch book to cover and I'm thinking how I'm in big trouble."

The next day, Ellison did his tutoring in front of a blackboard covered with terms, Jones reviewed the important points, and Kern ended up passing the course. He would go on to earn a master's degree, then a doctorate from Ohio State. But he wasn't alone in suffering the transition from high school to college.

John Brockington was terrified of flunking out. His first college class—American History—had 500 students. He saw some of them writing.

"Why are you writing?" he finally asked.

"We're taking notes," one said.

With Jones's help, Brockington learned to take notes. Chuck Hutchinson, a National Honor Society student in high school, was so homesick and out of place as a freshman, he managed only a 1.65 grade point average his first quarter. "It was two weeks before I found the biology class," he said.

Hayes called Hutchinson into his office and told him that if his GPA didn't improve, he would be off the team. But "if you get a 3-point or better," Hayes added, "I'll give you five bucks." With the coach looking over his shoulder, Hutchinson earned a 3.2 grade point the next quarter.

"I expect more of the same," Hayes said when he handed over the five dollars.

That was Woody, the same Woody who drew attention to something the professor said in that Illinois molecular biology class, something that didn't sound quite right to him. Stillwagon and Kern watched in amusement as their coach walked down to the blackboard to make his case.

"Well, yes," the professor said, "you are right."

Hayes spoke to the class for fifteen minutes. When he finished, the students gave him a standing ovation.

(2)

It was homecoming weekend at Illinois and, as part of the festivities, the bedsheet signs hanging from dorms were especially entertaining:

"Go Illini! Hold 'em to 50!"

"Good luck Illini—you'll need it!"

"Illinois vs. Ohio State: The Impossible Dream!"

Illinois had won the two previous meetings between the schools. The last time the Buckeyes were in Champaign, Hayes had his players take off their suit jackets on the morning of the game and do a walk-through on the hotel lawn, making a few last-minute adjustments before busing to the stadium. This time, Illinois students approached some Ohio State players as the Buckeyes walked across the campus and asked them what numbers they wore so the students could cheer for them. Their team was winless and Ohio State was a 20-point favorite.

The Buckeyes scored on four of their five possessions in the first half. Kern had touchdown runs of 11 and 16 yards. Jim Roman made the only field-goal attempt from 21 yards. Even Hayes must have exhaled just a bit in a 24-0 game, because at halftime he didn't give his normal There's-Thirty-Minutes-Still-Left-in-the-Game speech. Instead, he conjured up the ghost of Abraham Lincoln.

"Right up and down the riverbanks outside this stadium, the sixteenth president of the United States talked to people about . . . "

Meanwhile, in the Illinois locker room, coach Jim Valek made a minor technical adjustment that had a major impact on the rest of the game. He widened the split between his guards and tackles on offense, which widened the gap between the Ohio State defensive linemen covering them. Illinois' slot back bulldozed his way through the gap, blocking whatever linebacker was in the way, followed by the fullback carrying the ball.

Offenses, up to this point, had tried to outrun Ohio State's defense, but they couldn't match the quickness of Dave Whitfield and Jack Tatum on the wide side of the field, or escape Stillwagon's hot pursuit and the speed of Anderson and Sensibaugh. Illinois decided to try and outmuscle the Buckeyes in the second half, and with most of Ohio State's starters resting on the bench after getting the big lead, Valek's strategy worked. Stillwagon had his knees unwrapped. Tatum, who had twisted his ankle, was told to take the rest of the afternoon off as well.

The Illini racked up 218 yards in the second half after managing only 84 yards in the opening half. The offense scored two third-quarter touchdowns and made both two-point conversions to trail only 24-16. It was a game again. Hayes told McCullough to get the first-string defense back in the game.

"They aren't taped up anymore," McCullough said.

When Illinois scored its third straight touchdown, followed by a game-tying two-point conversion, Hayes wasn't passing along instructions. He delivered them.

"Get taped," he told Tatum, then Stillwagon, then the rest of the starters.

With just under five minutes remaining in the game, the underdogs had Ohio State on the ropes. On the first play following the Illinois kickoff, Kern was knocked unconscious. Trainers Ernie Biggs and Mike Bordner ran onto the field. Biggs bent down low to Kern's head.

"Rex . . . Rex . . ."

Kern didn't respond.

"Rex, how you doing?" Biggs asked.

Slowly, the Buckeyes' quarterback regained consciousness. But as the two trainers put his arms around their shoulders and carried him off the field, Kern was in some other area code.

Hayes put his hand on Bill Long's shoulder, as if to give his reserve quarterback instructions before sending him into the game. Long, however, saw a funny look on the coach's face.

"No, no, no, goddammit," Hayes said, looking past him. "Give me Maciejowski."

Long felt as if he were in some kind of bad foreign film, where the lips and words were out of sync. Wasn't he the Number Two quarterback? Did Hayes just say he wanted Maciejowski?

Maciejowski was equally surprised. Just a few seconds earlier, he had been secretly thankful he wasn't being called into this mess. Now he scrambled to the bench to find his helmet. He didn't even know the down-and-distance as he ran on the field. He thought it was first-and-10. It was actually second-and-17.

"Don't fucking throw an interception," Foley said in the huddle.

Was this welcoming line some ritual the linemen had?

After throwing a nifty 10-yard completion on his first play, Maciejowski was feeling pretty good. He thought he had a first down. He didn't know it was now third-and-7. When he began to run an automatic first-down play, the coaches went into a momentary panic.

What is the kid doing? Has he lost his mind out there?

Then the play broke down, and Maciejowski took off running. Twelve yards later, Ohio State was still in business, still trying to escape Champaign.

"We need a play, Hugh," Hayes said to Hindman on the sideline.

"Geez, I've been telling you to run 'Pipe' all day," Hindman replied.

And he had been, too. Dick Kuhn— the reserve tight end in case a two-tight-end set was called for—stood behind Hayes throughout the game. He heard Hindman saying, "Run the Pipe!" and "The Pipe's there, Coach!"

Maybe Hayes didn't hear him. Or maybe he reflexively ignored 99-Pipe because of the frozen afternoon in 1964 when Ohio State played Michigan for the Big Ten title. Scoreless in the second half, near midfield, Hayes called for 99-Pipe. The tight end goes 12 yards downfield and cuts outside. The opposite flanker goes down and out on his side of the field. The wingback is the primary target. With the other receivers taking the defensive backs outside, the wingback cuts in front of the isolated safety and can be open for a big gain.

That day against Michigan, tight end John Palmer didn't hear the call. He stayed in and blocked. The play failed, even though the wingback was wide open. Hayes still blamed Palmer so much that it contributed to him moving to guard the next year, where his leg was broken. But in 1966, with Palmer back in the huddle, Hayes would have Bill Long end many practices running 99-Pipe.

"Tight end, what's your assignment?" Hayes would say.

The tight end would answer he had to go 12 yards downfield and cut outside.

"We lost the goddamn Michigan game once because the tight end forgot his assignment," Hayes would say.

Years later, Long visited Hayes in retirement. On the chalkboard, half a play was drawn. Long recognized it as 99-Pipe. He went to the blackboard and finished drawing it.

"You know," Hayes said, "we lost the Michigan game once because our tight end . . ."

Maybe the bad karma explained why Woody wasn't listening too hard as Hindman kept suggesting the play against Illinois. Hayes called it, though. This time, it worked just as he drew it on any blackboard through the years. Jan White ran 12 yards and cut outside. Bruce Jankowski took the other side's coverage to the outside. That left the middle of the field for Zelina against the safety. Maciejowski purposely underthrew the ball, just a little, to hit a gap underneath the safety. Zelina made the catch and ran to the 4-yard line for a 44-yard gain.

"What'd I tell you, Coach!" Hindman said.

The next play, Otis pushed in for the touchdown, going over Rufus Mayes and Kuhn, who landed on top of the defender he was blocking. That was worth a Buckeye leaf. And now, with a 31-24 lead, the defense had only to hold the day. It was the first-team defense, too. Stillwagon stood at the line and stretched his arms out wide, telling Paul Schmidlin and Bill Urbanik to do the same at their tackle spots.

"Touch fingertips," Stillwagon said. "Don't get any wider than that."

That would narrow those gaps some.

When Sensibaugh intercepted Illinois' last hope, that was it. Ohio State didn't just have a win. They had an important lesson about playing out games. Maciejowski had a nickname, too. "Super Sub," they called him in the newspapers. This was the third game he had come into late and thrown a touchdown. This one saved the season, too.

He was now entrenched as the backup. Which meant . . .

Bill Long left the stadium that day and made the walk of shame to the AYO bus. *All You Others.* There was the bus for Bucks and Red One, the first team offense and defense. Then there was AYO bus. All his career, Long had ridden on Red One. Even as the backup quarterback this season, he rode among the starters, figuring it was where he belonged.

But after this game, after he had been demoted yet again, to third string this time, he had to face the facts. Just as several upperclassmen already had.

"Welcome to the club," said his friend, Tom Bartley, as Long came up the steps of the AYO bus.

Long couldn't believe his senior season had turned into this. He was crushed. "I thought my life was over," he would say of that day. And the life he had envisioned as a kid was indeed over. Being backup was one kind of disappointment, knowing you were just a great game or twisted ankle from the top job. But third string?

The truth was that his dream had begun to disappear, little by little, from the day he showed up for summer camp and found himself listed behind Kern on the depth chart. He always thought he was just a good practice away from regaining the job. That's how athletes think. Especially Long, the son of a coach.

So when he threw two interceptions against Oregon, he shook it off. And when he scored the big Purdue touchdown, he thought he was on his way back to winning the job. But now, after this Illinois game, as he took his seat on the AYO bus, it all began to sink in. He felt devastated. So did his family. "It was like a wake," he said.

He would never confront Hayes or say anything to a teammate about his feelings. Kern and Maciejowski, years later, would say what a great teammate Long was, how he could have created a scene and never did. That wasn't Long's way. He was a coach's son, a product of small-town America, the type of person who believed hard work and an optimistic nature would overcome anything.

"Hang in there," his father told him after Illinois. "It'll turn for you."

Long couldn't second-guess Hayes. A coach, he understood, had to make decisions that hurt someone. He just didn't like being the hurt guy. And he knew the talent of Kern and Maciejowski. He practiced alongside them every day.

What's more, the team would win every game that year. It would become the Big Ten champ and win the national title. "How can you challenge a decision when it works out perfect?" Long said.

Still, he felt humiliated. He would never shake the feeling, either. Decades later something burned inside him. "You'd think it would get easier with age and time," he said. "In a strange way, it's been harder. You think of how things might have been different."

His mind often settled on the Illinois game of his junior season. On fourth down, he threw a 9-yard pass to Billy Ray Anders that gave Ohio State a fourth-quarter lead. Then in the final minutes, Illinois went 77 yards for a touchdown and the win. It was Long's only loss as a starter that year. It was also the difference between Ohio State winning the Big Ten title and losing it. What if they'd won that game? What if—instead of people calling for Woody's job that winter—he had another Big Ten championship? Would Long's senior year have been different? *Well, would it?* he wondered.

As it was, that day in 1968, when the team buses pulled from the Illinois stadium, the former starting quarterback felt for the first time like a passenger, merely along for the ride.

Coach Emerson, *Buckeye*

On a plain, metal bookshelf in Woody Hayes's office at the North Facility, there were biographies of his heroes: Patton, Rommel, MacArthur, Sherman and Eisenhower. There were works to stimulate him by politicians, like Richard Nixon's *Six Crises* and John F. Kennedy's *Profiles in Courage*. There were anthologies of famous speeches, compilations of famous people and breakdowns of famous crises, like in Crane Brinton's *The Anatomy of a Revolution*.

There also was a small, tattered book he reached for while sitting with reporters in the week of the Michigan State game. It was a collection of essays by Ralph Waldo Emerson, the nineteenth century poet, author, philosopher, transcendentalist . . . and coach to Woody Hayes.

The hat-tearing, fist-pounding, emotion-spewing football legend read one particular essay by Emerson at least once a year. It was his touchstone. He had read, re-read, underlined, dog-eared, digested, recited, memorized, sermonized on, and generally toted around Emerson's essay called "Compensation," so much so that by 1968 the book enclosing it was held together by a rubber band.

He quoted it to future farmers in a speech in North Union, Ohio. He waved it at a North Carolina State coaching clinic, saying, "This is a book that every coach should read." He took the book to Harvard on the 100th anniversary of Emerson's death and told an audience, "My father gave it to me when I was

Bruce Jankowski

a college student at Denison, in Ohio. He told me that Emerson said that the more you give, the more you get in return. I was charmed by the fancy of this endless compensation. And doggone if it isn't true. It became the cornerstone of my coaching philosophy."

After hearing what Michigan State coach Duffy Daugherty said that Wednesday, he jumped to his feet while talking with reporters. Ohio State, Daugherty said, was a "great team with tremendous overall speed and quickness." Kern gave them "a lot more flexibility," while the receiving corps is an "excellent one to throw the ball to," Daugherty said.

Too young a team? *Ha!*

Daugherty said Ohio State's sophomores have "no limit to the amount of spirit they can generate Saturday after Saturday."

No one asked if Daugherty thought they could solve world unrest and hunger, too.

Daugherty was one of the great wits and fun personalities of the Big Ten. He invented the line, "A tie is like kissing your sister." Once asked how he knew twelve men were on the field, he said, "I counted the legs and divided by two." The Saturday before playing Ohio State, a laughing Daugherty told a laughing group of reporters he was going to try an onside kick against Notre Dame. He then did exactly that on the opening kickoff. Michigan State recovered and scored a touchdown in the opening minutes and sparked a 21-17 upset.

"Duffy said Ohio State is one of the truly great teams," *Cleveland Plain Dealer* sports writer Ed Chay said to Hayes.

"Oh, that's nice," Woody said, pulling out that battered book. "Let me see what Emerson says about that."

He began leafing through the book to a page that was dog-eared, underlined and yellowed.

"Page 84," he said.

He turned to the small group of reporters. "'Blame is safer than praise,'" he read. "'I hate to be defended in newspapers. As long as all that is said is said against me, I feel a certain assurance of success. But as soon as honeyed words of praise are spoken of me, I feel as one who lies unprotected before his enemies.'"

He turned a few pages over. "'Whilst he sits on the cushion of advantages, he goes to sleep,'" he read. "'When he is pushed, tormented, defeated, he has a chance to learn something; he has been put on his wits, his manhood.'"

He looked up at the reporters and stuck out his jaw. "Compliments take the edge off you and the kids. Once we had a winning streak going, I told our kids, any time somebody compliments you, you kick 'em in the shins unless it's a lady over 80."

He looked defiantly over the group of reporters, ready to kick *them* in the shins. This was Hayes's overriding philosophy in dealing with players, assistants, and anyone else who mattered to him. He never spoonfed them "honeyed words of praise." He always demanded the subject be "put on his wits, his manhood." Earle Bruce said that the only praise he heard in six seasons under Hayes was on his way out the door to Tampa.

Hayes pushed, demanded, and tormented to the limits a personality would allow. Sometimes even beyond. But that was the only way to get better, Coach Emerson taught him. Perhaps it explained why there were two Coach Hayeses in most players' lives: The one on the field and the one off it. There was the tyrant who prodded and annoyed and generally made half the team hate him. Then there was the one who helped, encouraged, befriended, counseled, and lobbied each of them to go to law school, or consoled them in crisis or drove across the state to meet for a few minutes a decade later, if a few minutes were needed.

In the coming years, as he climbed football's ladder of success, Lou Holtz noticed Hayes wouldn't return his phone calls. Time after time, he left messages at Hayes's office. Hayes wouldn't call back. Finally, in a message, Holtz said he had a problem and needed some advice. Hayes called back within minutes. When Holtz asked why he hadn't returned his other calls, Hayes responded straight off page 84: "You can get anyone around you to say you're doing a great job," he said. "You don't need me to tell you that."

After that, if Holtz wanted to talk with Hayes, he would say in the message that he had a problem. Hayes immediately returned the call.

Coach Emerson also taught Hayes how to deal with players. "I never talked down to them," Hayes said. "I learned that from Emerson. He said, 'Treat men as pawns and ninepins and you shall suffer as well as they.' I never did that to my players. I remember one year early in my coaching career I made that mistake. And we had a terrible season. I never made that mistake again. Even when I thundered at the players, I thundered that they could do better."

He would pull a line from Emerson in practice: "Our strength grows out of our weakness." He would quote the writer's words on self-reliance: "The harm that I sustain I carry about with me, and never am a real sufferer but by my own fault."

When author Robert Vare was writing his 1974 book on Hayes called *Buckeye*, Hayes discovered Vare had read "Compensation."

"Isn't it one of the greatest goddamned things ever written?" Hayes said. "Y'see, Thoreau was a cop-out. He spent the last thirty years of his life in seclusion because he didn't want to live in the world of men. To me, that is a cop-out. Even when he went to jail it was only for a night and his aunt bailed him out the next morning. Now Emerson was a doer. He could talk to people on all levels. He could talk to the Phi Beta Kappa society one day and to a bunch of farmers the next. He was a man of action who believed in working within the system."

One catchphrase Hayes seized on, and embraced in his own life, was often ascribed to Emerson but actually came from Benjamin Franklin. This was the principle of "paying forward." Giving of yourself. Helping those ahead of you. In 1842, Franklin wrote about lending a small sum of money to a man who promised to pay it back. Franklin said he couldn't do that. When he met "another honest Man in similar Distress," he said, "you must pay me by lending this Sum to him, enjoining him to discharge the Debt by a like operation, when he shall be able, and shall meet with another opportunity. I hope it may thus go thro' many hands, before it meets with a Knave that will stop its Progress. This is a trick of mine for doing good with a little money."

"You can't pay back," Hayes would say in speeches and locker room talks. "You can only pay forward."

In his office with reporters that Wednesday, Hayes put Emerson's essays back on his shelf and tied up his week's thoughts to reporters. It wasn't just Michigan State and Duffy Daugherty's honeyed words he had to battle. Nixon was on the ballot.

"'Things will not be mismanaged long,'" he said, quoting Emerson. "I hope the electorate remembers that Tuesday."

(2)

Saturday. One o'clock. Forty-two degrees. On the field before the game, stretching, Bill Urbanik and Jim Stillwagon looked up and saw Daugherty, wearing a cardigan sweater and a smile, walking to their side of the field.

"Hey, Bill, how you doing?" Daugherty said.

"I'm doing pretty good," Urbanik said.

Daugherty asked about Urbanik's brother, who had starred at Penn State. He then asked Stillwagon how he was doing, how classes were going, what . . .

"HEY!" Hayes shouted, hurrying over to Daugherty.

. . . Stillwagon was going to . . .

"WHAT THE HELL ARE YOU DOING OVER HERE!" Hayes screamed. "GET THE FUCK OUTTA HERE!"

Hayes, always looking for a winning angle, recognized when he thought an opponent was doing the same. He turned to his players. "Don't you talk to that sonuvabitch," he said. "He's trying to soften you up."

Daugherty smiled at Hayes.

"You get the hell back there!" Hayes said. "Don't you understand that's why I always kick your ass?"

Daugherty was still smiling at Hayes.

"You're too nice a guy," Hayes said. "You're just too nice. And I kick your ass because you are."

After the coaches left, Stillwagon and Urbanik laughed at the scene. That was Woody. Every conversation was analyzed. Every rock was turned over. Every detail studied. In his pre-game speeches, he always had a diagram of the stadium to show which way the wind was blowing.

"It'll come through this stadium porthole here, come this way across the field and go out this porthole here," he'd say.

The players would listen, wondering about the purpose of such things. But never the passion. And it was exactly this passion that allowed Hayes to notice the same flaw in Michigan State that Purdue had. Its big players were too big. They looked out of shape. He called for the no-huddle again. This time, he put in two scripts of plays, one called "Duffy," and the other "Spartan." Each consisted of a half-dozen plays.

The offense ran on the field after the opening kickoff, ran right into position, then ran the ball right down Michigan State's throat. Threw it, too. Three straight Kern passes racked up 25 yards. That was followed by an 18-yard run by Kern. Then another pass, this one for 39 yards. And Jim Otis running off tackle for a 1-yard touchdown.

Ohio State 7, Michigan State 0.

All of 1:43 was gone.

When the defense immediately got the ball back, it was more blitzkrieg. This time, Kern threw 14 yards to Jankowski for the score.

By this sixth game, it was clear that a new offensive era at Ohio State was underway. Anson Mount, the sports writer at *Playboy* magazine, said how Hayes had opened his attack to, "seven yards and a cloud of dust." Sometimes when asked about the difference in this offense, Hayes would answer with an Ara Parseghian joke: One buddy asks another, "How's your wife?"

"Compared to what?" the other said.

The comparison was: In 1967, Ohio State didn't have a game with over 375 total yards of offense. In 1968, its final eight regular-season games all had over 410 yards.

In 1967, its most productive passing game consisted of 139 yards. In 1968, it had six games beyond that.

In 1967, it averaged 16.9 points.

In 1968, it averaged 32.9 points.

For Chaump, these results were especially gratifying. It showed his concepts worked. The I-formation and downfield passing weren't high school concepts, as Hayes had yelled months earlier in that first meeting in which Chaump had been temporarily fired.

The strain of working for Woody didn't lighten for Chaump. Each day, he felt Hayes looking over his shoulder. At each decision, he wondered what Woody would say. And the film sessions? Hayes ran the projector back and forth, back and forth, over any fumble or interception, even ones in practice, ranting to Chaump all the while.

"Aren't you coaching these guys?"

"Where did they learn that?"

Even: "Go stand in the corner."

By the next season, Chaump would decide not to put up with it. Well, some of it. He would have the student manager in charge of films edit out every fumble and interception in practice. Out of sight, out of mind, out of the discussion for good. Meetings, he found, became quieter and more productive.

If Woody didn't trust success, the Michigan State game showed why. Despite the two early touchdowns, the Buckeyes couldn't pull away from the Spartans. Kern left the game in the second quarter with a sprained ankle. Maciejowski came in and directed a second-half drive, which ended with his two-yard touchdown run. Still, Michigan State refused to quit. Ohio State's defense would have to win the game. The defense had caused five turnovers through three quarters, including three interceptions. In the end, two unlikely heroes emerged.

Mike Radtke, the father of five-week-old twins, lined up at the defensive end on the short side of the field. Dave Whitfield lined up on the other side. Whitfield was a marvel to his teammates. He played the wide side of the field, despite not being especially fast. He wasn't big either—188 pounds—yet somehow he controlled blockers, often being asked to occupy two at a time, which freed up Tatum on a blitz.

Whitfield relied on technique and agility. He had been a standout wrestler at Massillon and knew how to leverage his opponents. Whitfield anticipated playing football at a smaller school like Kent State, but Hayes wasn't deterred by his lack of size. Over a meal of soul food, Woody convinced Whitfield's parents that Ohio State was the right school for their son. He became an All-Big Ten defensive end, never weighing more than 190 pounds.

Twice in the fourth quarter, Radtke crashed the line and knocked the ball loose.

Twice, Whitfield pounced on it.

Final score: Ohio State 25, Michigan State 20.

Now the spotlight was shining on Ohio State, at Number Two in the polls. The 6-0 Buckeyes were on a collision course with Michigan for the Big Ten title. Hayes, after years of anonymity, appeared to have reinvented himself. And the fans were back; the Michigan State game had been another sell-out.

Bruce Jankowski was hurrying across the Oval on his way to class when a student yelled, "Hey, Bruce! You got your picture on the cover of *Sports Illustrated*!"

The Buckeye receiver waved and said, "Okay, great." He thought it was a joke until he arrived at class and saw someone with the magazine. "The Buckeyes Are Back," read the headline.

Jankowski was on the cover, hauling in a pass.

"Ohio State's Jankowski Catches Touchdown Pass Against MSU," the caption read.

It wasn't his TD catch, but he didn't quibble over the magazine's mistake.

"We've got a celebrity here in our class who managed to get his picture on the cover of *Sports Illustrated*," the professor said, holding up another copy.

The naturally shy Jankowski didn't quite know how to react to his sudden fame. Just a few months earlier, with so many talented running backs on the team, he wondered how he would ever get his hands on the ball. Now everywhere he went, Buckeye fans asked him to autograph their copies of *Sports Illustrated*.

Magazine covers were one perk of being on a winning team. Movie passes, which they all got, were another. But if anyone at Ohio State was getting money on the side, no one seemed to know about it. They figured other schools did such things. Leo Hayden went to see friends at Michigan State and marveled at the cars the players were driving. He wasn't saying anything was going on. He didn't have to, either. Lots of people higher up than Hayden saw what was happening, and in 1976, Hayes turned Michigan State in to the NCAA, on so many violations that head coach Denny Stoltz and some assistants were fired.

Hayes didn't duck the issue, either.

"Integrity!" he said at a Big Ten luncheon in Chicago. "We've got to keep the integrity of our sport. If someone gets out of line, by god, you've got to put them back in line.

"Did I turn in the team that cheated in our league? Yes, I turned them in. You're damn right I did! And I'll do it again if necessary."

But while Ohio State players weren't paid, there were ways for enterprising young capitalists to make some money off the system. And, make no mistake, several players fit under that heading. The primary way was game tickets. Each player received four season tickets in 1968. On the black market, they were golden.

A graduate assistant ran the ticket business inside the team, dating back to his playing days. It was all hush-hush. He would come around before the season and collect season tickets.

Where did they go? Who bought them? No one asked.

"All you know is he'd come back a few days later with $800 for you," Urbanik said. "That was some good money then."

Also, if you were a starter, you could buy four more tickets for individual games. They cost $6 apiece. They could sell for up to $50, if you knew where to go. And some players did.

Even on road games, a good and profitable system was organized, depending on the opponent. The schedule didn't work that way in 1968. But in 1969 they played at Minnesota and Northwestern, two big cities where the best tickets could fetch good money. Several players pooled their extra tickets, say, twenty-five in all. A scalper was flown up from Columbus. Flights were only $70. And, let's see, if you could get $50 a ticket, multiplied by 25 tickets . . .

Mace, *in your* *face*

On Saturday morning, as he waited in his hotel room in Madison, Wisconsin, Ron Maciejowski felt the earth move. Pictures shook. Walls trembled. If at any time in his Ohio State career he felt that only a force of nature would provide him a chance to start, here was the necessary proof.

"Did you feel that earthquake?" he asked teammates.

"What earthquake?"

"Naw, I didn't feel anything."

But there was one that morning, measuring 5.5 on the Richter scale and centered 400 miles away in Mt. Carmel, Illinois. Wisconsin hadn't felt an earthquake in nineteen years. This one was felt across twenty-three states. Nor, it seems, would that be the only time Maciejowski sensed things others didn't. Maciejowski had no illusions about himself or his situation. He felt talented enough to start at this level. He had confidence that he could do the job. He also knew by this seventh game of his career that he would never be Ohio State's regular quarterback. Not with Kern in the same class. No way.

Kern, Maciejowski felt, embodied everything Woody wanted in a quarterback. He understood that. He didn't have an overriding problem with that part of the equation, considering Kern's talent and how he handled himself. They became great friends right from their first practice as freshmen. Hayes was short of varsity quarterbacks that day and had the two freshmen come over. They stood to the side waiting for their turn.

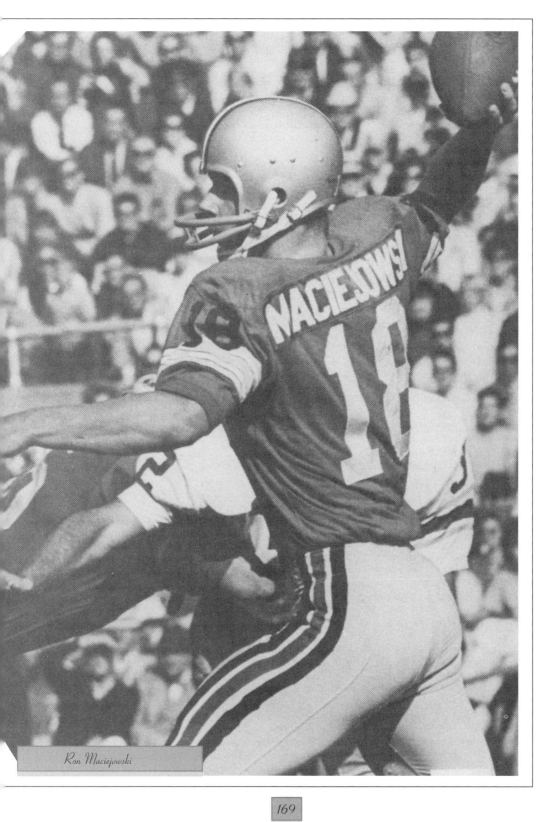

Ron Maciejowski

"You should go in first," Maciejowski said.

"No, no, you should have the first turn," Kern said.

They never did get in. But from then on they were kindred spirits, knowing they were in a competition but somehow never letting it leak into their friendship. It was a difficult juggling act. It spoke of the two players involved, perhaps the backup more than the starter, since his position was more difficult.

But if Maciejowski was fine with Kern, what he never understood was Hayes's constant need to remind everyone who was the starter and who wasn't. If Kern made a mistake in practice, Maciejowski felt, Hayes wouldn't say anything until Maciejowski made a similar mistake. Then a megaton would detonate. The proper point would be made, but not at the expense of his starter's confidence.

Soon, Maciejowski came to believe Hayes wanted to pound the reality into everyone that Kern was The Man. His guy. *Their* guy, actually. Hayes wanted to show that this was the quarterback who best inspired the team's faith and confidence toward victory. Again, that was fine. But Maciejowski didn't like being typecast as the ugly step-quarterback.

It had been like this from the start of this season, too. In the first practices of August, with Kern resting to protect his back, there was a scrimmage in which Maciejowski was on fire. He threw strike after strike, completing by his count 17 consecutive passes. But when his 18th pass was thrown intentionally high to put it where only a receiver could possibly get it, and as it ticked off the receiver's fingertips, a group of Big Ten writers watching practice got a show.

"Goddammit, quarterback!" Hayes yelled.

He then caused such a scene that Maciejowski was kicked out of the practice. It was as if all his other work was discredited. So it went, he felt, through much of his career. In 1969, in an easy win when Kern was hurt, he and Kevin Rusnak played well. Hayes, speaking to the team afterward, addressed their performance in an odd manner.

"Now, Rex was out," Hayes said, "but what's-his-name and the other guy did a great job for us today."

Maciejowski and Rusnak began calling each other What's-His-Name and The Other Guy. When the team autographed footballs, they even signed some that way. A weaker personality might have been sunk by all this. Maciejowski, in fact, saw several players with great talent wither a little more with each passing season simply because they didn't know how to deal with Hayes's manner. But he was not insecure in any way nor did he measure his self-worth by any coach's approval, even that of a legendary one like Hayes.

He felt the aura of Hayes, of course, the power that seemed to pour off him. In all the time they spent together, he saw Hayes appear lost just once, and it wasn't in the presence of a president or four-star general. It was with Vince Lombardi. This was in 1968, after a Green Bay Packers exhibition game in Cleveland, which Hayes attended with his coaches and quarterbacks. He began his introductions as if he were an awestruck teenager.

"Coach," he said, when he got to Bill Long, "this is . . . uh . . . uh, goddammit, he's been the starting quarterback for the last two years, tell him your name son."

Then it was Maciejowski's turn.

"This is our sophomore quarterback, Ray Maciejowski," Hayes said.

"It's actually Ron," Maciejowski said. "It's nice to meet you."

"You know, Ron," Lombardi said, "last year in the Super Bowl we had a play where Bratkowski handed off to Grabowski, who fumbled and Skaronski recovered. We like you guys."

As time went on, Maciejowski rebelled against the rough treatment in small ways he himself would come to label as "childish." He wouldn't shave, for example, just because he knew Hayes liked clean-shaven faces. Then Hayes would say he needed to shave. That would guarantee Maciejowski would let his beard grow for that much longer. It was the same thing with his hair. Hayes didn't like long hair, which was part of the 1960s scenery. So naturally Maciejowski let his grow longer than usual. Just to stick it to the coach.

What compounded their personality clash was all the time quarterbacks spent with Hayes. There were the pre-practice meetings. The rugged practice hours. Sometimes post-practice reviews. The Saturday pre-game session. Various discussions in between. All the time, Hayes was asking, testing, cajoling, pushing. Years later, at a New York event announcing Kern's election to the College Football Hall of Fame, a handful of teammates sat around a hotel room afterward. Kern and Maciejowski told Woody stories, back and forth, one after the other, feeding off each other's memory to the point where one of the wives said, "Doesn't anyone have a story about Woody Hayes besides Rex and Ron?"

No one spent nearly as much time with Hayes as his quarterbacks did. But while Maciejowski would get along well with Hayes after football, and in time, come to appreciate some of his methods, they didn't have a good relationship during his playing days.

Kern understood. He looked with some sympathy and even greater appreciation at how Maciejowski didn't turn his issue with Hayes on him. He was the one in the way, after all. But Maciejowski never let it interfere with his relationship with Kern.

If Hayes didn't feel Maciejowski was the best starter, he had a valuable insurance policy for three years. And in light of Kern's injuries, it was a needed one. Already this season, Maciejowski sealed the Oregon and Michigan State games and provided the winning points against Illinois. So it would go, all through his career. In Maciejowski's senior season, after starring against Purdue, he even got a call in the locker room from President Nixon.

"Hey, I saw the game on TV, and you did a great job," Nixon told him.

That was a nice moment for him. What he wanted most of all was to have all the feel of being the starter. Get the majority of snaps in practice. Have the game plan molded to him. See how it felt to walk onto the field, first.

The way the quarterback issue was framed in the public discussion was that Kern was the better all-around quarterback but Maciejowski the better pure passer. Maybe that was so. But years later, when Troy Smith won the Heisman Trophy, he became the fourth Ohio State quarterback to run for 100 yards in at least two games. The other three: Cornelius Greene, Kern . . . and Maciejowski.

He would start just twice in his Ohio State career, too.

His first chance came in Madison, Wisconsin.

(2)

When Ohio State arrived in Madison on Friday, the team went directly to Camp Randall Stadium to practice. There, the future awaited them. It was new. It was shiny. It was called Tartan Turf. And it covered Wisconsin's football field.

"Mod Sod," some called it.

Wisconsin joined the University of Tennessee as the first to lay one inch of synthetic grass and a tartan surface over a slab of concrete. A few other schools and Houston's Astrodome had bought fields from its competitor, Astro Turf.

"Sometime in the next ten years we'll have one, too," Hayes said. "I look for a great improvement in football. A good back will be able to cut faster and sharper. Ends and backs will be able to run sharper pass patterns.

"The new turf will definitely cut injuries. It will be great for football."

This wasn't a unique opinion to scoff at through the porthole of time. It was

the prevailing idea of the day. Michigan State's Duffy Daugherty said
that by 1973 every school would have synthetic turf. Alabama's Bear Bryant
said it represented progress that "can't be avoided." NFL commissioner Pete
Rozelle said the turf solved the problem of playing championship games in
cold-weather cities.

Injuries? No one was concerned. Just the opposite, as Hayes suggested. The
University of Houston, playing in the newly carpeted Astrodome, reported eleven
knee injuries on grass in the 1968 season and none on the Astro Turf. Monsanto,
one of the synthetic field makers, said teams with real grass averaged 9.6 ankle
and knee injuries a year while teams using their product had 1.6 such injuries.

A voice in the wilderness, such as Green Bay coach Vince Lombardi, didn't
argue about injuries or progress. He was a purist. "Football is supposed to be
played on a natural turf," Lombardi said.

The overriding concern was cost. Wisconsin spent $210,000 on its tartan
field. Hayes said it was worth the problems it would solve. Ohio State's players
weren't so certain. It was fast, sure. But it felt like concrete. And it ripped skin
if you fell on it. But they heard Hayes say it was "great for football."

"I don't know if I want to say," Jim Otis told reporters when asked what
he thought. "I want to play my senior year."

(3)

Ohio State led 10-0 after a ho-hum first half. The star, so far, was on a
defense that couldn't be dented. Wisconsin would run forty-five times on the
afternoon. It would gain 88 yards. It ran in the middle, and ran, and kept running
into the same problem.

Jim Stillwagon.

If there was a perfect body for middle guard, Stillwagon had it. At 6-0,
he wasn't especially tall. At 210 pounds, he wasn't especially big. In street
clothes, the combination didn't seem too imposing. After one game, he was
told a prominent Ohio State booster wanted to meet him, and Stillwagon
walked over to her recreational vehicle in the parking lot. As he stepped inside,
her face dropped.

"Oh," she said. "I'm really disappointed in you."

Not knowing quite what to say, Stillwagon asked why.

"You play so much bigger," she said.

What Stillwagon did have was long arms and uncommon speed for a lineman. That combination allowed him to gain crucial leverage on almost any opponent that dared block him one-on-one. In his stance, teammate Bill Pollitt thought, those long arms on that thick body made Stillwagon look like a "rabid frog."

Still, the overriding physical characteristic for Stillwagon's game was power. No one had seen an assembled body quite like his. Linebacker Doug Adams came the closest. Stillwagon had muscle flexed on top of muscle to the point that when Kern first met him during a recruiting trip, he was awestruck as Stillwagon changed shirts at the fraternity house where they were staying. Kern had never seen muscles like that.

"He had a little piece of fat on his ear lobe," said Vic Stottlemyer, who played behind him at middle guard.

Weights were a novel concept at the time, and one Hayes didn't trust. "We don't need weightlifters," he often said. "We need athletes." When Stillwagon arrived on campus, he was taken to a room in the athletic center and shown the school's weighlifting equipment. It consisted of a Universal machine with its eight interlocking stations.

"That's *it*?" he said. "That's something you have in an apartment."

Stillwagon brought in his own set of free weights. His older brother, Tom, a center for Miami University, was the first to tell him about their effectiveness. So Stillwagon began pumping iron at Augusta (Virginia) Military School, where he followed Tom's path. Their father was an executive at Continental Can, the major employer in Mount Vernon. He hired half the town, it seemed to his son who, as a youth, attended the Catholic school in town but regularly clashed with the nuns and priests. One nun told his parents to prepare themselves, because their son would be spending his life in a penitentiary.

So, at age 15, Stillwagon was shipped to Augusta. After his first year, he was called into the office of one of the school's officers. He was reminded that his brother had been voted the top cadet among the 600 at the school. "You've just been voted the second-worst cadet," the officer said. "What are we going to do with you?"

By his senior year, he tied for tenth-best cadet. He played every sport he could at Augusta. Football. Lacrosse. Baseball. Anything, he said, that would let him get through the gates to glimpse the outside world. He enjoyed the school and its remoteness. He just enjoyed seeing what the rest of the world offered.

Stillwagon's roommate was from York, Pennsylvania, home of a renowned weightlifting company, and had his own set of weights. Soon, Stillwagon did as well. On quiet nights with nothing to do, while other students frittered away the time, he and his roommate lifted weights. Soon, Stillwagon had the perfect body to go with the perfect mindset.

After a two-a-day practice as a freshman, Dick Kuhn was getting tape cut off when Stillwagon came over to the trainer, Ernie Biggs. He wanted to know if Biggs had any more weight plates to put on the Universal machine.

"Yeah, there's a couple of 100-pound plates in the closet," Biggs said.

Stillwagon added those plates to the maximum 250 pounds on the machine. Suddenly, some of the seniors began to whisper. "Do you see that?" they said. "He's got 450 pounds on it." They watched as Stillwagon whipped off five bench press repetitions.

Stillwagon's game flowed from this strength. He decided the best way to beat the guy in front of him each game was to offer a demonstration right from the start. And so, no matter what defense was called, Stillwagon spent the first three plays of every game helmet-butting the opposing center as fiercely as he could. That sent the proper message. Often, it immediately settled who was king of the jungle.

Bill Urbanik, who lined up at tackle beside Stillwagon, would go on to coach the likes of Hall of Fame lineman Howie Long with the Oakland Raiders and All-Pro Tim Krumrie with the Cincinnati Bengals. Stillwagon, he said, was the toughest lineman he ever saw. Nothing fazed him, Urbanik said. Double teams. Triple teams. Injuries. Nothing.

"He came to practice every day and his jaw was locked, he was so intent on playing hard," Mallory said.

With some players, Mallory said, you had to push and prod and find the right button to push. With Stillwagon, if anything needed to be said, it was a simple, "Jim, let's get it cranked up."

Most days, like this one, Mallory just watched him play.

(4)

By the third quarter of his first start, whatever nervousness Maciejowski felt had evaporated. Everything he called worked. Five times, Ohio State's offense got the ball in the second half. Five times, it scored.

Maciejowski had a day of days. He passed for 157 yards on the day and a touchdown. He ran for 124 more yards and three touchdowns. Granted, it was against a winless Wisconsin team. But when you've sat listening to the music for so long, you don't complain about your dance partner.

"You know the most amazing thing about the football season to date?" Hayes said while waving the statistics sheet after the game. "The greatness of it is right here. Look at the pass receiving—how doggone many ways we've got to go. Name me two other sophomores in the country who are over 50 percent in completions."

He was asked if there would be an issue over who would start at quarterback the next day.

"Well," he said, "that's a good problem to have. And Ron played well. But I think we know who our quarterback is."

Maciejowski knew, if the reporter didn't.

In the post-game locker room, Hayes took out page 84 of Coach Emerson's playbook.

"Where is George Chaump?" he said.

Chaump was at the back of the locker room by the showers, in the crowd of players, nearly out of view.

"WHERE IS THAT GODDAMN GEORGE CHAUMP?" Hayes yelled.

No one moved. Dave Brungard, upset over playing hardly at all in the game, turned around to spot Chaump. Earle Bruce, standing beside Chaump, wondered what this was about, after such a big win.

"That was the worst gameplan I've ever seen," he said. "YOU'RE FIRED!"

Silence.

"You're fired," he said again.

This would be firing Number Two of a dozen in Chaump's nine-year marriage with Hayes. He reacted the same as the first time, which was that he wasn't sure he heard correctly. Hadn't they just won 43-8? And now, in front of the entire team, he'd been *fired*?

Hayes was upset over a second-half mix-up that left no fullback on the field. Paul Huff had been told that Brockington was going in the game. But Brockington didn't. And Hayes began screaming at Huff, kicking him out of the game, making him walk across the field to the locker room. Which was locked. Huff, with family in the stands, felt humiliated standing there. Especially when he did nothing wrong.

Hayes felt angrier when told it wasn't Huff's fault.

And Chaump?

He felt confused. Earle Bruce tried to console him. It would go like this all season, one trying to pick up the other. Bruce, in his first season on the offensive side, was reminded again how little the defensive coaches actually knew Hayes. The entire staff would meet at 8 a.m. for ten minutes. The defensive side then went on its way while the offensive assistants sat with Woody. All day. All year.

He was such a presence to the offense that, in the first on-field huddle of the season against Southern Methodist, a gap was left where Hayes stood in the practice huddle. The players looked at each other and chuckled. Then they closed the gap.

And the hours? The offensive coaches told their defensive counterparts to make a lot of noise on their way out of the offices. Maybe, they hoped, Hayes would get the hint at 10 p.m. Or 11 p.m. Or whenever. But Hayes's competition with McCullough carried over to who worked more, too. He wouldn't leave until an hour after McCullough did.

Another scene in the Wisconsin locker room offered an example of how Woody dealt with the defensive staff. Holtz diagrammed a play on a small blackboard. Hayes watched with his arms folded. This was Wisconsin's only big pass of the day, and watching the scene, student reporter Ray Dyson was struck by Woody's obsessiveness. After such a lopsided win, Hayes was demanding that Holtz show him how Wisconsin could possibly have completed one pass against his secondary.

"See, their guy went here," Holtz said, moving the chalk.

"Mmm-hmmm," Hayes said.

"Then our coverage went like this," he said, drawing lines.

"Mmm-hmm," he said.

"It won't happen again, Coach," he said. "It won't happen."

Hayes said nothing. Which is how Chaump would have preferred it. Bruce tried to console him on the flight home.

"You know Woody, you'll be fine," Bruce said.

"I don't know what to do," Chaump said. "Tomorrow's Sunday. Do I come in?"

Chaump did go to the office the next day. The offensive coaches met in a different room, away from Hayes, as if to show their unity with Chaump. Near the end of the workday, Hayes asked to see Chaump.

"Don't make it easy for him," Bruce told Chaump.

Chaump went into Hayes's office. The rest of the coaches snuck to just outside the door. Chaump wasn't fired. He had his job back. He left that day, grateful to have his job while wondering how to improve on 43 points.

Increasingly, as Hayden and Brockington began to play more, Dave Brungard began to disappear. The junior who scored three touchdowns in the opener against Southern Methodist didn't score again all year. Score? He didn't even play against Michigan State. Or Iowa. Or Michigan. Or . . .

"We've been in meetings all day," said his friend Bo Rein, a graduate assistant, as they walked to practice one day.

Brungard looked over at him.

"The best thing I can tell you is you'd better go somewhere else," he said.

He said it as only a good friend could. It still hurt. Brungard had been the prize a few years earlier. All-Ohio. All-America. Woody came to his first high school game as a senior in Youngstown and called seemingly every week thereafter. He spoke at the post-season banquet of Brungard's team, all with the idea of staying on top of his big recruit. How intoxicating that felt!

Brungard's father played on Ohio State's 1935 Big Ten championship team, but George Brungard didn't affect his son's college decision as much as Woody did. Only now, everything had changed. Now, if Brungard did something wrong, he'd hear Hayes say, "That's why he can't play for Ohio State."

Now he knew that if he wanted to keep playing, he'd have to leave Ohio State. And he did want to keep playing. Football was important to him. He would finish out this 1968 season, then go to Hayes and say he wanted to transfer.

Already, he heard, Alabama's Bear Bryant would welcome him. He would start his final college season at Alabama and gain 500 yards on a team that won the Bluebonnet Bowl. It wasn't the Rose Bowl. It wasn't a national championship team.

But he played. Football became fun again. And he became a trivia answer: How many players were coached by both Woody Hayes and Bear Bryant?

Just one.

The Ten Percent
rule

When Bill Mallory was hired as the defensive line coach in 1966, he was taken aside by Lyal Clark, the retiring assistant he would replace.

"Let me tell you about the man you're about to work for," Clark said. "Ninety percent of the time, he's as fine a person as you'll ever meet, the kind of man who will do anything for his players and make you a better coach.

"But there's that other ten percent of the time. When that kicks in, get your ass out of the way."

This is about the other ten percent.

They all discovered it, everyone down the roster. Many felt the fists that proved it. After Roman missed an extra point against Michigan State, Hayes was waiting for him on the sideline.

"You sonuvabitch, now next time we've got to go for two points," he said, then balled his fist and punched Roman hard in the sternum, right beneath where the protection of the shoulder pads ended.

Roman nearly puked from the force.

"You all right?" Hindman said from the press box phone, when Roman made his way to the bench.

"I swear, I'm gonna kill him," Roman said.

Jim Otis

"Just stay away from him," Hindman said. "Go stand on the other side. Don't go near him."

That was the advice they all heard. Sensibaugh heard it after he shanked a punt in the opener and walked by Hayes and—*Bam!*—felt that fist. Oppermann heard it when he missed a field goal and—*Pow!*—passed Hayes on the sideline.

In the Northwestern game, guard Alan Jack lost his starting job. Even when called to go into the game, he felt dejected, and Hayes must have noticed. So he delivered three left jabs straight to Jack's gut, right there on the sideline. It was his applied coaching philosophy on how a player's dejection could be changed into anger.

"I could hardly breathe when I went running on the field," Jack said.

There were two rules passed down through the years to incoming Ohio State players, like Native Americans passing down how to fish or to dance a ritualistic dance:

1. *Don't do anything to tick off the Old Man.*
2. *If you break Rule Number One, remember he's left-handed.*

One common freshman mistake was standing within range of his left fist. Anyone who had been around for any length of time knew to stay away from it. Early in 1968, the quarterbacks shifted the open spot in the huddle so Hayes had to stand to their right. This kept the left fist too close to be unloaded quickly.

After guard Randy Hart once made a mistake in practice, he moved away from Hayes's left, and kept moving away from it, to the point where both he and Hayes had turned in a full circle. When they rejoined the huddle, and Hart relaxed, a Woody backhand slapped his gut so hard it left an imprint for three days.

"Don't pull that shit again," Hayes said.

Even at 55, Hayes's left hand was dangerous. As a teenager in Newcomerstown, he had developed it by earning $5 for boxing on the farm of former pitching great Cy Young. His father, a school superintendent, once arrived to give a speech to a near-empty auditorium, asked where everyone was, and was told they were at a big fight. He went and saw his two sons fighting under assumed names. At Denison University, Hayes fought regularly in intramural bouts, with a string of knockouts on his reputation.

There were stories up and down the roster. While practicing a new blocking pattern on the 32-Trap play, Oppermann forgot his assignment. He did, however, get his man to the ground by merely shifting his weight, basically giving no resistance, and letting the defensive lineman's forward-leaning momentum make him fall.

Oppermann was laughing over his prey—"You fell for *that* old trick?"—when Hayes, upset over the missed assignment, began screaming, "You think that's funny, you sonuvabitch?" he asked.

Hayes proceeded to tear off Oppermann's helmet, jersey, and shoulder pads. Oppermann was standing in only his football pants when Hayes, "began punching me in the face," he remembers. It was part of such a traumatic time for Oppermann that upon graduating he left the school bitter. He remained so for more than a decade, until an intermediary reintroduced him to Hayes and patched up everything.

Some of this seemed a product of the coaching times as much as the work of an uncapped temper. A freshman practicing on the scout team, Tom Bartley intercepted a pass against the first-team offense. The next play, the same play was run. Bartley intercepted it again. "Before I could look up, Woody was on top of me, swinging his fists," he said. The scene flashed in Bartley's mind years later, when Clemson's Charlie Bauman intercepted an Ohio State pass in the Gator Bowl and Hayes, in the final act of his era, punched him.

In the spring practice of 1968, with Kern's back hurting and two-year starting quarterback Bill Long playing baseball, Maciejowski ran the offense much of the time. One day, the offensive players walked out of the huddle to the line of scrimmage. Maciejowski tried to prod them to jog, as was expected. But the next time out of the huddle, the same thing happened. This time, Hayes jumped in.

"GODDAMMIT, QUARTERBACK!" he yelled to Maciejowski. "YOU GET THEM MOVING!"

Everyone still walked out of the next huddle. At this point, Hayes grabbed Maciejowski and delivered a left uppercut into his stomach. That got everyone moving. But as the offense stood at the line and waited for the quarterback's signals, it stayed silent. No call came from Maciejowski.

"GODDAMMIT, QUARTERBACK!" Hayes yelled.

Hayes had hit Maciejowski so hard he had knocked the wind out of him. He couldn't walk, much less talk.

(2)

Hayes's temper was, in such moments, inexcusable to some players. It hardly mattered whether it was calculating or not. Two weeks into his Ohio State career in 1967, Jerry Tabacca didn't catch a bad pass during a scrimmage. Hayes must have felt he didn't give full effort. He ran up to Tabacca, yanked off his helmet, and punched him in the face.

Hayes must have recognized immediately that he had broken some personal protocol.

"Sorry, I shouldn't have done that," he said.

He yanked Tabacca's helmet back onto his head.

"This is what you deserve," Hayes said, and then started punching him again.

In one practice, working on the Sprint Draw-14 play, the backside guard stepped around the center and led through the hole to block the linebacker. The fullback would follow. Cheney, who was white, ran the play twice and tripped over the center both times. Strickland, who was black, then ran the play from the other side. He screwed it up, too.

Hayes ignited. He grabbed Strickland by the facemask. He was cursing him. Then, Cheney said, "It was like a light bulb went off in his head."

He grabbed the black player who screwed up once? And didn't the white player who did twice? In these turbulent 1960s?

He yelled to Strickland. "IF IT'S NOT YOU . . ."

Hayes threw a fist hard into Cheney's chest.

" . . . IT'S *THIS* DUMB SONUVABITCH!"

The players talked afterward about that. It was how Hayes dealt with black and white issues. Cheney, even though he was the one hit, respected him for that. It said they were all treated like equals in Hayes's eyes. All like dogs.

There was also a line out there with Hayes, somewhere. No one knew exactly where it was, though everyone had different ideas on how often Hayes crossed over it. Many players figured Hayes's punches were simply "exclamations points to what he was saying," as defensive lineman Bill Pollitt said. Paul Huff said the punching didn't hurt much.

"It was when he got to kicking you that it could really hurt," he said.

Many players felt Hayes was in control most of the time when he threw his punches. As a senior in 1969, Chuck Hutchinson jumped offside on consecutive plays. Woody stomped up to him, yanked his facemask to bring him in close, and said, "Son, you're the dumbest sonuvabitch I've ever coached. In fact, you're the dumbest sonuvabitch in the Big Ten."

He threw his left into Hutchinson's solar plexus. All the wind went out of Hutchinson's body. As he stood gasping but not daring to flinch, Hutchinson heard Hayes scream how he didn't deserve to play at Ohio State and kicked him out of the practice. Walking alone to the locker room, Hutchinson thought that was it, he had enough—"The Old Man can have this place to himself," as he said.

Hayes called Hutchinson into his office after practice. "You know why I did that?" he said. "I did that to make you mad. You play a lot better when you're mad. I expect you to have a great year."

Did that make things square with Hutchinson? He said it did. Often, this make-up session actually brought the coach and player closer. Often, it came in the shower, of all places, in a trademark manner. Tight end Dick Kuhn felt the wrath and fists of Woody one practice. While showering afterward, "All of a sudden, I felt someone's hands on my back," he said. "It was Woody. He said, 'Dick, I'm just washing your back for you here.' He does it awhile, then he goes, 'Okay, now you wash my back.' "

This was part of the Hayes experience. He would regularly wash the back of the player with whom he had a megaton moment earlier. How could you stay mad at someone who was washing your back? And then asking you to wash his? Often, shower time turned into a calmer coaching session. That day with Kuhn, Hayes began talking about the technicalities of catching a pass.

"Here we are, buck naked, and he's trying to show me how to put my fingers for catching," Kuhn said. "He says, 'Now, goddammit, Dick, when you're catching a pass above your chest, you've got to put your thumbs together.' He showed me how. Then I did it. And we stood there in the shower doing this after we'd washed each other's backs."

After being punched, Hart was trying to ignore Hayes in the shower. Hayes called him from ten showers away. Hart said nothing. Hayes moved to four showers away and called out. Still nothing. Now Hayes was in the next shower.

"Randy, I understand you're upset, " Hayes said. "But if you had made that same mistake in the Michigan game and cost us the Big Ten championship and an opportunity to win the Rose Bowl, you would feel a whole lot worse than you do now. That's why I got mad at you."

Hurt by the punch and humiliated by the outburst, Hart stood there somehow feeling he should thank his coach.

Often, after a loss, Hayes simply lashed out at whatever was closest, animate or inanimate. "When we lose a game, nobody's madder at me than me," he once said. "When I look into the mirror in the morning, I want to take a swing at me."

After a loss at Minnesota in 1966, he entered the locker room and put his fist through a plywood door. His coaches couldn't believe the power behind that rage. When Ohio State played there next, the door hadn't been replaced. Instead, it had become something of a George-Washington-slept-here landmark around Minnesota football for everyone to notice.

See what we caused Woody Hayes to do?

In that vein, Kuhn stood behind Hayes on the sideline, ready in case a two-tight-end set was called. Sometimes, after a bad play, Hayes simply turned around and punched Kuhn in the stomach. Kuhn quickly learned to stand a few feet farther away.

Players and coaches came to realize there could be the on-field Woody and the off-field Woody. They weren't always the same people. Hayes, off the field, would do anything for anyone. Hayes, on the field, had an intensity beyond what any of them had seen or could comprehend.

Steve Crapser, a reserve lineman, knelt next to Hayes on the sideline during the spring game in 1968. Hayes took off his wire-rim glasses and held them. At some point, he became so involved in the game he clenched his fist and kept it clenched. When he finally opened it, the glasses were crushed and his hand was cut and bleeding. Occasionally, in practice, Hayes's hand would be wrapped in a towel from doing the same thing. Then there were the regular reactions: Hayes biting the palm of his hand; Hayes punching himself in the face, often with a championship ring on his finger accentuating the damage.

(3)

Many of the tantrums belonged on Broadway. Maybe they all did. No one could figure him out completely. Especially after they had been around for a while, players saw a slight cut in his shirt or cap and knew something was coming.

The first time Jim Coburn saw Hayes rip his shirt over some missed practice assignment he was stunned by the power of the coach's rage. But he soon learned the tricks of the shirt torn just a bit to help it go or the hat stitches cut with a razor blade. He once stood next to Huff as Hayes began screaming about some missed assignment.

"He's gonna tear his hat," Huff whispered.

Hayes tore the hat, threw it to the ground, and stomped on it.

"Watch, he's gonna tear his shirt," Huff whispered.

Hayes grabbed and ripped his T-shirt.

"Oh, my god, he's gonna throw that watch," Huff whispered, actually surprised.

Every upperclassman knew Hayes wore cheap watches for the effect of throwing them on the ground and leaving them. Occasionally, a player would pick one up after practice. Hayes, they came to realize, threw only old watches. But on this particular day, Huff had noticed Hayes was still wearing his good watch, the expensive one. Hayes grabbed it and with flushed face ripped it off his wrist. He reared back to throw it. Then, still cursing loudly, he threw the wristband across the field.

Huff looked for it after practice. All he found was the watchband. Hayes, he figured, had palmed the watch itself and slipped it into his pants pocket. Sleight of hand, Woody style.

"Damn, I wanted that watch," Huff told Coburn.

Still, even in this era, smashing watches and ripping hats was one thing. Hitting players was another. It was a dark magic, accepted by the older coaches on the staff. Hayes might change his recruiting pattern. He might add the I-formation. But that left fist remained as integral to his coaching as the off-tackle play.

"You suppressed your favorite dramatic technique this spring about as well as can be expected," Tiger Ellison wrote in a staff report in the spring of 1968. "You kept your hands off your players and you did not lambaste your coaches in front of players and such control has to contribute to a thing called morale. However, the 'X' factor in our formula for victory respects only one thing: Power applied fairly. So the velvet glove you wear must still enclose an iron fist."

The iron fist was wielded that season. Once at halftime as Hayes calmly pointed out all the mistakes his players were making, Strickland stood up to adjust his shoulder pads. That was another mistake. The tone of Hayes's voice didn't change as he "lashed out with four or five jabs to Phil's head," Tatum wrote in his book, *They Call Me Assassin*. "Then Woody went on talking as if nothing had happened, but Phil had been knocked over backward from the punches to his head."

Still, no single incident involving these players displayed that Ten Percent Rule more than one at halftime of the Illinois game in 1967. It wasn't just the schizophrenic rage that came out of this legendary coach. It was also the player he went after.

(4)

They all had nicknames. Doug Adams was "Cowboy," because he wore cowboy boots. Holloway was "Sugar Bear," after the mascot of the cereal Sugar Crisp. Urbanik was "Choo-Choo," because he sounded like a train when running. Gillian was called "Cheese," from his high school days as a big cheese. Sensibaugh was "Baugh," because half the tape bearing his name on his helmet wore off and those letters remained.

Jim Otis was "King."

He carried himself like one, players felt. He strutted. He posed. He came with the attitude of royalty, which served him well, because if any position cried out for an imposing amount of confidence in Hayes's system it was the fullback. His star. His centerpiece. And, well, his target, too, when things went bad.

In some sense, Otis was bred for this spotlight. His father met Hayes when both were students at Denison University in 1933. They became roommates, fraternity brothers, and lifelong friends. When Hayes boxed in school, James Otis introduced him and was his second in the ring. When Hayes began dating Anne Gross, he made sure Otis met her. When their son, Steve, was born, it seemed a bonus that the day fell on Otis's birthday.

Each year, Hayes brought Anne and Steve to visit the Otis family in Celina, Ohio, and receive a physical from his old roommate, a physician. Each year on those visits, young Jim Otis asked Woody to watch him run the football or catch passes.

At 7, Otis played on the Ohio Stadium field and had a photo taken with Hopalong Cassady. By 10, he was telling everyone he would grow up to play fullback at Ohio State. Other friends imagined running like Jim Brown on the sandlots. Otis would be Ohio State's Hopalong or Bob Ferguson. When he was a senior, his coach warned other recruiters he was going to Ohio State. Otis told Bo Schembechler, then coaching Miami University, that if he didn't attend Ohio State he'd play at Miami. They joked about that later. Schembechler said he never had a shot.

Following Otis's senior season, Hayes spoke at the Celina football banquet. Afterward, talking privately, Hayes offered him a scholarship. It was on full merit. Otis could have gone to any school he wanted. But there was concern that the family relationship not be misconstrued.

"We've recruited a couple of other fullbacks," Hayes told Otis. "One is bigger. We don't know, they might be better."

"Coach, you offered me a scholarship, right?" Otis said.

"Yes," Hayes said.

"We'll just have to find out how good they are, won't we?" he said.

That was Otis. He didn't fear competition. He dripped with a tangible measure of confidence and self-reliance. It was a big component of his game, considering that he wasn't particularly big or shifty. As Huff said with full respect: "Jim did more with less than anyone I know."

What Otis did have was balance and quickness and unmatched determination. The balance was developed through his diving as a kid. He never lost a competition in northeastern Ohio. One day, while Otis was jumping on the trampoline in high school, Ohio State swim coach Phil Peppe observed that he could be a diving champion if he worked at it. Otis told Peppe he'd rather be Ohio State's fullback.

Otis was quick enough so he lined up a fraction behind the normal fullback position rather than slowing down for a handoff from the quarterback. It was that quickness—and an innate ability to find seams in the line—that enabled him not to lose any yardage on a carry at Ohio State until his senior season.

Still, if his effectiveness wasn't a question, his relationship with Hayes sometimes was. It could be a burden to both, especially as events played out with Brockington in 1968 and more so in 1969. "Woody's boy," Otis was considered by teammates. With it came the suggestion he got something he didn't deserve.

"I get sick and tired of hearing people say I'm the starting fullback because my dad and Woody Hayes were college roommates," Otis said during that 1968 season.

"I get sick and tired hearing people say I start him because his dad was my best friend," Hayes said.

The halftime incident in 1967 should have changed any such thoughts.

With Ohio State at 2-2, with one losing season already in 1966, with that plane circling with the "Goodbye Woody" banner and Ohio Stadium fans singing the same, the team trudged into halftime in October of 1967 losing to Illinois.

It was the low-water mark of the Hayes era, and no one felt lower than Otis.

In high school, he hadn't fumbled in more than 300 carries. He would never again fumble more than once in a game and rarely at that.

But he had fumbled twice that first half.

"Freakish," Otis called it.

Hayes entered the locker room in a rage. It wasn't surprising to players who had seen Hayes throw every possible emotion at them across practices and games. No one expected what came next, though. As Hayes ranted down the litany of errors, he came to the subject of fumbles and snapped.

"WHERE'S THAT GODDAMN OTIS!" he screamed.

Then, in a scene replayed for decades among these players, Hayes launched himself over the first row of players at Otis—"like Orca going after a penguin," Oppermann said. Suddenly, it was bedlam. Suddenly, a bucket of oranges was flying through the air and the six-ounce bottles of Coke being passed around exploded "like firecrackers," Otis said.

Suddenly, Hayes's fists were flying on Otis, too. Or around him. Otis said no fist connected. But Hayes was on top of him, throwing punches, still screaming. Players scrambled out of the way. Assistant coaches came running in.

"C'mon, Coach!"

"Coach! Get hold of yourself!"

"Get off him, Coach!"

Otis sat, stunned, as Hayes kept yelling. "He told me in front of the whole team I'd never play at Ohio State again," Otis said. "Not only was he talking to me, he was telling everybody on the whole team he wouldn't tolerate mistakes. Fumbles set him off. I thought my playing days were finished."

Sitting beside Otis, Dave Brungard put on his helmet and snapped the chinstrap as Hayes picked up with the halftime talk. He had fumbled once in the first half, too. Woody, he figured, was coming after him next. "He's not hitting me in the head like that," Brungard thought.

"That might've been the worst of anything he did," Worden said. "It wasn't right. I think it cost us that ball game. It deflated the team. At least for myself, it was demoralizing, and I think we went out and played like that in the second half."

Ohio State lost to Illinois, 17-13, and fell to 2-3. Otis didn't play the second half. He was certain his days at Ohio State were finished. Larry Catuzzi talked with him for more than an hour in the parking lot the next week, trying to lift spirits that couldn't be lifted. Otis mentioned transferring. Catuzzi remembered Otis as being "depressed, upset, confused."

For the next two games, Otis sat on the bench and Huff starred, as if confirming that their Ohio State careers had switched tracks. During that time, Hayes said nothing to Otis. But then Huff suffered an injury. The day before the Iowa game, Hayes asked Otis, "How're you sleeping?"

"Normally, I don't sleep well before games," Otis said. "I've been sleeping just fine lately."

Hayes told him not to expect much sleep that night. He was starting. He carried thirty-five times for 140 yards against Iowa. The next time he was out of his team's lineup, he was in the NFL.

(5)

Now, a year later, it was the Iowa game again. No Big Ten peer knew about Hayes's Ten Percent Rule better than Iowa athletic director Forest Evashevski. As Hayes—during a 1965 Big Ten meeting—talked about the purposely high grass on Iowa's field, Evashevski became so upset that he called Hayes a "disgrace to coaching."

Hayes whipped off his suit coat, knocked over his chair getting up, and ran around a table with fists cocked.

"I don't take that from anyone!" he yelled.

Their peers became a buffer, holding each coach back. Still, as they prepared to play, one Iowa newspaper wrote it would be more entertaining to watch Evashevski and Hayes in a three-round fight than these teams. No site paralleled a boxing ring more than Iowa's Kinnick Stadium, too. As Hayes gave his pre-game speech, an Iowa ball boy came into the locker room.

"What do *you* want?" Hayes said.

"I'm supposed to tell everyone to wear their helmets when they go on the field," the boy said.

As the Ohio State players ran up the stairs to the field, helmets on, Iowa fans rained boos, drinks, cups—whatever they had to offer—down on them. As he got to the field, Muhlbach turned and looked back. Hayes never led his team on the field like most coaches. His way was to be last out of the locker room, the last on the field.

And as he came out, the storm of boos and thrown cups increased. Hayes didn't seem to notice. If anything, Muhlbach thought, he seemed to thrive on the idea that he stirred this passion in another crowd. It would be this kind of fistfight of a game, too. Stillwagon's face became bloodied. Mud caked the players. Stier got punched by an Iowa player, and Urbanik kicked the guy back in the helmet.

Blood.

Guts.

Iron fists.

They could survive that way.

Ohio State 33, Iowa 27.

(6)

A tradition wasn't always a tradition. One day it was just a new idea sprung on people. And what might later be treated with respect, even reverence, could be welcomed with a smirk or amusement or some United Press International reporter calling it "schoolmarm tactics."

So it was with the Buckeye Leaf.

On the Monday after the Iowa game, Hayes called deserving players in front of the team and slapped a leaf on their game helmets. He then released to the media the names of those so awarded. That way, the recognition factor added to the luster. Players were soon lobbying for them as they watched film with coaches.

"Rewind that and tell me that doesn't get a leaf."

"Did you see that block right there?"

"Come on, my grade should be higher after that game."

The concept of the Buckeye Leaf was just a year old. Hayes and trainer Ernie Biggs concocted the idea, but the decals weren't ready for the first game in 1967. So after the second game, a 30-0 win against Oregon, Hayes awarded the first fifteen leafs, covering two games. Talk about stingy.

Provost got three for his three interceptions.

"Teddy the Tree," Hayes called him for getting that many leafs, thus delivering the nickname that followed Provost ever after.

"Every boy who intercepts a pass, recovers a fumble, blocks a punt, or makes a great play gets a Buckeye Leaf on his helmet," Hayes said that first day to the media. "So do the top back and top linemen on offense and defense each week."

The early response was, well, understated.

"It may never take the place of little gold stars on 'A' papers, but if you're an Ohio State football player, and you're good, you'll get a little Buckeye leaf decal on your helmet," the UPI wrote that first week in a story picked up by newspapers across Ohio.

Later, at the Rose Bowl, they were such a novelty to the national audience that NBC did a close-up of an Ohio State helmet. "Those are Buckeye Leafs," announcer Curt Gowdy explained. "If they make a touchdown, they get a full leaf. They get parts of leafs for outstanding defensive plays or offensive plays throughout the season. Sort of like the old World War I and World War II airplane men."

Over the course of the first couple of seasons, players became accustomed to the idea, as well as the motivation behind it. After the Iowa game, Hayes passed out twenty-five leafs. Stier got three, Hayes said, for being a "tremendous football player as a leader and a sticker." Cheney, who started a couple of games and played regularly at tackle, got his only leaf that season, for recovering an onside kick.

Then again, there was an economy to how they were handed out. By that Rose Bowl, after nine undefeated games, Kern and Otis each had nine Buckeye leafs. Tatum had eight.

And *they* were the stars.

The team up
north

*F*or Ohio State football, two words have written history, defined eras, spelled success, catalogued failure, regulated emotions the rest of the year and specifically, marked the rise and fall of coaches.

These two words:

Michigan Week.

And in November of 1968, Hayes strode into the North Facility on that Monday before the week's first practice and did something he never had before and never would again during these players' careers. He told them to sit down. He passed out pencils and paper.

"Write down what you are going to do differently this week to get ready for this game," he said. "I don't care if you're a starter or not. Come up with one thing you will do this week that will make this team better prepared for this game."

Ohio State was ranked Number Two. Michigan was Number Four. Both were unbeaten. The winner was off to the Rose Bowl. Not since 1964 had either team played for the title in this game (Michigan won). Not since 1955 had both had a chance for at least a share of the title (Ohio State won).

"It's like old times," Paul Hornung wrote in the *Columbus Dispatch*. Scalpers were getting $50 a ticket. Ticket director George Staten, who just a couple of months earlier was answering questions about dwindling attendance, was saying now an attendance record could be set for the third time this season.

Michigan, 1968

So the players sat at the start of this week and wrote something. Anything.

"Run extra sprints."

"Concentrate more."

Mike Sensibaugh composed a letter that began: "Need it be said? This is probably the biggest week of your life. How can one game have more at stake than Saturday's? The only way the Rose Bowl can live up to its reputation (which hasn't been the best in recent years, because the best teams haven't played) is by having OSU represent the Big Ten.

"A game between the Number One and Number Two teams—both undefeated—would be perhaps the greatest college game of 'all time.' There is one game between you and that . . . "

No one needed to tell Hayes the significance of this week every year. He understood from this Darwinian angle: It's why he got the job. In 1950, in the famous Snow Bowl, during a blizzard of such white-out proportions the teams punt forty-five times—often on first down—Michigan upset eighth-ranked Ohio State. That put Wes Fesler out as coach. Hayes rode in.

And while by 1968 some could question his offensive ingenuity or his recent seasons, no one questioned his 11-6 record against Michigan. In 1957, he won before Michigan's first crowd of over 100,000. In 1958, he won when Dick Schafrath forced a goal line fumble on the final play. In 1961, he won to go to the Rose Bowl That Wasn't.

In 1954, he summed up what it meant to beat Michigan by getting up on a chair and shouting to a room of reporters, "Boys, this is how I feel!"

He then jumped in the air.

WHOOP-EEEEE!

His highs and lows became North and South poles by Michigan. In 1955, he told reporters the Michigan win was "the very best game any team has ever played for me. Did you ever see anything like it? Ever?"

Before beating Michigan in 1967, Hayes became so impassioned during his locker room speech that Tom Backhus, then a sophomore still getting his introduction to Woody, expected a fistfight to break out before the game. The two locker room doors at Michigan Stadium were across from each other in a long tunnel that led to the field. Hayes pointed toward the Michigan locker at the end of his speech and began shouting to his players.

"WE'LL FIGHT 'EM RIGHT HERE IN THE TUNNEL!" he yelled. "LET'S GO! WE'LL START IT RIGHT HERE!"

Players started moving with him.

"LET'S GO FIGHT 'EM!" Hayes yelled.

The emotion was somehow turned to the field. Again in this Michigan Week of 1968, with another sophomore class to indoctrinate, Hayes raged against Michigan in a manner only he could.

"I despise those arrogant sons of bitches!" Hayes said to his players. "I despise them all! I don't hate them. I'm not a hater. You can't be a hater i n life. But I despise them. It's okay to despise."

As the sophomores tried to register that difference . . .

"Those arrogant sons of bitches tried to break Hoppy's leg!" Hayes said.

The sophomores looked at each other.

Hoppy?

"Ron Kramer put a cheap shot on Hoppy and . . ."

They quickly learned it was Hopalong Cassady. The famed Ohio State runner in the 1950s. The disdain for everything Michigan became part of the genetic code at Ohio State. As a freshman, Ralph Holloway once wore a yellow-and-blue tie to a team meal. It wasn't Michigan's maize-and-blue colors. But it was close enough that Hayes said, "Ralph, I've got to get you another tie." The next time Hayes saw Holloway, he gave him a red, black, and gray tie.

That week, a Michigan rug was put in the middle of the locker room for players to wipe their shoes on. A decal with a Michigan insignia was put in the urinal. In his practice, Woody turned the dial a few notches higher, too. That Wednesday, Maciejowski threw a high pass that ticked off Jankowski's fingertips. Hayes threw his intricately made, color-coded play cards in the air. He began shouting how no one cared, how everyone's work habits were weak.

"DO YOU KNOW WHAT WEEK IT IS, GODDAMMIT!" he screamed.

Hayes tore off his cap and tried to rip it in half. But it wasn't the old wool cap he could split whenever he wanted. This was serge material, sewed up well. It wouldn't tear. That made Hayes madder. He took his watch and smashed it to the ground. He took his glasses and smashed them, too. He tore his T-shirt down the front and briefly tried to tear the whistle cord before giving up and deciding to punch himself in the eye instead.

That five-star megaton took fifteen seconds.

Even the seniors were impressed.

Two years later—the season after 1969's crushing loss to Michigan—Ohio State players walked into the locker room on the Monday of Michigan Week and their normal music wasn't playing over the speakers. It was the Michigan radio announcers' play-by-play of that '69 game. They were giddy about Michigan's domination. They were mispronouncing the names of Ohio State players, most glaringly that of Maciejowski, whose name sounded like it was something going through a disposal. That Monday, while changing for practice, players shook their heads and chuckled over the lengths to which Woody would go.

That same play-by-play greeted them as they returned from practice. And as they got out of the shower. And as they left the locker room. It was there Tuesday, too. And Wednesday. At some point as the week went on, their amusement at Woody turned to anger at Michigan.

"Can you believe they said Michigan was tougher?"

"I'm tired of them 'winning easily.'"

"They're still butchering Maciejowski's name?"

Every year, Woody had a Michigan angle. In 1973, while Jim Stillwagon was playing for Toronto in the Canadian Football League, Hayes asked him to speak to the team after the light Friday practice. Stillwagon began by saying that no matter where football took them, this was the greatest game they would play, that every play would matter, that . . .

"No, no, no," Hayes interrupted. "Tell them what it's *really* like!"

"Well," Stillwagon said, "this will be the biggest game of your life and . . ."

"NO!" Hayes interrupted again. "TELL THEM WHAT IT'S LIKE!"

"Uh," Stillwagon said, fumbling around, "you won't play a big . . ."

"NO, TELL THEM IT'S A WAR!" Hayes yelled. "IT'S A WAR!"

Hayes threw a left hook into Stillwagon's back to punctuate his words. Stillwagon was wearing a leather jacket, so each punch reverberated like a drumbeat that was accompanied by his yells.

". . . IT'S A WAR! . . ."

Punch.

". . . IT'S A WAR!"

Punch.

The players caught the emotion and began yelling, too. The speech was over. The task was done. Stillwagon, his back bruised, watched Ohio State win the next day.

The emotion spilled into the public, too. In 1970, an Ohio State student named Thomas Harrington was arrested for public obscenity while driving his 1962 Volkswagen. His bumper sticker read: "Fuck Michigan."

Lawyers went to work. The prosecution argued no word was more offensive than this verb, which was slang for sexual intercourse. But Judge James A.

Pearson in the Franklin County Municipal Court considered this dictionary definition and reasoned it "absurd" to think the bumper sticker meant to "have sexual intercourse with the state of Michigan."

"Mr. Harrington's bumper sticker accurately expressed the derogatory nature of this mood toward the University of Michigan football team and the state of Michigan as a whole," Judge Pearson wrote in his decision. He added: "Most of the people of Ohio would say that Mr. Harrington's bumper sticker also had redeeming social value."

Next case.

Mark Stier, in his final Michigan Week in 1968, surmised all along that Hayes was play-acting this villain's role for Michigan. It was too over the top, too irrational, even for him. With each passing year at Ohio State he believed in it less. His belief—or lack of it—continued while he became a graduate assistant and Hayes's rejection of all things Michigan became even more pronounced as the Ten-Year War began with Hayes's former assistant Bo Schembechler.

Hayes publicly referred to Michigan as "That School up North."

"The Fat Man," Schembechler privately called Hayes to his players.

Years later, when his son was being recruited by Michigan, Stier felt his theory checked out. He went into Schembechler's office and there, in the most prominent place on the wall, the center spot where a picture of a wife or loved one typically hung, was a picture of Hayes.

To tell that same story from Hayes's side, Bruce Smith remembers sitting in Hayes's office in 1986, years after he had left coaching. Schembechler phoned. It was the week Dave McClain, the Wisconsin coach and Hayes's former assistant, had a heart attack and died. As Smith sat there, Hayes told Schembechler, "Dave was too young. It should've been me." He then asked if Schembechler, who had a heart attack at the 1970 Rose Bowl, was seeing a doctor.

"Now, goddammit," Hayes said, "you've got to go and see the man and do what he tells you."

After they hung up, Hayes looked off into space for a few seconds, contemplating something. Then he said, "You know, I really love that guy."

(2)

Such sentiment was nice. But Hayes's players never saw it on Michigan Week. As thirty-degree weather settled on Columbus, players thought they might go inside the warmth of the French Field House. Hayes kept them outside for a two-hour-and-fifteen-minute practice.

"I bet those sons of bitches up north are indoors!" he said. "I'm sure they are! They aren't as tough as you are!"

It didn't matter if players knew he was planting some psychology on them. It still worked. Come Saturday, many couldn't help looking across the field and feeling they actually *were* tougher. Four decades later, each could quote Hayes as saying throughout their college careers: "As Admiral Nimitz said, 'If you're going to fight in the North Atlantic, you have to train in the North Atlantic.'"

Once, with a small blizzard and icy winds raging, Bill Pollitt sat in the locker room with teammates, agreeing that if practice was held outside Hayes was indeed insane. They practiced outside. "We said, 'Yup, he's insane,'" Pollitt said.

Hayes wore just a gray T-shirt on those days, too—his trademark. Often he had another T-shirt or even a thermal shirt under it. But the T-shirt was his way to scoff at conditions, and more important, tell his players to do so as well. If he were dressed like that, what player dared complain?

On game days, sun or snow, his patented uniform was a white short-sleeved dress shirt. He was so famous for this shirt that the week before the Michigan game that year Purdue assistant Ron Meyer wore a white dress shirt for *his* snowy game.

"I really wasn't trying to be like Woody Hayes," Meyer said. "I just thought it might pep the fellows up."

In 1970, when these sophomores were seniors, Hayes would surprise everyone in the Michigan State pre-game locker room by appearing in a jacket. He understood the stir this caused inside the team. "Dr. Bob said I can be a better coach if I wore this," Hayes said. "So if it can help me be a better coach, I said I'd better try it."

There was no such suggestion on that cold Wednesday evening as Hayes left the practice field.

"Pretty nice night, wasn't it?" he said—in his T-shirt—to two reporters.

"You're kidding, you mean you're not cold?" Jim Braham of the *Cleveland Press* said.

"Naw, wasn't nearly bad as last night, and the kids didn't mind it," Hayes said.

The spirit of Admiral Nimitz lived.

Kern showed up early for practice to meet with coaches and watch some film. His back was bothering him. George Chaump looked at him. "Rex, you don't look so good," he said. "Are you okay?"

Kern said he was a little tired, that he had been in classes from 8 a.m. to 2 p.m. and didn't have time for any lunch.

"We'll send out," Chaump said. "We'll get you something to eat."

Kern was going through the daily routine of practice drills when he saw a manager running up with a McDonald's bag. The manager stopped and talked for a second with Hayes and Chaump.

Uh-oh, Kern thought. *This is going to set off a megaton from Hayes. A McDonald's delivery? In practice?* Hayes took the bag from the manager and looked at Kern.

"Rex, come over here," he said.

Kern grew more uncomfortable with each step.

"Here," Hayes said, handing him the bag. "You go over there and eat this. Then you get back in when you're done."

So as practice for Michigan continued, Kern sat on a rolled-up tarp beside the field and ate a cheeseburger and fries. Never had a meal tasted so good. This didn't go unnoticed by the rest of the team. Kern's status again was confirmed. After practice, Rufus Mayes chuckled at Kern.

"I don't believe that," he said. "If it had been an offensive lineman who was hungry, he'd say, 'Get down and eat grass.'"

Late Friday afternoon, as thousands cheered and the band played, a slice of Ohio State tradition capped Michigan Week: The Senior Tackle.

Hayes, in his game day trademark of black block "O" cap, loosened tie, and short-sleeved white shirt, stood by the scarlet-and-gray tackling dummy.

"This is it, seniors," he said. "This is your last chance to hit the dummy for Ohio State."

School president Novice Fawcett talked briefly. So did Ernie Godfrey, who supposedly began the tradition in 1934 when the idea came to "get that old dummy out at the last practice and hit it one more time," as he told everyone.

Godfrey then prayed for the seniors: "Dear Lord, enter my heart and give me strength to play my greatest game and whip Michigan."

One by one, each of the sixteen seniors was introduced. Each shook hands with his teammates and the coaching staff. Each hit the blocking dummy one final time. Mark Stier awaited his turn, thinking, *Wow, is it already over?*

He had entered four years earlier with thirty-two recruits. Now sixteen were left to hit the dummy. Some fell to grades. Some lost interest. Some, like Jerry Tabacca, ran into trouble with Woody. But the ones who survived got to see the program turn from awful to awesome. In Ohio State history, there might never be a three-year turn like it.

To John Muhlbach, the emotion of the day was tangible. Five years earlier, he had entered the stadium for the first time with his father while they were in Columbus watching the high school basketball championships. They talked of what might lie ahead.

Now it was his final time to . . .

Ooomph!

. . . hit the dummy.

(3)

Dear Jim,

My heart is with you. Thank you for the two chin straps you gave me. I thought it only fair to give you the one your hero Bob Ferguson gave me after his best game as an Ohio State football player. The game was his last against Michigan. The score: OSU 50, Michigan 20.

I hope you carry it for good luck tomorrow.

Your Number One pal,

Scooter Hall

On the eve of the game, a campus bonfire roared. About 5,000 fans chanted, "We're Number One." A Michigan player was burned in effigy, which, of course, was better than the Woody Hayes effigy that had been burned here a couple of years earlier.

And Scooter Hall, a 12-year-old fan from Upper Arlington, approached Jim Otis with his letter and the enclosed chinstrap. It was from Ferguson's 1961 game against Michigan in which he scored four touchdowns.

Otis was touched. Better yet, he was fueled. No one on the team could have embraced the involved history of this artifact like him. Hadn't he been Ferguson on the sandlots of Celina? He watched the bonfire roar, thinking he'd tape the chinstrap to his shoulder pads the next day, wondering if there was another touchdown in it. Or two. Or . . .

Hayes stood until the final speech was made, the final cheer given, then drove off to another stop. He was never big on parties, especially the night before a game. He made an exception this Friday night. John Galbreath was throwing a party at his Darby Dan Farm. This was a friend he wanted to keep. Hayes was asked to speak to the crowd of 200 that included boosters, officials from Ohio State and Michigan, newspaper reporters . . . and Big Ten Commissioner Bill Reed.

Right at the front table.

Right where Hayes could welcome him.

"The Ohio coaches look at ten thousand feet of football film a week," Hayes told the assembly. "That's why we know so much about Big Ten officiating. I'm tired of other teams taking a cheap shot at my quarterback."

No one could miss whom Hayes was addressing. No one knew Kern hadn't practiced much again that week. Hayes was doing what any good coach would, what he had been trying to do ever since that Northwestern post-game when he went after Alex Agase.

"I asked Reed how many times I had been reported for playing dirty football in my eighteen years at Ohio State," Hayes said. "He never told me. Look what's happening in pro football. Who's quarterbacking who with the pros? They haven't got any left."

If Reed minded, he didn't show it. Going back to 1961, when Hayes showed a controversial call three times on his television show, the commissioner was used to it. After Hayes finished, Reed went before the crowd to determine whether Ohio State or Michigan officials would leave the party with a huge armful of roses. He flipped a coin, then secretly looked at it on his forearm.

"You call it," Reed said to Michigan athletic director Don Canham.

"Heads," Canham said.

"It's tails," Reed said.

So Dick Larkins walked out of the party with the roses and a promise to carry them into the Michigan locker room if Ohio State lost.

(4)

That Saturday, Charles de Gaulle stunned the western world by refusing to devalue the French franc, Julie Nixon and David Eisenhower announced they would be wed in New York by Dr. Norman Vincent Peale, and none of that mattered in Columbus. It was the Michigan game.

On the line was the Big Ten title, a trip to the Rose Bowl, a tip-top national ranking, and more important than all of that, the satisfaction of beating Michigan. A city had its game face on.

Getting off the AYO bus a couple of hours before kickoff, Vic Stottlemyer walked into the stadium with the other reserves. He went past a solemn Hayes in a weekly event that seemed like a military pass-and-review between soldiers and a general. And on this day of days, as the clock ticked toward kickoff, Hayes locked eyes with Stottlemyer as he passed.

"Vic, did Jeff get his ticket?" Hayes asked.

"Uh, well, I don't know," Stottlemyer said.

Earlier in the week, the senior had needed a ticket for his 12-year-old brother, Jeff. Hayes, hearing this, said he'd leave a ticket for Jeff to pick up. He would then be allowed behind the bench, to watch the game sitting on the roll-up tarp.

Now, a couple of hours before the biggest game of the year, the one that could triumphantly erase the past couple years of pain, Hayes was worried about a reserve player's kid brother getting his ticket? Woody grabbed a student manager. He ordered him to the gate where Jeff's ticket waited. He was told to escort Jeff to behind the bench.

"Don't worry, Vic, it's all taken care of," Hayes said.

When Stottlemyer walked onto the field, Jeff was sitting on the tarp, beaming.

As if the week hadn't brought everyone to enough of an emotional peak, one more script was played out. Normally, to enter the Ohio State locker room, one must pass a couple of armed guards who, on one memorable occasion, wouldn't let invited legend Red Grange pass. But this day a delivery boy carrying a box entered just as Hayes was finishing his pre-game talk and the players were moving out the door.

"I've got roses for Mr. Woody Hayes," he said.

Hayes came careening through the players. He grabbed the box out of the boy's hands. He took the roses and began thrashing the kid with them. And thrashing. And yelling. And, for those players who weren't yet out the door, the scene created such bloodlust they began chanting . . .

"WOOO-WOOO!"

. . . and jumping . . .

"WOOO-WOOO!"

. . . and yelling to the point it took the emotion even higher. Looking back on his way out the door, Bob Smith, a senior tight end, saw Bill Mallory grabbing the roses from Hayes and stepping in to protect the delivery boy.

On the field, just before kickoff, Hayes approached Jim Otis.

"You're going to carry the ball a lot today," Hayes said.

Otis smiled. He tapped Ferguson's chinstrap, which was taped to his shoulder pad. This is what he had wanted. It's what he expected, too, considering what they had practiced, all the way back to last spring. As for the Purdue game, Hayes had something special planned for Michigan. But if the no-huddle against Purdue showed Hayes at his most futuristic, the strategy for Michigan appealed to the old Woody, the Robust-formation one, the one who all his life was a bare-knuckled brawler.

As Ohio State's offense ran onto the field and lined up on the ball for the first time, here is what Michigan's defense saw:

Guard Brian Donovan, tackles Dave Foley and Rufus Mayes, and tight end Jan White on the left side of the ball.

Guard Alan Jack, and one step back, wingback Larry Zelina, on the right side.

The line was so unbalanced the field seemed to tilt. More than 900 pounds of beef were to the left of Muhlbach at center. Less than 400 pounds were to the right of him.

Naturally, Otis ran to the left—*wham!*—for five yards.

On the second play, the line flipped. The field tilted the other way. Foley, Mayes, and White were on the right beside Jack. Zelina went to Donovan's side.

Bam! Four more yards for Otis.

This is how it would be much of the afternoon. What's more, Michigan never adjusted. It never moved an extra defender to compensate for Ohio State's lopsided line. Not during that first series. Not for the second one. Not at half. Never. And so, even at 14-14 midway through the second quarter, Woody was in his element.

He had bought into all this wide-open, downfield-passing, spread-the-field philosophy for much of the season. Now he would show flexed muscle could still carry the day. And this day turned on a second-quarter drive that started at the Ohio State 14-yard line. Hayes called fifteen running and two pass plays. Otis ran the ball nine times. All of them were over the lopsided side of the line.

Hayes was beaming inside. With each off-tackle run of "26" or "27," it was confirmation of who he still was. Of how his punch still worked. Couldn't everyone see that? After seven minutes was eaten off the clock, on fourth down and inches, Otis plunged four yards for a touchdown. It was 21-14. Thirty-six seconds were left in the half.

And the game was over.

The code had been cracked.

Kern didn't throw a pass in the second half. To start the third quarter, Ohio State got the ball and its drive consisted of eleven consecutive runs. Six were to Otis. The final one was six yards by Zelina for the touchdown. And so a second-half scoring flurry, the likes of which no one had seen, toppled down on Michigan.

Roman kicked a field goal, Kern scored from three yards. From two yards, Otis scored his third touchdown of the day.

All without passing the ball.

Unimaginative? Maybe for some. Unexciting? Maybe for Michigan. Unstoppable? Definitely.

There was no feeling quite like this, Foley thought, coming to the line. Knowing the day was moving on your muscle. And seeing Michigan outmanned each play. The extra blocker on the side caused a "swinging gate" effect on the defense, essentially sealing it off and allowing a runner to move freely. What did World War I's General von Schlieffen remind Hayes before the Purdue game? *Keep your flank strong.* Didn't Michigan study its history?

Ohio State ran 79 times for 421 yards that day. Otis gained 142 yards. Kern ran for 96, Zelina for 92. Everything broke Ohio State's way. Once, after kicking off, Jim Oppermann was running downfield, trying to ward off blockers like a mailman with a bad dog, when he ran face first into Michigan return man Ron Johnson. He didn't even see Johnson. He certainly didn't brace for a collision. But it was a hit of such force that Johnson fumbled and Ohio State recovered.

Oppermann, in such a daze that his world went black, called out to Jim Stillwagon, "Wagon! Carry me off the field! I can't see!"

The day had bent so far backward on Michigan that Hayes's just running out the clock with reserves proved too much. Ray Gillian ran up the middle, through the line, into the secondary, and was hauled down 40 yards later at the Michigan 5. That set up Otis's third touchdown. It was 44-14 with more than three minutes of celebration left that would resonate forever.

On the very next Michigan play, safety Art Burton intercepted. Ohio State was in business again. When it got to first-and-goal at the 3-yard line, another touchdown looked as simple as opening a door. But after three downs, they weren't any closer. Jim Otis approached Hayes on the sideline.

"Coach, you want the score?" Otis asked.

"Go get it," Hayes said.

So he would become exactly like four-touchdown Ferguson. In 1961, Ferguson was given a standing ovation as he was taken out of a 50-20 game in the final minutes. The next play, Woody sent him back in the game.

Otis, too, was put back in the game. As he buckled his helmet, he asked what play to run.

"You pick the play," Hayes said.

It wasn't like Otis had a thick catalogue in his mind. His repertoire consisted essentially of three plays. Fullback to the left. Fullback to the right. Fullback up the middle. Take your pick. So when Otis ran into the huddle—now composed of all reserves—he picked out left tackle Dave Cheney.

"Woody wants a touchdown, and he wants it over you," he said. "So you'd better make it." Otis then called the play in the huddle: "Twenty-seven."

Fullback to the left.

It was the same play Otis had just run for a touchdown. It worked the same this time, Cheney pile-driving his man back, Otis plowing into the end zone, and, exactly as before, heaving the ball high into the crowd as rolls of toilet paper flew across Ohio Stadium.

It was now 50-14. Done. Won. But the play that defined this rout, the one that would ring for years, was about to happen. For most of these years, Otis was considered the instigator, since he ran off the field saying, "Let's go for two!"

Go for two? Winning by this margin? That would be running up the score beyond anything reasonable and rubbing Michigan's snout in the embarrassment. George Chaump looked to see what Hayes would do.

"One! One! One!" Hayes yelled from the sideline, holding up a finger for his players to kick the extra point.

On the field, no one heard. They were having practical confusion. The long-

snapper on extra points, John Muhlbach, was hurt and out of the game. The
backup long-snapper, Jim Roman, was the kicker. Maciejowski, who had done
the honors at Wisconsin, wasn't on the field.

"You can't hold it *and* kick it," Bill Long said.

"Aw, piss it, let's go for two," Roman said.

With that, they did. And that was how a play that lingered forever—like bad
air—actually came about. The backup center and third-string quarterback made
the decision. Earle Bruce, who had just arrived on the sideline from the press
box, saw the offense lining up in formation for a play instead of an extra point
and felt his heart skip. He thought what any coach would: *Michigan would use
this as motivational fuel next year! This play would never die!*

"Don't go for two!" Bruce began yelling frantically on the sideline, looking
for Hayes. "Don't go for two!"

Hayes quit holding his finger up and yelling for the extra-point kick as he
saw the offense line up.

"Aw, hell," he said, turning to Chaump. "Let 'em go for two."

Long's pass fell incomplete. The conversion failed. But the damage was
done. After the final seconds melted away, after thousands rushed the field, after
the band played "California, Here We Come," after Hayes had been carried on
his players' shoulders and run through the human maze off the field, he sat at his
locker when the late-game intentions were brought up.

"Woody," a reporter asked, "why did you roll up the score?"

"The way these young kids pass and catch today, I've gotten to the point
where I need 50 points just to feel safe," he said.

The way it works, when the legend becomes fact, you print the legend.
Especially when the legend is better. And the legend in this case has Hayes being
asked why he went for two points.

"Because I couldn't go for three," he said.

Good answer.

Bad facts.

Instead, Hayes soft-shoed something about there being a mixup and changed
the subject. "We deserve to be Number One," he said. "Kern had some back
trouble this week. He couldn't even practice Thursday, which is why I closed
the session to the press. I'm like a good general. I'm not going to announce any
weaknesses to the enemy."

The military allusion bounced the conversation to Vietnam. Hayes said he
would fulfill his promise of the summer before about returning if Ohio State

went to the Rose Bowl. He even offered a suggestion to end the war: "Get television over there," he said. "Let those Vietnamese watch our shows and pretty soon every one of them will be toting a six-shooter and whipping those Charlies."

You go to talk football, and you get a full worldview.

Meanwhile, in Michigan's locker room, a 365-day wait had begun. Assistant coach Tony Mason's words came out in a hiss.

"Listen, we were beaten by a better team," he said. "I wouldn't have minded so much except for that fat hog going for two points. Did you get that? I said 'FAT . . . HOG.' He'll get his. We waited a year for Michigan State. Now we'll wait for that guy."

(5)

That night, a call went out to Bob Grossman, Jim Essian, and other members of the Ohio State Marching Band: *Get to the stadium. Pick up your instruments.* The celebration was stumbling out of control on High Street and authorities wanted the band to calm it.

Already, some shop windows had been smashed. The fifteen-foot statue outside the BBF Hamburgers restaurant had been toppled. So an hour later, after they got the phone call, right there on 15th and High, dozens of band members straggled together, out of uniform, and began to play music to soothe the savage mob. "Hang On Sloopy." "Carmen, Ohio." All the big hits.

One of the sousaphonists, drunk himself by that point in the celebration, fell flat to the ground and crunched a new horn. *Oops.* But the band began moving down High Street while playing. Thousands of people followed. Ralph Holloway, the sophomore tackle, walked along, caught in the wave of fans now singing the lyrics:

> *We don't give a damn for the whole state of Michigan,*
> *The whole state of Michigan,*
> *The whole state of Michigan,*
> *We don't give a damn for the whole state of Michigan,*
> *We're from O-hi-o.*

They sang and played and celebrated a few miles downtown to the

Statehouse. There, they deposited part of the torn-down goalpost. They stood on the Statehouse lawn singing awhile longer. About 2 a.m., the party broke up. Everyone went home happy.

For the first time in eleven years, Ohio State was going to the Rose Bowl.

That week, for Thanksgiving break, Ohio State exhaled. Classes stopped. Students went home. Most players did, too. They went home for the first time since summer. Some of the out-of-state players spent Thanksgiving at a teammate's Ohio home. Jack Tatum, for instance, went up to Oberlin to Holloway's home.

One was left in Columbus. John Brockington, married, with a baby, and a long way from his and his wife's Brooklyn parents, had nowhere to go. They lived in a one-bedroom apartment and had only the basic needs of a young couple. This was good, because Brockington had little money.

It was amazing how far a $20 weekly grocery bill could stretch if it had to. Frozen fish. Hamburger and fries. Chicken. Waffles. Pizza. John and his wife, Jackie, became experts at making do. Thanksgiving would be just another day of that, they figured.

Far from home, with their friends gone, John and Jackie were planning nothing special when there was a knock on their apartment door.

"Happy Thanksgiving," Woody Hayes said.

He entered the apartment carrying a big turkey, fruit and nuts.

"I want you to enjoy your day," Hayes said, setting them down on a table.

Within thirty seconds, he was gone.

California, dreaming

*O*utside, the snow fell, the wind blew, and Old Man Winter gripped Columbus. Inside the locker room before their first Rose Bowl practice, the mood was much warmer. Their final exams were done. They hadn't practiced in nearly two weeks. They could look ahead now and see the sun and beach and girls, and oh yeah, the game, too. California Dreamin', as the Mamas and the Papas sang.

Then they walked into the French Field House that first day and the mood instantly changed. They could barely breathe. The Field House was a greenhouse. It was set to broil. Someone walked over to the thermostat. *Ninety degrees!* They looked at each other, wondering what was going on.

At one of the first meetings addressing the Rose Bowl trip, guard Phil Strickland had asked if they could go out a couple of days early, you know, *wink-wink*, "To get acclimated to the weather," Strickland said.

Woody liked that idea, except for the leaving early part.

"This is Southern California weather," Woody greeted them at the French Field House that first day of practice with the thermostat set to high. "This is what you have to get used to."

And, with that, they met his California corollary to "If you're going to fight in the Atlantic, you have to practice in the Atlantic."

Hayes knew about his players' sun-filled thoughts. He wanted to knock those out of their heads. The best way he knew to do that was to knock heads.

Rex Kern

From the first practice, he set the tone of what was coming. They ran. They hit. And, man, did they sweat in this sauna. The coaches loved it. They'd been waiting to get going again. In fact, as this first practice went on, Hayes had an idea.

"Hey, George," he yelled to Chaump. "Bring your quarterbacks down here."

Hayes stood at a tackling machine, a set of padded dummies used to practice tackling form. Not that the quarterbacks practiced tackling much. None of them had really worked on it since they were high school safeties. But that didn't matter on this day of tone setting.

"Let them hit the machine," Hayes said.

Kern was the first one up. He launched himself into the machine in particularly rusty form, his head down, his shoulder down. Upon striking the pad, he felt such pain in his left shoulder that his body froze and slid down the pad to the ground. Hayes came running over.

"I think I've dislocated my shoulder," Kern said.

"OH, SHIT!" Hayes yelled. "SHIT! SHIT! SHIT!"

Ernie Biggs, the team trainer, hustled over. He reached under Kern's shoulder pads and felt around the bone and muscles.

"Hold on a minute," Biggs said,

He popped Kern's shoulder back into place.

"Coach, I think he's dislocated his shoulder," Biggs said.

"Oh, shit," Hayes said, hands on hip, cap tipped back, face full of frustration. Too late, he turned to the others and said, "Okay, that's enough for you quarterbacks for the day."

Kern's shoulder was immobilized and his arm put in a sling. He watched the rest of the practices in the Field House. The hope was he would be healed enough to practice in California. The prayer was he'd be able to play. The truth was there couldn't have been a much worse way to begin preparing for the Rose Bowl.

The players thought that maybe now the practices would be ratcheted down in intensity. They thought health would become the Number One priority. The coaches thought otherwise. At the end of that first practice, McCullough lined his defense up and had them run sprints. And run them. And . . .

"I'll tell you one damn thing," Urbanik said to him when they kept going, "if I wasn't here, I'd kick the shit out of you."

"Get on the line and run," McCullough said.

And so their Rose Bowl experience began. Two-hour practices. Twice a day. It was like summer, all over again, right down to how much the coaches were pushing. Drills. Technique work. And constant conditioning. All in that oven of a field house. One practice, during a megaton moment, Hayes grew so disgusted by the work that he ordered everyone to start running. And kept them running for a couple of miles.

Kern's injury had a painfully residual effect. With Bill Long imitating Southern Cal quarterback Steve Sogge to get the defense ready, Maciejowski had to throw double his normal allotment of passes to make up for Kern. And throw. At some point, Maciejowski threw so much the ulnar nerve in his elbow began to ache. The pain wouldn't go away. The elbow would hurt all the next season, too. He began taking cortisone shots, but his arm was never the same.

The quarterbacks weren't the only ones hurting. Ed Bender, a senior reserve running back who wouldn't even make the trip west, was picked to be Southern Cal running back O.J. Simpson in the field house practices. Bender didn't have O.J.'s speed—who did?—but he had a similar slashing style of running.

And the coaches instituted the O.J. Rule: Every defender had to touch him before a play officially ended. If he was down, it didn't matter. If he went out of bounds, it didn't matter. Every defensive player had to touch him before the whistle blew. The coaches wanted to underline how the whole defense had to come after this guy and bring him down.

Since players couldn't tackle on the rubberized surface of the French Field House, they popped Bender with an initial hit, then wrapped him up with their arms, often squeezing his back with their hands. Or, if he'd already been popped, they slapped him on the back. All eleven of them, every play, just like the O.J. Rule said.

So Bender went from being a guy no one typically noticed to someone put in a Number 32 jersey, which stood out in these practices like a "Most Wanted" sign. Practices became brutal for him. Every play, he got hit eleven times. One day, after another two-a-day workout, Bender was in the shower when his roommate, Mark Stier, said, "What happened to you?"

"What do you mean?" Bender said.

"Your back's all black and blue," Stier said.

Bender looked in the mirror. There were bruises all over his back. Actual handprints could be seen. It was tough playing O.J. in practice. It would be tougher, Bender figured as he inspected his back, being him in this game. If they ever got to the game.

The days dragged. The practices burned. Occasionally, there would be a moment. One practice, the defensive linemen had to run through a Blaster machine, which was a gauntlet of spring-loaded arms that jostled you as you ran. It was designed for running backs. But there was only so much to do inside and so on this particular day, the defensive linemen worked on it. As they did, either in boredom or anger or team unity, they began to chant: "Rose Bowl. Rose Bowl . . ."

It picked up volume . . .

"Rose Bowl! Rose Bowl!"

. . . and more players . . .

"ROSE BOWL! ROSE BOWL!"

Soon, it was echoing inside the Field House. Players were clapping. They were getting into it. Outside, the weather howled and the snow blew. Inside this cocoon, they were tired and confused and they felt overworked. But California was calling.

(2)

As a reward for their regular-season achievement, New York's Downtown Athletic Club awarded Ohio State the MacArthur Bowl as its national champs. Never mind that some polls had USC on top. Never mind the Rose Bowl had yet to be played. It was a prestigious award, and Ohio State was going to act the gracious winner. With Foley already in New York for an All-America banquet, Hayes invited his other captain, Dirk Worden, to fly with him.

In his four years at Ohio State, this would be the only time Worden met alone with Hayes. The offense and defense had that church-and-state separation. So Worden, whose senior year had been ruined by injury, looked forward to this trip to New York. Hayes surprised him by talking about his family. How did Hayes know so much about them without talking to him much all these years? Then Hayes launched into a discussion of the team, and then current events.

The coach was talking so much, in fact, Worden couldn't get a thought in edgewise. He had something on his heart to tell Hayes, too. Worden remembered those times as a sophomore in 1966 when the team was losing, the crowd was hostile, and the plane flew around the stadium with the "Goodbye Woody" banner.

Now the whole world had flipped for Hayes. He was king again. People were praising him again as the biggest name in college football. He would win two Coach of the Year awards. Worden was happy to be part of the turnaround, happier still for Hayes.

Finally, as they flew to New York, Hayes quit talking for a second. There was actual silence. "Now's the time," Worden said to himself. He already had prepared the little speech in his head, and he turned in the seat to face Hayes.

Hayes had fallen asleep.

He was human, after all.

Through the years, Worden remembered the words he wanted to tell Hayes and never did: "Hey, Coach, I really want to thank you for all you've done. I know it's been a tough road. But all your work is coming to fruition for you and I couldn't be happier for you."

(3)

One December day, Kern answered the phone in his dorm room.

"Hi, Rex?" a voice said. "This is *The Dating Game* calling from Hollywood."

They wanted him on the show. He'd be the special guest to pick one of the three dates. Kern couldn't believe it. *The Dating Game!* In Hollywood! But as they talked, as the show's representative said what the show would entail, a cloud settled over the conversation that prevented Kern from growing too excited: What would the Old Man think?

He told the show he'd have to check with his coach for permission. He then plotted what he'd say to Hayes and, as important, when he'd say it. There was no sense asking Woody after a megaton moment. Or even after a generally bad practice. No, he had to wait and find the proper time to measure Hayes's mood, then slip in the idea. So he waited. And one day, after practice and a team meal when Hayes was in a good mood, Kern sidled near him.

"Coach, can I talk with you?" he said. "Hollywood called and asked me to be on *The Dating Game*."

Looking back, Kern figured that wasn't the best way to pitch the idea: "Hollywood called."

"Rex, we're going out there to play football," Hayes said. "We're not going out there to be on a TV program or to eat beef or anything like that."

"I know, Coach, I just wanted to ask," Kern said.

"What do you think?" Hayes said.

"I thought it might be kind of fun."

"I think you should tell them thanks for asking, but you're going to be tied up."

Kern, no dummy, nodded in agreement, even if he was disappointed. Hayes, no dummy, made it a point several days later to find Kern on the flight to California. He asked the player sitting beside his quarterback to move, so they could talk. Kern inwardly groaned that a four-hour play-calling session was coming. Instead, Hayes said he had reconsidered *The Dating Game's* proposal. Kern should do it.

"Coach," Kern said, "I already told them I couldn't do it. I think it's probably too late to set it up now. You were right anyhow. We need to be focused on football."

This, Kern reflected later, was Woody at his finest. He got his way. But he ensured that no feelings were hurt.

Besides, as it worked out, Kern would have no problem finding a Rose Bowl date.

(4)

As the plane left Columbus, all the news stories discussed in sober terms how the top-ranked team in college football was heading to the Rose Bowl. Inside the team, the reality was different. For now, they just felt like midwestern college kids thinking what Midwestern college kids do on most trips to California. *Venice Beach! Sunset Boulevard! Good Vibrations!*

That suddenly changed as the plane flew over the Rocky Mountains. Trainers began walking down the aisles, and one by one, tapping players on the shoulder and telling them to come to the back of the plane. They needed to get their ankles taped for practice.

"Wha-a-at?" players said as the news spread. "Practice?"

"Right when we land?"

"Is this trip a reward or a punishment?"

When the players got off the plane in California—met by the Rose Bowl Committee and the Los Angeles media and ushered to a reception at the Huntington Sheraton Hotel—their ankles, under their dress pants, were taped. When they got into a playful orange-throwing fight with the Rose Bowl queen and her court at the hotel, equipment was being wheeled to the bus. When they stepped on the field at East Los Angeles Junior College, they had been in California all of ninety minutes.

It was cold, too. Forty-eight degrees! It was snowing in the Los Angeles foothills! All that work in all that heat of the Field House. And now this?

Hayes said the idea of this first practice was to show the local media this was a working trip, and thus send a business-only message to Southern Cal. But he didn't just send a little message this practice. His players lived it in a big way. Sprints. Drills. Scrimmage. And when the offense misfired, he had a megaton.

"Okay, everyone, get running!" he said. Everyone began running around the field. Hayes looked to the sideline and pointed at Paul Huff, who was sitting out with a bad back. "That goes for you, too," he said. "And you run until I tell you to stop."

As the team went back to practice, Huff kept running. He clocked maybe six miles that day. The next day, with his back in worse shape, Hayes saw him at the start of practice and said, "Just get started." So Huff started running at the start of practice while waiting for the signal that he could stop. He was running when the team did drills. He was running as they scrimmaged. He was even running as they left the field for the showers.

In the cramped facilities, Kern's locker was beside Hayes's locker. After everyone had showered and was dressing, Kern overheard equipment repairman Phil Bennett whisper to Hayes, "Coach, do you want Paul Huff to stop running now?"

"Yeah, yeah, tell him to get dressed," Hayes said.

The next day, as Hayes told Huff to get going again, Ernie Biggs intervened. "There's only so much," he told Hayes.

This wasn't a vacation for Long, either. Playing Steve Sogge, he had been wearing a protective yellow jersey. But McCullough went to Hayes and said, "We can't get a good look at what Sogge's doing. We've got to be able to hit him."

Off came the yellow jersey. For the next nine days, Long would be pounded like breaded veal by the country's best defense. By then, the message had been sent—and amplified—to the players how this was a business trip. That first night in California, after being taped on the plane, after a tough practice, the players still expected some free time. They could get out. See some sights. Meet some girls. Find some fun. At the team dinner that evening, they were discussing where to go. After all, by 7 o'clock California time, they'd be finished eating.

"What time is it in Ohio, Lou?" Hayes asked McCullough.

"Ten o'clock," McCullough said.

"Curfew's in half an hour," Hayes said.

So much for the players' night-time plans.

Still, this was their first bowl game. Everything was new. They made the best of everything. As the team continued practicing hard, as players got battered and bruised, as the blondes and beaches might as well have been a continent away, the planted seeds of discontent didn't bloom until two years later when this sophomore class had become seniors.

Stillwagon, by then a captain, suggested to Hayes the team leave a day early that 1971 Rose Bowl trip. Relax a bit out there, he said. Have some fun. He also got Hayes to promise that no ankles would be taped on the flight out nor would the team be overworked. To a concerned team, Stillwagon announced they wouldn't overdo everything—as they had the previous trip.

Of course, he might as well have asked a fish not to swim. On the same pass over the Grand Canyon, Hayes ordered that the ankles be taped. Stillwagon barged up the aisle to Hayes, who said it was raining in Los Angeles and he didn't want anyone to twist an ankle in the light workout that was planned. It wasn't raining when they landed. It wasn't a light workout, either. Hayes ordered them out in full pads. Again, Stillwagon spoke for the seniors and asked what was going on.

"We want to look big for the photographers," Hayes said.

They practiced for two hours in full pads. The opening days became the 1969 Rose Bowl all over again, except for the fact this wasn't their first time around the block. That second time, they weren't merely happy to be there. They had by then developed ideas on what helped and hurt preparation for a game. That second time, they thought, Hayes was hurting the team more with his tough practices than helping it. They bordered on mutiny. The seniors asked for a meeting with Hayes, kicked the underclassmen out of the room, and listed their grievances. Hayes wrote them on a blackboard as they came up.

1. Getting taped on plane.

2. Two-a-day practices.

3. Too much scrimmaging.

On and on, Hayes wrote, until in the heated discussion McCullough said, "As far as I'm concerned, we can load these guys on the plane and send 'em all home."

"What do you think of that?" Hayes asked.

"If that's how you feel, get the airplane," a senior said.

All the seniors were ready to walk out. They had discussed it before the meeting. A couple of assistants cooled down emotions, but the battle lines were drawn. Hayes told Stillwagon, "If we lose this game, you sonuvabitch, it's your fault."

"Okay, but you did more to lose this game than anyone ever could," Stillwagon said.

Ohio State would lose that game to Stanford, 27-17. The players always felt it was lost in the days beforehand. But in the final days of 1968, that was far ahead of them. Everything on this trip was new and different. Even the seniors had never been to a bowl game. If the coaches wanted to overwork them, well, maybe they were right.

Besides, they found a bar around the corner from the hotel and several players sneaked out at night. They were still in California, too, as Brockington marveled, staring out the bus window and wondering how a kid from Brooklyn got here.

Look at the sunshine. Look at the palm trees. Look at the girl walking down the sidewalk in a fishnet shirt. And no bra!

"HEY, LOOK!" Brockington shouted to his teammates.

A roar went up from those at window seats. Others rushed across the aisle to look. They began laughing and pointing and shouting.

"WOW!"

"DO YOU SEE THAT?"

"UNBELIEVABLE!"

They weren't in Ohio anymore, Toto.

(5)

Woody Hayes is a dinosaur. Such recurrent insanities would be inconceivable from coaches like John McKay or John Wooden. How do his players stand him?—Jack Hastert, Bellflower, California, in a letter to the *Los Angeles Times*.

You better watch out,
Better not pry;
Better not ask,
He'll spit in your eye.
Woody Hayes is coming to town.

   —*Los Angeles Times* story, words sung to the tune of "Santa Claus
   Is Coming To Town"

Ah, California. The soft sun. The ocean breeze. The morning paper, where through the years Columbus was described as a place where if you buy a piano, "they throw in a free shotgun," where Ohio's foreign policy was described as "Beat Michigan!" and Hayes was described as "an American institution who belongs in one."

And that was just from Jim Murray, the star columnist of the *Los Angeles Times*, who had a special affection for all things Hayes. At various times, Murray called Hayes the "Scarlet Scourge," "Football's Attila The Hun," and "The Last of the Cavemen."

It was one thing to be a writer in Columbus, the heartbeat of the Buckeyes, where every written word was viewed through a scarlet-and-gray prism. It was quite another to work from the outside, where Hayes could merely be the next column's fodder. In this regard, he was a gold mine, especially for writers from Southern California.

After Ohio State's Rose Bowl win in 1955, Hayes either told the truth (his side) or belittled the USC team (its side) by saying, "There are four, possibly five, Big Ten teams I'd rate ahead of the Trojans." He also scolded the Rose Bowl Committee for allowing the marching bands to parade over the wet field at halftime. "They turned it into a quagmire," he said.

In the 1959 season, after Southern Cal beat Ohio State in Columbus, Hayes took a swing at a couple of Los Angeles writers, missing both but allegedly hitting the brother of one of the writers. Hayes denied hitting anyone. He "pushed" them, he maintained to the Ohio State Athletic Council, whose report stated: "The council is assured that there will be no reoccurrence of such incidents."

Ahem.

In this timeline, 1968 was a quiet blip in the contentious Hayes's West Coast portfolio. At the 1973 Rose Bowl, 1955 and 1959 continued. As a photographer took a picture of the Ohio State pre-game huddle, Hayes rushed over and shoved the camera into his face, causing him to need medical treatment.

And so through the years Hayes was greeted by headlines in Los Angeles papers like some wacky uncle had come to visit: "Woody Hayes Show Hits Town"; "Ho! Ho! Ho! Ol' Woody's Coming to Town Again!"; and "Same Ol' Woody Hayes."

There were also the regular one-liners from Jim Murray's typewriter:

On Hayes's demeanor: "A loud, loveable character who (goes) through life the way his fullbacks go through a line."

On his military bent: "He never really forgave the world for making him a football coach instead of a field marshal."

On Hayes and the media: "Sports writers had better learn to take a 9-count. And to duck."

On first impressions of Hayes: "The first look you get at Woody Hayes, you're surprised he's not wearing a bearskin loincloth and carrying a club with spikes sticking out of it."

On Ohio State not making the Rose Bowl one year: "So Woody Hayes is not coming to the Rose Bowl. Dad rat it! Somebody's always spoiling the fun."

On the words *forward pass*: "They were dirty words to Woody, hard-core porno."

On his attraction to controversy: "A guy who even sleeps with his foot in his mouth."

On his taskmaster ways: "When someone wanted to know which way the team got back from the Rose Bowl practice session each day, an observer said, 'The usual way—by goose step.'"

On his consistency: "Graceless in victory and graceless in defeat."

On Hayes' personality: "Occasionally discursive but never dull . . . Woody is one of the rarest specimens in nature—the non-hypocrite."

(6)

Before his players got off the plane in Los Angeles, Hayes warned them to ignore the women sent to greet them. He described them like modern-day Sirens, hoping to lure them closer and watch Southern Cal rip them to pieces.

"They're here to make you soft," he said. "Don't pay any attention to them! They've sent the cutest girls to goo-goo and ga-ga and soften you up!"

Butch Smith chuckled at this. And, naturally, with such an advertisement, all the players inspected the locals more closely. One did even more. Rex Kern got in one of the courtesy Chrysler cars with Dave Foley and Ted Provost just as it began to rain. The Rose Bowl queen and several princesses sent to greet them began to hop out of the rain into different cars, too.

"Tree, grab that one over there!" Kern said to Ted Provost. "Get her in our car!"

Provost jumped out and invited her in. Her name was Nancy Henno, she was a freshman at Pasadena City College, and to these midwestern football players, she was the very ideal of California cuteness. She also had taken her job as host seriously enough to do some homework. She had gone over the Ohio State roster, for instance, and said she noticed one player was from Lancaster.

"Hey, that's me," Kern said.

"How do you like coming home?" she said.

"Home?"

"You're from Lancaster."

"Lancaster, Ohio," Kern said. "I've never seen palm trees before."

They began talking. When they got to the hotel, she threw him an orange. He threw it back. That sparked the orange-throwing flurry. In the coming days, they saw each other at various Rose Bowl functions—Disneyland, the Christmas party—and made a point to talk with each other. A friendship was struck up. Something more was, too.

After the Rose Bowl, the quarterback visited the bowl princess in her home. Met her family. Spent some time. They began to talk about where this might lead. She was planning to enroll at Southern Cal and suggested he transfer there. Couldn't he play football at Southern Cal just as easily as at Ohio State? *Hmm.* Kern thought it more practical for her to come to Columbus.

In 1969, she became an Ohio State student.

In 1973, they were married.

In 2008, Rex and Nancy Kern celebrated their thirty-fifth wedding anniversary.

(7)

As a Christmas gift, Hayes gave the players the day off. He said they could take a trip on their own, as long as they returned for the party that night.

Go explore the mountains, he said. Go see Los Angeles, he said. Go as far as San Diego, a couple of hours away, he said. *Don't* go to Tijuana, he said.

Kevin Rusnak looked at Foley. They knew where they were going. They asked a couple of others, like Sensibaugh and Sam Elliott, a graduate assistant coach and former team captain. There were just a couple of issues: how to get to Mexico and how to stay out of trouble if they were caught. Rusnak said he'd take care of the former. Elliott took care of the latter. He spotted Kern.

"Hey, Rex, you want to go to Disneyland?" Elliott asked.

The day before, Kern had a great time at Disneyland. He had never seen anything like the rides and attractions. Sure, he said. He had nothing planned. He'd love to go back. As for how they would get there, well, Rusnak had that taken care of.

"Walk to the corner," he told everyone outside the hotel. "I'll meet you in ten minutes with a car."

He walked to the garage where the Rose Bowl's complimentary Chrysler cars were kept. Players could ask to go somewhere and one of these chauffeur-driven cars would take them. Rusnak, however, didn't want a chauffeur. He just wanted a car. No one said anything when he got in one. He drove it to the corner where his buddies awaited. The adventure began.

As they drove south out of Los Angeles, and kept driving, Kern didn't remember it taking so long to get to Disneyland. He asked how much farther it was. The car went silent. Then, as if on cue, everyone burst out laughing.

"DISNEYLAND?"

"We're not going to Disneyland!"

"We're going to Tijuana!"

Kern said Hayes would kill them.

"Why do you think we brought you?" he was told. "You're our insurance policy."

He asked to be let out of the car. He'd walk back, he said. But they kept driving. And driving. Kern felt as if he'd been kidnapped. A few hours later, they were seeing the sights of Tijuana. Rusnak bought a bottle of tequila. Kern, figuring since he was there, looked at a sombrero.

"Twenty dollars," the guy said. Kern began walking away. "Ten dollars," the guy said. Kern didn't really want one, but the guy kept badgering, and lowering the price, so Kern returned to the hotel that night carrying a five-dollar sombrero. Hayes's room was right by the stairwell, door open, so he could see players coming and going.

"Have a good time at Disneyland, Rex?" Hayes called out to him.

Kern just kept walking. He knew better than to answer. Thank goodness the Christmas party was about to start. Bob Hope was there. So was a magician who, blindfolded, took on Lou Holtz at tic-tac-toe.

"Nobody beats me at tic-tac-toe!" Holtz said.

He lost in something like three moves.

That morning, Hayes had started to hand out gifts to the players—thin, black neckties. Some of the players giggled and told Hayes they were out of style. That's all he needed to hear. He gathered them back up and then passed out a fashionable wide tie with stripes.

So there.

The players, in turn, gave Hayes a dark turtleneck sweater just to see him in something other than that white, short-sleeved dress shirt. He put on a turtleneck and black sunglasses and—*click!*—had his picture taken for the papers, the essence of Hollywood cool.

Through the party's laughter, the Tijuana trip seemed forgotten. It wasn't, though. When Rusnak and Elliott went walking by Hayes's door, the coach came out. He grabbed Elliott, threw him inside, and shut the door.

Why get mad at your players when a graduate assistant's around?

(8)

On December 26, the players' wives flew to Pasadena with Anne Hayes. At least this brought a smile to the faces of the married men on the team. In fact, that night, John Muhlbach and his wife, Bobbi, pulled the two twin beds of their room together. They climbed into them and were making love when they heard a quick rap on the door, followed by an immediate twisting of the knob.

The door flew open.

There stood Woody Hayes.

He was making his nightly bed-check rounds at 10:30 p.m. But as he looked at the scene before him, and realized what he had done, he was struck speechless for the first time Muhlbach could remember.

"Oh, no . . . I forgot . . . the wives came . . . oh, geez," Hayes said.

He apologized and quickly backed out of the room. Muhlbach looked at his wife. They laughed.

The next morning, Hayes approached Muhlbach and apologized again. But later that day, after the team had a lackluster practice, Hayes called everyone together. He blamed the bad practice on the players' wives joining them. He said the "soft bodies" beside them had taken the focus away from the football.

"If the practices don't improve, we're going to move the wives out of the hotel," he said.

Most players wondered what he was talking about. Muhlbach listened to Hayes and chuckled to himself.

(9)

Landing from a goodwill U.S.O. tour to Vietnam a few days earlier, comedian Bob Hope, in his role as Grand Marshal of the Tournament of Roses, unfurled the one-liners.

"I started out as a boxer," he said. "They called me Rembrandt Hope, because I was on the canvas so much."

Deadpan look.

"In football, I was a lonesome end," he said. "Until I discovered Right Guard."

Wry, sideways glance.

"O.J. Simpson," Hope said, "gets in the end zone more than penicillin."

It was no surprise that Simpson, by his final collegiate game, was part of Hope's monologue. He was a star in a town of stars and the rarest commodity in college athletics: a talent accompanied by the fellow traveler of celebrity. There was talk of movie offers. He had agreed to appear in the TV series "Medical Center" the next spring. Chevrolet, Royal Crown Cola, and ABC-TV were waiting for the end of this game to sign him to endorsement deals. He was the subject of an Arnold Friberg painting, "O.J. Simpson Runs For Daylight."

As an example of his public position, Simpson was being asked if he would challenge pro football's draft system and shop his services to the highest bidder. He shrugged and said, well, he just might do that. Simpson had won the Heisman Trophy a few weeks earlier by what remains the widest margin of victory. Married, with a month-old baby girl, he suggested the baby's name would be "Heisman J. Simpson." (She was born the week of the Heisman presentation, and "in his excitement over the Heisman award, he forgot to ask his wife the baby's name," wrote *The New York Times*.)

In November, twenty-five of twenty-six professional scouts polled by *Sports*

Illustrated said Simpson would be the Number One pick in the draft. Ten said he was the best running back they had ever seen in college. He had a fullback's size (6-1, 202 pounds), a sprinter's speed (9.4 seconds in the 100) and such large features that the following season he had to go through several practices at Buffalo without a helmet until they could locate one that would fit him.

Even before he lined up in Southern Cal's backfield, he had starred for the school as a member of the 440-yard relay team that set a world record in the NCAA Championships. The only question coach John McKay wrestled with when Simpson arrived in 1967 was how to make full use of his talent. At first, he learned the flanker and split end positions, besides that of running back.

"We wanted to see if he could take it inside," McKay said. "We ran him seven straight times in one scrimmage and that was it. He busted people backward."

Only now was the nation realizing O.J. didn't stand for Orange Juice but instead Orenthal James (Orenthal, the family story went, was the name of a French actor that Simpson's aunt liked). He grew up in the projects of San Francisco, the second of four children whose father left when he was 4. His mother raised the family on her nurse's salary.

He grew up wanting to be hometown hero Willie Mays. That changed to a Southern Cal running back one day when he saw the school's mascot—a white horse galloping with a sword-carrying Trojan on its back. High school grades kept him out of USC. But after mind-bending seasons at City College of San Francisco, he took a spot in the USC backfield in his first season in 1967, leading the nation with 1,451 yards rushing. In 1968, he led it again, rushing for 1,709 yards and 22 touchdowns.

John McKay considered it funny when reporters asked why he'd run Simpson a staggering 355 times that season. He first repeated a line Paul Brown once used regarding Jim Brown: "When you have a big cannon, shoot it."

Then he tried humor.

"We will continue to operate from only two plays," he said. "I will nod, 'Run left' or I will nod, 'Run right.'"

"I plan to give the ball to O.J. on the first fifty plays of the game," quarterback Steve Sogge said that week.

This is what Ohio State feared. Okay, maybe that's not the proper verb.

"I don't fear a damn thing," Hayes said.

He went straight to his mentor: "It was General Patton who said, 'Never take counsel of your fears,'" he said.

One Ohio State player involved in the O.J. Factor actually *was* afraid. With Ed Bender left off the travel team, Leo Hayden became Simpson in the practices at East Los Angeles Junior College. Hayden put on Number 32. He ran the student-body-right sweep. He gained 19 yards on his first carry posing as Simpson.

That, he quickly learned, was a mistake.

The coaches jumped on the defensive players so hard that for the next several days Hayden went through exactly what Bender had gone through in the French Field House. Only now they could tackle him. And did they ever.

"Brutal," Hayden called those practices.

The good news: Ohio State coaches were so impressed by Hayden's hard running that they put him in the game plan.

(10)

That week, Anne Hayes was asked if she would visit Vietnam after the Rose Bowl with her husband. She dismissed the idea with a wave of her hand.

"Why would he want me to go after he was there before with Lana Turner?" she asked.

She was the perfect midwestern counterbalance to her famous husband, a pillar of good sense and better humor, a personality who didn't covet the spotlight but refused to shrink from it or let it change her.

When a reporter asked to talk with her, she said, "You want to hear the story of a plump little gal like me?" When someone asked what she did, she said, "I'm a full-time housekeeper who is Woody's part-time mistress."

When a stranger expressed sympathy for her being the wife of a football coach, she'd answer, "Don't feel sorry for me. I like being a coach's wife. If you want to feel sorry that I married Woody Hayes, well, that's different."

They were the first couple of Columbus, but with such little pretense their phone number was listed in the book. Anyone could call. Everyone often did. Fans. Rivals. Monday morning quarterbacks. Saturday-night drunks.

"Your husband is a fathead," someone said when she answered the phone.

"I agree with you," she said. "I think he is at times, too."

"You're leaving town," someone called to say during the losing season of 1966.

"No, I'm here talking with you," she said.

They had met in 1936 when Anne Gross was hanging May Day baskets in her hometown of New Philadelphia. "You over there," the new football coach in town called over. "What have you got in those baskets?" That, she would say, "started a whirlwind romance that lasted six years."

In Granville, while Woody coached Denison, they lived in the basement of an apartment building and were responsible for stoking the furnace. "And you know who that meant," she said.

Where Woody was confrontational, Anne was disarming. Where he was loud, she was funny. Where he was strong, she was equally strong. When she went to women's clubs and someone asked how to be a good coach's wife, she said it was simple.

"Marry a good coach," she said.

Nothing was off topic.

"I know you all want to know my age," she would say. "I'm 55. I'm proud of it. But I'm not proud of my weight. You can all see it's on the upside."

She once told a Massillon ladies society that she knew it wouldn't be a good day when she was three blocks from home before realizing she'd forgotten to put in her partial plate. Stockings, she told a group in Elyria, were something she never wore. Which reminded her of something else.

"Tell Forest Evashevski he's wrong about Woody wearing thermal underwear under his shirt," she said. "Evy doesn't know. I do Woody's laundry. I know."

Just like her husband, she was invited to speak all over the state. Like him, too, she refused to profit from it, answering groups who asked what she charged, "How much can you afford to give the American Cancer Society?"

She knew why she was in demand. It wasn't her lively personality that made her the first woman to speak at the weekly Big Ten sports writers luncheon in Chicago. That's why she was invited back annually, though.

"Does Woody own a long-sleeved shirt," one writer asked.

"No," she said.

"Can Woody walk on water?" another did.

"He tries, but he's not a good swimmer," she said.

Michigan athletic director Bump Elliott made the mistake of saying he was substituting for a busy Bo Schembechler, "just like Mrs. Hayes is substituting for Woody Hayes."

Her eyes flashed. "I'm not substituting for anyone," she said loudly. "I was invited here."

In that regard, she was a woman in full, someone who understood that Woody was the star of the family but didn't defer to him. She supported him. They were in it together. They had to be, the way he coached. Occasionally, when a player was in academic trouble, Woody would move him into the home. He and Anne became tutors. Sometimes, when a coach interviewed for a job, Woody and the prospective hire might show up unannounced for dinner. That was fine, too.

Bill Mallory, just days from his first head coaching job, said Anne was the football role model for his wife, Ellie. How to act. What to see in situations. When it was time to support the husband and where to draw a line in protecting your children.

Anne came by her love of sports honestly. Her parents' honeymoon consisted of nine days of baseball games in Detroit and Cleveland. She watched football so intently that someone might mention a move by the running back and she might say she had missed it. "I was watching the line," she'd say.

Always, Anne had the ability to line any path with humor. When her friend moved to Michigan Boulevard in Chicago, she wrote on an envelope, "Ugh, can you move?" When their son, Steve, who had just graduated from Ohio State's Law School in 1968, was looking for a college he was told he could go anywhere except one place.

"I told him, 'If you choose Michigan, I'll pack up your bags and throw them on the sidewalk,'" Anne said.

It was Anne who wrote the witty headlines on the family Christmas card ("Merry Christmas Anyhow!" it read after the Board of Trustees voted against Ohio State attending the 1961 Rose Bowl). It was Anne who told coaches' wives when they talked of loneliness, "While Woody's absorbed with eighty boys and their problems, I don't have to worry about one thin blonde in an apartment."

She could help out, if needed. On a speaking engagement in New York, she took a side trip to help recruit Kevin Rusnak in Garfield, New Jersey. Within two minutes, she felt like family, Rusnak said. She didn't have to recruit the mom, like Woody. She was the midwestern mom Rusnak's parents wanted him to have so far from home.

She was that, too. In one hand in the lobby of the Huntington Sheraton, she was carrying a bag with a shoe in it and in the other hand were some children's books. The shoe was a player's that needed a new sole. The books were for some of the assistant coaches' children. She demanded they call her their "associate grandmother."

"I have a hobby," she told people. "I collect pictures in newspapers of Woody with other women being referred to as 'Mrs. Hayes.'"

At the Rose Bowl, she added a new one. Woody's sister, Mary North, had gotten off the team plane with him. She clipped out the new "Mrs. Hayes."

At the foundation of her marriage was an understanding of her husband's obsessive passion to work.

"If Woody had to do something besides coach, even digging ditches, he would dig bigger, wider, and deeper ditches than anyone," she said.

She understood him. That didn't always mean she agreed with him.

"During the football season, I am so nice," she said. "I never bother him. After the season I have what I call my bitching week. I cleanse my soul. I tell him everything he's done wrong. Then I become a normal wife again. It's interesting."

(11)

As the big game came into view, as the tension ratcheted up, as game plans were finalized, Lou Holtz called over Tim Anderson.

"Woody wants to start Mike Polaski," Holtz told him. "This can be his only Rose Bowl."

Anderson was surprised. He had been a regular starter. Now, in the biggest game of the year, one even people on Anderson Hill could watch on television, and because of a Big Ten rule that denied Ohio State the chance to return to the Rose Bowl the next year . . . he was on the bench?

He thought about this for about one second. "Well, you might as well put me on a plane home," he said. "I don't even want to play if that's the case."

As Holtz and Anderson talked, Hayes walked over and asked what was going on.

"He wants to go home," Holtz said. "If he's not starting, he doesn't want to be around."

They led to a longer talk. Anderson didn't budge. Holtz went to Jack Tatum and tried to get him to talk with Anderson. As the word filtered out to them, the African American players began talking about it. And taking issue with it. And the question was raised: Maybe they all should go home. Maybe this was an issue they should rally around.

It was the end of the year in which other players were taking stands at schools, of gloved fists being raised on Olympic medal stands, of the African

American athlete finding a voice in society. Or trying to find it. Or sometimes just exercising their voices after so many years of prejudice.

These players went to Rudy Hubbard, the lone black assistant who was just finishing his first season. By the time they got to him, they were becoming more strident. They were leaning toward going home. Hubbard began talking with them, asking what they expected to gain from doing that. He told them to keep calm. Let him try to deal with it.

That day, at a staff meeting, Hubbard took a deep breath and said, "Here's what's going on . . ."

In the years before an African American coach could lend some perspective, maybe this issue would have mushroomed into something bigger. Maybe until battle lines were drawn, the coaches would have missed it altogether. Maybe the players would have harbored resentment even if they had stayed.

As it was, even Hayes decided doing something out of loyalty for an upperclassman wasn't the smartest thing to do. It certainly wasn't worth this fight. A decision was quickly made. A crisis was averted.

The next day, Holtz went up to Anderson.

"Okay, you're starting," he said.

More problems were avoided than Holtz could imagine in that moment. Provost had hurt his ankle in practice. He wouldn't finish the first quarter of the game. All four healthy defensive backs would be needed.

(12)

The drama wasn't done. A couple of days before the game, in a workout with no pads, no contact, not much of anything, McCullough put his linebackers through a simple drill. They dropped into coverage. He threw the ball. They caught the ball.

While they were, for the most part, taking it easy in practice, McCullough wanted more effort than was being shown. There was a standard, after all.

"Show some hustle!" he barked. "Start getting to those balls!"

His next turn, Stier dropped into his zone. The ball was thrown a little beyond him. Stier ran for it and—he wanted hustle?—dove for the ball. He caught it, too. But he also landed on his right shoulder and felt something crunch. His shoulder was separated.

He lay, wincing in pain. McCullough came running over, screaming,

"WHAT'D YOU DO THAT FOR? WHY'D YOU DIVE?"

Hayes came over, too. He began yelling at McCullough for running a drill that could get someone hurt so close to the game. Stier lay on the field in pain. He was the team's leading tackler, the Most Valuable Player, the acting captain and a senior. He had looked forward to ending his career in style. Now this?

"Get Radtke ready," Hayes said.

"Coach, Radtke's been playing end all year," McCullough said.

Hayes didn't care. McCullough thought he didn't actually know Radtke was an end, confirming how little attention he paid to defense.

Good Lord. Get a defensive end ready to play linebacker? For the biggest game of the year?

(13)

Hayes arrived for the final news conference before the game in his trademark short-sleeved white shirt and tie. He answered without incident all the requisite questions about how he felt, about how his team felt, and whether he thought they'd be too high, too low, or just right by kickoff.

"We'll be just right," he said.

It was, by Hayes's standards, a completely subdued thirty minutes. Everything had become an issue to him. The swimming pools around the city concerned him. ("You don't get football players out of soft living like that.") The morning grass at the practice field was too heavy because of the dew. ("Back home we keep a tarp on it.") He forfeited the traditional beef-eating contest at Lawry's Restaurant to Southern Cal. ("Our guys were getting too fat out here.") He also missed a scheduled TV show with USC coach John McKay ("Practice took priority," he said), and he demanded to appear in another television program—out of turn—to maintain *his* schedule. ("That only required switching around a few nonentities like Chief Justice Warren and Bob Hope," wrote Jim Murray.)

On the night before the game, Hayes wasn't taking any chances, either. He had made advance plans. On the afternoon of New Year's Eve, he sent out immediate orders: *Pack up. Meet in the lobby. We're moving out.*

Buses took the team from the plush Huntington Sheraton Hotel up the Sierra Madre mountains outside Los Angeles. The players looked out the window as civilization disappeared behind them, wondering where they were going.

Ten miles into the foothills, they stopped at a place that was officially called "The Mater Dolorosa Passionist Retreat Center." To the players, it became known by a simpler name: The Monastery. That's exactly what it was, too.

The Passionists were a group within the Catholic Church who had built this isolated refuge. There were fifty priests and brothers in black habits who served the players dinner. There were cell-like rooms with only a bed, a table, a lamp, and a Bible where the players would sleep, one to a room. There was an olive grove, perfect for meditation, where some of the Ohio State players walked.

There was no television, no limo drivers, no intrusive tourists—and no mischief to uncover. Exactly as Hayes planned. He would come to like it so much he passed on the word to Michigan's Bo Schembechler. The next year, it became the site where Schembechler suffered a heart attack.

So maybe it wasn't always so peaceful.

It wasn't even relaxing for McCullough and Radtke. McCullough called for a meeting and began by pointing at the statue of the Virgin Mary.

"You better pray to her, because if you make a mistake Coach Hayes is going to be mad at me and I'm going to be mad at Sark and Sark's going to be mad at you," McCullough said. Then he broke the news: "Sark won't even be your coach. You're going to be a linebacker this game."

"A linebacker?" Radtke said.

McCullough reminded him that Stier was hurt, and how they were scrambling for a fill-in. "Coach Hayes thinks you've been playing linebacker," he told Radtke.

If that wasn't insult enough, Radtke now had to learn a whole new position. Overnight. And he was going against the Heisman-winning running back. Past nine o'clock, ten o'clock, eleven o'clock, he and McCullough pored over the playbook. They got up the next morning and began again.

Meanwhile, through friends of the program, Hayes had finagled some notable eve-of-the-game entertainment: the world premiere of *Hellfighters*, a John Wayne movie in which he plays a macho oil-well firefighter, based on the life of the famed Red Adair.

One problem: no one brought a movie screen. And the monastery didn't have one. So the world premiere of Wayne's latest movie was shown on a bed sheet hung on a monastery wall.

Another problem: even here, Hayes was antsy. He wanted his players thinking about the game, not some firefighter. Certainly he didn't want them thinking of the firefighter's daughter, who was played by Katharine Ross in her first movie since playing the daughter in *The Graduate*. Would this movie never end? Shouldn't these players be getting some sleep?

After the second reel finished, Hayes asked how many more reels there were. Four, he was told.

"Goddammit, it's all the same," he said. "All they're doing is putting out fires. Just put on the last reel."

Even The Duke, at the height of Hollywood fame, in the premiere of his latest movie, was no match for Woody.

After the movie, some coaches wandered to the veranda and talked with the priests. The players got the normal snack of hot chocolate, cookies, and an apple before going to their solitary rooms. Alone, in a strange place, on a mountain in California, some players lay in the complete darkness and listened to a sound they never forgot: the howling of coyotes.

"Oow-oow-OOWWWW!" the eerie sound came.

"Oow-oww-OWWWW!"

What they didn't know was, up in the mountain, Stillwagon was doing the howling. Everyone had been told there were coyotes around the monastery. He just wanted to make sure their presence was heard. Even here, he could make his own fun.

Meanwhile, Rusnak sat in Ted Kurz's room with a view that stretched from the Sierra Madre across the entire Los Angeles Valley. They watched fireworks pop up into the night sky across the valley. They poured each other a shot of tequila Kurz had stored in small mouthwash bottles.

At midnight, they toasted.

Happy 1969.

(14)

Early on New Year's Day, Bill Mallory sent word across the monastery that he needed to see Stillwagon. A student manager hunted down the player and took him to Mallory's room. Mallory sat on the bed. This would be their last father-son, coach-player, mentor-mentee—however their good relationship was phrased, this would be the last game.

Stillwagon sensed it, too. When he went in the bathroom, he saw among Mallory's toiletries a hair net and coloring. There must be a reason for that, Stillwagon figured. He was getting ready to be a more public figure. Good detective work, you might say. Just that week Bo Schembechler had been named Michigan's coach, and within a few weeks, Mallory would be named his replacement at Miami of Oxford. He would get his dream job.

That wasn't on Mallory's mind this morning, though. This game was. He wanted to impress its importance on Stillwagon. He wanted to impart how significant Stillwagon would be. He hardly needed to say anything, however, because Stillwagon already saw Mallory was foaming at the mouth. Eight hours before kickoff! Maddog was ready!

"You won't play in anything bigger than this," Mallory said, leaning in close. "You've got to make sure . . . you've . . ."

"Hey, Coach," Stillwagon said, pointing over Mallory's shoulder and out the window.

"What're you looking at?" Mallory said.

"Isn't that the blimp?"

"Wha-a-a-t?" Mallory said.

Mallory turned and there, indeed, was the blimp flying above the mountains. It was a surreal sight. It also was something the coach didn't want intruding on a pep talk with his star player. And to show the intensity involved in this day, Mallory ran to the window, flipped up his middle finger in each hand and began pumping his arms up and down.

"FUCK THE BLIMP!" he began yelling out the window. "FUCK THE BLIMP!"

This, Stillwagon decided, was better than the Michigan State talk. It was the best one yet! It did the trick, too.

Man, was he ready to play now.

(15)

As the TV picture came alive, as the sunshine splashed the field, as the camera panned the Rose Bowl Stadium from afar, the voice entered America's living rooms: "The San Gabriel mountains overlooking the Rose Bowl in Pasadena. Happy New Year, everybody. I'm Curt Gowdy with Kyle Rote. The only time two undefeated teams have met in Rose Bowl history. The Number One and Number Two teams in America. The Heisman Trophy winner, O.J. Simpson. An enthusiastic, speedy, talented group of Ohio State sophomores. Kyle?"

"Well, it'll be O.J. Simpson against Ohio State's Jim Otis," Rote said. "And, of course, Rex Kern, their fine, young quarterback from Ohio State, against Steve Sogge for Southern Cal. Ohio State is favored. Southern California doesn't believe it. We'll see."

"All right, let's go down now for the toss of the coin at the 50-yard line," Gowdy said.

That, in twenty seconds, was the pre-game show.

Already, 100,000 American flags had been passed out to fans. Already, President-elect Nixon sat beside Ohio governor Jim Rhodes for the first half. Already, the crowd had applauded nineteen members of the *U.S.S. Pueblo* who were released a few days earlier after eleven months of North Korean imprisonment.

The sun sat high in a cotton-ball sky, and the temperature was a sweaty eighty-five degrees. So Hayes was proved right once again. The weather was just as he had predicted, way back in the French Field House sauna. In the pre-game workouts, the players' heavy cotton jerseys felt like wet blankets on them.

"This isn't gonna work," Otis said.

He told the trainers they needed a change. Off went the heavy jerseys. On went the light, fish-net jerseys that looked so fashionable. This was a team that appreciated fashion, too. In their Ohio State time: the silver helmet would replace a scarlet helmet; the sleeker, trendier jerseys with the black numerals on the sleeves would be introduced; and they'd move from high-top to low-top shoes.

The change of jerseys had nothing to do with fashion, though. It was survival. It was the small decisions, they all agreed, that affected the bigger moment.

As did this: The morning of the game, the doctors reexamined Stier's shoulder and said he couldn't do any more damage to it. There were two options: (1) don't play; (2) shoot up the shoulder with a numbing agent so he wouldn't feel anything for a few hours of football.

That, Stier thought, wasn't too tough a decision.

He had the shoulder put in a harness that the medical staff had designed for Kern. He couldn't raise his arm above his shoulder, he didn't have full strength in the shoulder, and, come kickoff, he didn't feel a thing on the entire right side of his body, either.

Zelina kicked off to start the game. That made him the fifth player to kick off this season. The others felt Zelina won the weekly competition for both kickoffs and placekicking because he was resting a sore ankle all week. His leg was rested. The legs of Roman and Oppermann, meanwhile, had been literally run into the ground.

Through the first quarter, the two teams traded thrusts and punts and zeroes on the scoreboard. At the start of the second quarter, though, Zelina lined up for a 17-yard field goal. To continue the saga of Ohio State kickers—and unbeknownst to even him at the time—he had suffered broken ribs on a punt return. He just knew breathing was becoming difficult. And kicking?

"He boots it at the 17," Gowdy said, "and . . . "

Way left. Way ugly.

". . . no good."

You can take the kicking game out of Ohio, but you can't take Ohio out of . . . well, whatever. They all had to wonder: would this be the game where their Achilles' foot finally cost them?

Especially because Southern Cal took the ball right down the field, throwing short passes to Simpson, which he turned into nice gains. On the final one from the Ohio State 19-yard line, Tatum picked up the wrong man. He finally chased down Simpson and knocked him out of bounds at the three-yard line.

Now it was first-and-goal. Guess who got it? When you have a cannon . . . Sensibaugh collided with Simpson in the hole for the tackle. No gain.

Again, Simpson got the ball on second down. Again, Sensibaugh met him in the hole. Loss of one.

On third down, Simpson went to the right, stopped, and overthrew on a sure touchdown in the end zone. No problem. It was a simple 21-yard field goal that, yes, Southern Cal made look simple. It was 3-0. But not for long.

The next time Simpson got his hands on the ball, it was on Southern Cal's famed student-body-left sweep. It began like a dozen other plays that game.

"Sogge pitches to Simpson," Gowdy told America.

But on this particular play, the strength of the Ohio State defense became its weakness. It was too quick. Its players overran the play. What was Coach Emerson's line? *Every excess causes a defect?*

Defensive end Mark Debevec, as planned, forced Simpson inside. But Simpson changed directions. He cut back across the field. Jim Stillwagon had run too far and could just hold out an arm as Simpson cut through it. Mark Stier, too, was in no position to help. Sensibaugh got an arm on him, but nothing more. Tim Anderson and Jack Tatum got caught in traffic.

". . . Twenty-five!" said Gowdy. ". . . Thirty! . . ."

Simpson was all shaking hips and dipping shoulder pads in front of Mike Polaski, who spun to the ground, as if the grass had turned to ice.

"Look out! He runs a 100 in 9.4!" Gowdy shouted.

Suddenly, a defense intent on stopping Simpson was chasing him. Anderson, Tatum, and Polaski sprinted five yards behind him.

"They won't get him!" Gowdy said.

Three Southern Cal receivers were escorting him.

"He's being convoyed in!" Gowdy said.

Simpson flipped the ball to the ground in the end zone and began to decelerate.

"Eighty yards for O.J. Simpson!"

On the Ohio State sideline, Hayes had an involuntary reaction with that left fist. He punched Tiger Ellison in the chest, knocking him to the ground—"like I'd been kicked by a Georgia mule," Ellison said. He jumped right up and stood in Hayes's face.

"Did I hit you, Tiger?" he said.

"Damn right, you hit me," Ellison said.

Hayes put his arm around Ellison for a second, then got on the phone to Holtz in the press box. "Why'd he go 80 yards?"

"Coach," said Holtz, in a line repeated in speeches for years, "that's all he needed."

Holtz wasn't so flippant with his players. He sent word through a student manager to Polaski. Polaski said he didn't want to talk. Holtz insisted. Polaski put on the headset.

"Dammit, son," Holtz said. "We can't have that happen. I don't care how you get there, but you've got to get there."

"Wait 'til you see the film," Polaski said. "It's the best move I've ever seen."

"I don't care, just get there," Holtz said.

That summer, Hayes would run film of Simpson's run back and forth. He drew "that thing exactly on graph paper—to the exact yard," as he told reporters later. Then Hayes recreated the play on a blackboard for the reporters. The "relative motion" of Simpson to his Ohio State players, he said, was like his Navy experience in World War II. Simpson, he said, was like a German U-boat. His safeties were like sub chasers. Simpson escaped, Hayes said, due to "high relative speed, equal to the sum of the two speeds when the sub and the sub chaser are traveling reciprocal courses."

The reporters looked at each other.

Huh?

Down 10-0 on the biggest stage any of them had been on, no one on the Ohio State sideline felt panic. At least not in the manner most fans would have expected. Kern thought: *Oh, man, I don't want to fly home with the Old Man, losing a game like this.*

This was like the Southern Methodist opener, he thought. They were just missing. *He* was just missing. Once, he had Zelina open deep on a downfield pattern. And overthrew him. Another time, near the end zone, he had Zelina open over the middle. And missed him. Other times, a run was just one block from busting open.

But as he looked at the game from a wide-angle lens, Kern settled on one thing that suggested they'd be okay: Their offensive line was dominating Southern Cal. Never mind the size difference. The line was pushing Southern Cal back, opening holes, doing everything with the intelligence and quickness that they had all season. This told Kern they should be okay.

Up in the broadcasting booth, Gowdy was telling America, "The Buckeyes, who have averaged 33 points a game, have been held scoreless so far. We have six minutes and thirty-four seconds to play in the first half. O.J. Simpson already has made 131 yards rushing. The record is 194 in a Rose Bowl game."

Down on the field, Kern was telling teammates in the huddle: "Okay, look guys, we've screwed around too long. It's time for us to put the machine in gear. Let's go."

Kern had some limitation in the game. After his shoulder separation, the training and equipment staffs sat around trying to figure out how to help him play. They came up with something no one had invented: a shoulder harness. It consisted of two four-inch leather straps. One went from his shoulder around his chest. The other connected around his biceps area. They were connected by strands of rawhide, like a shoelace. And, *presto*, he could play without fear of his shoulder popping off like a bottle cap every down.

With a simple run up the middle by Leo Hayden, the machine began to slip into gear. There was three yards. Then Otis went up the middle for five more. Then Otis got four and a first down. Then he got nine, and Ohio State was in Southern Cal territory.

"This is some fullback, this boy," Gowdy said. "Woody Hayes said, 'I've never quite built this boy up to where I should, for fear people think I'm prejudiced, because his father is my best friend.'"

Ray Gillian gained six yards, and they all began to feel the rhythm coming to them. Gillian did, especially. He replaced the injured Zelina. On third down from the Southern Cal 21-yard line . . .

"Kern to throw," Gowdy said. "Wide open! Gillian! First down, Ohio State, to the 3-yard line! Gain of 18!"

Gillian got up clapping. This would be the start of his big day. Two off-tackle plays later, Otis ran behind guard Alan Jack and tackle Rufus Mayes for a touchdown.

"A 69-yard drive," said Gowdy, "and they just powered their way down."

The drive took fourteen plays, and they weren't done for the half, either. With just over a minute to play, Kern was back on the field, throwing 17 yards to Jan White.

"Boy, he laid that one right in there," Gowdy said.

Now, for the first time in the game, Kern felt the full arsenal was working. The rust was off. He threw a couple of yards to Bruce Jankowski. Then Otis gained six up the middle. On third-and-two, with thirty-four seconds remaining, he threw down the middle.

"Complete to Gillian!" Gowdy said. "Gillian on the 16. Ray Gillian has caught two big passes today!"

Now came the real issue. Do they dare try a field goal? With this kicking game in flux? Already in the game, Zelina had missed one. Now he was hurt. Jim Roman came to kick.

"From the 16-yard line of Southern Cal," Gowdy said. "The kick is . . ."

The state of Ohio held its breath.

"Good!" Gowdy said.

There, the game had swung. The players felt it. Down 10-0, they had rallied to a halftime tie. From that point, they felt more confident, back in rhythm. Simpson had shaken loose for one long run and had gained 136 yards at the half. Maybe, as they said later, they had been awakened by O.J.'s run. Maybe, too, he didn't get another because at halftime, the coaches adjusted to the defense they'd practiced so hard leading up to the game. The one that involved Stier shadowing O.J. Simpson. They hadn't used it in the first half, to see how Stier played on that shoulder.

At halftime, he said he was fine. He was assigned to Simpson. The players, meanwhile, were so energized by the finish of the half they could barely listen to the coaches. They just wanted to get back on the field.

"Okay, let's go out," Hayes finally told them.

They practiced in the end zone, knocking against each other, trying to hold that momentum as the band finished its performance on the field.

(16)

On the Rose Bowl field at halftime, a fifth-year sousaphone player in the Ohio State Marching Band was about to get his five seconds of fame.

Jim Esswein had first picked up the clarinet in his Columbus elementary school. In eighth grade, he was in the music room when, just for something to do, he squeezed his lanky frame into a rack of sousaphones, found a mouthpiece, and blew on it.

"Would you like to play that?" the music director asked, entering the room.

The moment led to private lessons, a spot in the high school band, and, once he improved his marching by his sophomore year, a place in The Best Damn Band In the Land. And not just *any* place. As a sousaphone player, Esswein was a candidate to dot the "i" in the famed Script Ohio formation.

The use of a sousaphone player as punctuation artist went back to 1937, the second year Script Ohio was performed. In the first season, a trumpet player had dotted the "i." But in rehearsing it the next season, band director Eugene Weigel shouted to a sousaphone player named Greg Johnson to try it. An idea was hatched. A tradition was born.

Seniors got to perform the honor, and in 1967, Essewin dotted his senior season. In 1968, back as a fifth-year senior, he stepped aside so the five other senior sousaphonists who hadn't dotted the "i" would get the chance. Five seniors. Five home games. That worked.

"I'll do it at the Rose Bowl," he said.

Now here he was. He had furiously practiced the move that accompanied the dotting. He grew increasingly nervous, too. What if he slipped? What if his legs got tangled? What if he actually embarrassed the band on this national stage?

That halftime, the Script Ohio went perfectly. Esswein marched to the top of the "i." He then came to a standing stop and made the required series of dance steps for the exclamation point: throwing his right leg straight out to the right, throwing that right leg back to the left and allowing the momentum to turn his body 180 degrees, and swinging the foot to the front and down to the side.

He took off his hat.

He bowed deeply.

And, from this position, face low to the ground, he heard an applause that echoed for decades.

(17)

Midway through the third quarter, Ohio State got the break it needed. It came one play after Stier had met Simpson, *mano a mano*, on a swing pass wide in the flat. If Simpson got by, it would be a big gain. And Simpson nearly did get by. Stier stuck out his leg and tripped him.

Whew.

"Good thing Stier had long legs," Kyle Rote said.

The next play, Simpson fumbled a pitchout. He was looking for his pathway upfield, and he just didn't catch it. It bounced off his chest, onto the ground, and Sensibaugh was the first to it. Or "Sessibaugh," as Gowdy called him most of the game.

"That's the first significant break in the game by fumble or interception," Kyle Rote said. "Now we'll see how young Rex Kern takes his club."

At half, the offensive staff noticed Southern Cal was overplaying Ohio State's speed by taking away the outside. This was fine with Hayes. He reverted to his personality. He hit them up the gut. First, it was Otis up the middle for six yards. Then Otis for two. On third down, Kern went around left end for five yards.

Then Gillian gained nine over the left side. Otis, out of the Robust-T formation, gained six . . .

"This is what Southern Cal—in talking with their coaches before the ball game—this is the one thing they've got to stop," Rote said as Ohio State lined up at the Southern Cal 33. "They've got to stop these runs right up the middle, where Donovan and Strickland, those two guards, and Alan Jack as well, they're just blowing them out of there."

Hayden for five. Otis for one . . .

"This is the type of ball control, power football, Woody Hayes is famed for," Gowdy said.

Hayden for five . . .

"The Ohio State band strikes up the Battle Cry with their team now threatening," Gowdy said.

Finally, on third-and-three, from the Southern Cal 10, Kern was stopped for two yards. Fourth down. In came Jim Roman. He laid his piece of tape on the ground just so. Billy Long held the ball. And after Roman kicked the ball through, as Long ran off the field holding two palms out for Kern to give him ten, the coaches breathed in relief. The kicking game had come through again.

It was 13-10. Everyone felt the game had shifted. Now it would capsize on Southern Cal. Sogge would drop back to pass on the next possession and be swamped by Dave Whitfield, who beat two blockers. Sogge fumbled. Stottlemyer recovered at the Southern Cal 21.

The offense was on the field again. Hayden up the middle for three yards. And Hayden up the middle yet again as the NBC camera followed him and . . .

"Kern fools everyone in the ballpark," Gowdy said.

On the final play of the third quarter, Kern kept the ball, dropping to pass, then scrambling down to the four-yard line. Up to this point, Kern's shoulder felt fine. His movement was restricted. But he could throw. He could run. He could play without constantly thinking about what might happen with the wrong hit.

But on this final play of the quarter came a painful reminder of his injury. As he was tackled, his shoulder popped out. Lying on the field, wincing in pain, he looked to Southern Cal safety Mike Battle for help.

"Pop it back in, pop it back in," he said.

Battle walked away. So much for sportsmanship. As players switched ends of the field for the fourth quarter, Kern dragged himself to the sideline. Bozich wrenched Kern's shoulder back into working order. (After returning home, Kern would have surgery to repair the shoulder and ensure the injury didn't become chronic.)

He returned without missing a play, and on third down from the Southern Cal four-yard line, Kern stumbled back to pass and . . .

"Throws to Hayden," Gowdy said. "Touchdown, Leo Hayden!"

White picked up Hayden. Gillian jumped on them. It was now 20-10. Victory was calling. History, too.

"Come on! Don't let up!" the defensive players told each other.

Three plays and the offense had the ball back. Hayes went into a time-killing shell now. He couldn't help himself. Hayden went up the middle twice for no gain. On third down, Sensibaugh came on and Ohio State lined up in punt formation. The ball was snapped to Otis for a three-yard gain, but everyone understood what Hayes was saying: No mistakes meant no chance for Southern Cal.

That's not to say all drama had leaked from the game. Running downfield on the ensuing punt, John Muhlbach was clipped. His leg and ankle broke immediately. He ran the final 15 yards of his career on pure adrenaline, before collapsing to the ground. As he was carried off the field to the locker room, he passed Bob Hope, who placed a dozen roses on his stretcher. When his wife came to the locker room, she got the roses. Thanks for the memories, right?

On Southern Cal's next play, Sogge threw a little swing pass in the left flat to Simpson. There was his shadow, Stier. Together again. This time Stier didn't need his leg. He hit Simpson just from the right angle to cause the ball to pop loose. Again, Ohio State got it.

Hayes decided what the heck. Go for the kill. On first down, Kern threw a simple pass over the middle to Gillian, who—to his surprise—found that no one was around him. He was free. For so much of this season Gillian was relegated to playing first behind Brockington, then Zelina, wondering if his chance would ever come.

Finally, it had. Finally, he could show his talent. Four of his season's six catches would come this day. So would six of his 16 carries.

And his lone touchdown.

This touchdown.

He took Kern's pass, accelerated down the middle, and went into the end zone untouched. He flung the ball high into the crowd.

"What an arm!" Rote said.

Gillian had watched a Southern Cal game on television earlier that season and seen O.J. fling the ball in the end zone. So they were even turning Simpson's tricks on him.

"Gillian has been some replacement," Gowdy said.

They all got a piece of the celebration. Sensibaugh—"Sessibaugh," Gowdy kept calling him—intercepted a Sogge pass. Anderson intercepted a Simpson pass in the end zone. Gowdy did some housecleaning, noting how there was only one senior starting on the Ohio State defense—Stier—and just three on the offense: Mayes, Foley, and Muhlbach.

"Think they might rank in the preseason rankings next year?" he asked.

With the game decided, a grab for memories was on. McCullough called down from the press box to Worden and told him to get in the game, "so you can tell your grandkids about it," McCullough said. Worden, who would undergo surgery on his knee within the week, hobbled around for a few plays.

Just when it appeared Ohio State would have a nice, tidy victory without the hint of controversy, Sogge, in the final minute, threw a ball to the back of the end zone. Polaski jumped with Southern Cal receiver Sam Dickerson.

"And it is Polaski who caught the ball," Gowdy said. "Now did he catch the ball in the end zone or not? They want to call in another official to look at it from (another) angle."

Polaski listened to the officials a second, then began clapping his hands and running away in apparent celebration. But when the referee walked away, he signaled a touchdown.

"Well," Gowdy said.

It hardly mattered in the outcome. But Hayes's passion never turned off. He charged down the field, yelling at the referees, walking off the sideline amid dozens of fans ready to celebrate the win.

"And now Hayes is arguing," Gowdy said.

What would the New Year be like without a Woody megaton? This one earned a 15-yard penalty.

"I don't know, maybe my eyes were deceiving me," Gowdy said. "I thought Polaski had the ball and the question was whether he was in the end zone or not. But it's now a Southern California touchdown."

All that meant was with forty-four seconds to go, Ohio State got the ball back. Maciejowski started to buckle up his helmet, but Hayes stopped him.

"Bill's a senior," Hayes said.

Long went in at quarterback to replace Kern. But Maciejowski wanted in, too. He bolted onto the field and approached tight end Dick Kuhn.

"You're out," he told Kuhn.

"Huh?" Kuhn said.

"I'm in," Maciejowski said.

Another replacement, Ted Kurz, appreciated being in the final three plays at guard. On the first play, as others rode out the clock, Kurz smashed into the Southern Cal lineman, then chopped his legs to knock him to the ground. When he started getting up, Kurz hit him again.

"What the hell you doing?" the player said to Kurz. "The game's over."

"You'd better buckle up," Kurz said. "This is the first time the people at home have seen me."

When he came out of the huddle for the second play, the guy had gone to the sideline. His replacement was in. He, too, got the full treatment. Two simple handoffs remained. Hayes and McKay began moving toward midfield.

Gowdy counted down: "Three . . . two . . . one . . . the Ohio State Bucks have won the Rose Bowl, 27-16, and strengthened their hold as the Number One college football team in the country!"

By now, the Ohio State fans were chanting, "WE'RE NUMBER ONE!" Soon, they switched it to: "O.J. WHO?" And then: "WE WANT WOODY!"

In the swirl of celebration, Ohio State players laughed and hugged their way to the locker room. Hayes sat on a bench with the game ball. Players stopped by to shake his hand.

"Now let them vote!" Kern shouted across the locker room regarding the pollsters.

"YEAH!" teammates yelled.

"ONE! ONE! ONE!" they began chanting, then: "ROSE BOWL! ROSE BOWL! ROSE BOWL!"

As that began to fade, someone by the door said, "Hey, guys, quiet! It's O.J.!"

Looking over, the Ohio State players saw Simpson standing just inside the door.

"Hey! It's O.J.! Quiet down!"

"SHHHH!"

They crowded around him. Simpson was still sweating and in full uniform. He raised a hand and said, "You're the best fucking ball team in the country and don't let anybody tell you you aren't. Congratulations!"

As players began shaking his hand or patting his shoulder pads, Simpson approached Foley. They had met at various functions. Simpson held out the coin the referee had handed him after winning the pre-game toss.

"Listen, this'll mean a lot more to you than to me," he said, handing it to Foley. That night, as they replayed the win, Foley gave the coin to his father. He put it in his pants pocket and carried it with him until the day he died.

Hayes walked over, shook Simpson's hand and said, "Thanks, thanks." Simpson then raised two fingers as he walked out of the locker room, indicating either peace or that his team was Number Two. It was a classy visit that crystallized the Rose Bowl trip for many of the Ohio State players.

Hayes began talking to his team, telling his players how well they played, how proud he was, all the things coaches say after big games. Then he said they were free for the night. There was a team meeting at 9 a.m., and immediately after it he was flying to Vietnam.

"And don't get arrested tonight!" he said. "I'm not getting you out of jail!

And, remember, be back at the hotel at 9 a.m."

The team laughed. Hayes held up a hand to quiet them. "Who gets the game ball?" he said. Names were shouted out. Mark Stier, for playing so well on that bad shoulder. Ray Gillian, for his touchdown. Dave Foley. Rufus Mayes.

"How about John Muhlbach?" Hayes said. "The little guy probably had his ankle fractured today. Doggone, he deserves it anyway. I guess we'll end up giving about five out."

He went over and gave Muhlbach a ball. He gave another to Long, the quarterback who had kept quiet all year. Long put the ball in his locker. And in keeping with his mood, he would leave it there when he departed the locker room.

Hindman hustled up to Hayes and said an important visitor might be coming to the locker room.

"President Nixon," Hayes guessed.

Hindman said no, not that big. But Nixon would call the hotel later to congratulate Hayes. For now, the head of the Helms Foundation entered the locker room carrying a silver trophy awarded to the game's outstanding player.

"This year," he said, "it goes to Rex Kern."

Players cheered. Kern moved to accept it.

"Don't hit him on this shoulder," Hayes said, covering Kern's left one. "It went out again today."

Kern shook the man's hand and turned to his teammates who would be his friends for life, just as Hayes had said in that meeting so long ago.

"Every part of this belongs to you guys!" Kern said.

He held the trophy in the air.

"The greatest team in the country!"

Epilogue:
the days after

PHU BAI, Viet Nam, Jan. 13 (UPI)—Woody Hayes, football coach of the national champion Ohio State Buckeyes, ignored monsoon rains today and flew to three fire support bases to visit troops.

Hayes, on his fourth tour of Viet Nam, was accompanied by Bill Hess, Ohio University football coach, on trips to the 101st airborne division bases some 382 miles northeast of Saigon.

After a 20-minute lunch with the acting division commander, Brig. Gen. Allen M. Burdgett, the coaches were presented with a lighter engraved with the unit's "Screaming Eagle" emblem.

They then flew by helicopter to three isolated fire support bases where they shook hands with the troops and showed the 45-minute film of the Buckeyes' Rose Bowl victory over Southern California . . .

In Vietnam during January of 1969, Hayes showed the film six times a day for twelve days. He discussed Kern's toughness with the shoulder, singled out Otis's determination in running, and quoted Lou Holtz on why Simpson ran those 80 yards—"Coach, that's all he needed"—each time. He answered soldiers' questions, too: Yes, Ohio State can be as good in 1969. Yes, O.J. Simpson was as talented as expected. No, he didn't think the New York Jets would upset Baltimore in the Super Bowl.

As always, he took a notebook, wrote down the names and numbers of Ohio soldiers, then called or wrote their families when he returned home. He saw again Paulette Ngan, who scheduled itineraries for American entertainers and personalities visiting the troops.

Woody with Bill Hess

In 1975, with Saigon on the verge of falling, Ngan got word to Woody and Anne Hayes. She asked them to be her family's sponsor so they could leave the country. Paulette and her sons, Huy and Thy, flew to Columbus and lived with the Hayeses for several weeks until they could be set up in a home of their own.

That was Woody Hayes.

So was this: On the morning after the Rose Bowl, a few hours before he left for Vietnam, he held a staff meeting that only Coach Ralph Waldo Emerson could love.

"Okay," he said to his assistants, "I think I can get all of you the same contracts you had this year. That should be no problem."

The assistants looked one final time that season for a wink, a smile, any hint of a joke. None came. There went any hopes for a raise after their achievement.

"And another thing," Hayes said.

He paused and looked around the room.

"If any of you sons of bitches are thinking of leaving, I want to hear about it now," he said. "I don't want to read about it in some newspaper while I'm over in Vietnam how you took another job."

The victory buzz was off.

"And if you are leaving, you should know I've got your replacement already," he said. "I've talked with some people and they're all ready to come here."

Class dismissed.

(2)

The following autumn flowed perfectly from that national championship season. By the final game against Michigan, Ohio State had won twenty-two straight games, was ranked Number One, was being called the best team in college history, and was causing a debate about whether it could beat the NFL's sickly Los Angeles Rams.

One afternoon in Ann Arbor, all that changed. When Bo Schembechler took over as Michigan coach that season, he set one goal: beat Ohio State. He said it in his first meeting with players. He worked on it all spring in practices. He had the advantage of knowing Woody, too. He used the same offense as his mentor, the same motivational tactics. He taped photos of Ohio State players to Michigan lockers. He put "50-14" on practice jerseys—the previous year's score.

THE DAYS AFTER
Epilogue

Michigan also benefited from two components Ohio State had sidestepped in 1968. The first was Kern's problematic back. He couldn't get out of bed the morning of that Michigan game. He still started the game, much to the debate of his teammates. But he was not the same player, throwing four interceptions before being subbed by Ron Maciejowski, who proceeded to throw two more.

The second problem was the kicking game. Ohio State went ahead, 6-0, but missed the extra point. It then failed on the two-point conversion after the second touchdown. Michigan led 7-6, then 14-12, and its kicker, Frank Titas, didn't miss any of his three extra points that day.

"I hope he breaks his goddamned leg!"

Yeah, *that* Frank Titas.

Shortly before he died, Hayes spoke at a private banquet that included several hundred of his players. No outsiders were invited. It would be one final, emotional thank you between Hayes and the players he had burped into manhood on football fields across several decades.

Amid the larger emotion of the evening, Hayes said the Super Sophomores were the best class he ever had and that 1969 team was the greatest he coached.

"It was the best offense I had," he said. "It was the best defense I had. It was the best everything I had."

He stared down at Bo Schembechler. He then repeated what he told Schembechler on that Ann Arbor field immediately after the game.

"Goddamn you, Bo," he said. "You will never win a bigger game."

So what was expected to be a run on national championships by Ohio State after the 1968 season instead became a lesson in just how difficult they were to win. In 1970, again undefeated, again Number One and having gotten by the Michigan barrier, it lost to Stanford in the Rose Bowl.

That, however, wasn't the legacy of the Best Class Ever. It had a 27-2 record. It won two Big Ten titles and the national championship. In so doing, it revived a grand football program and renewed the legend of Woody Hayes into its final triumphant leg.

Before the Super Sophs arrived, Ohio State hadn't won a Big Ten title in seven seasons.

Starting with 1968, it won at least a share of the Big Ten nine of the following ten seasons.

(3)

On NFL draft day in the spring of 1971, John Brockington sat by the phone in his Buckeye Village apartment. And sat. Why hadn't it rung? What pick were they on?

His future was inside that phone, it seemed. Finally, it rang and Green Bay Packers general manager Pat Peppler said, "Congratulations, John. You're a Green Bay Packer."

He was the ninth pick overall.

"Leo, I'm going to the Packers," Brockington said when he called Leo Hayden.

"What round are they in now?" Hayden said.

"The first round."

"Man, they're still doing the first round?" Hayden said.

With no televised New York party for first-round picks, no ESPN with wall-to-wall coverage, no draftniks, no gurus, no tip sheets, and agents only newly in vogue, the players didn't know what was happening until the phone rang. And so they waited. And waited.

"You heard anything yet?" Hayden said over the phone that afternoon to Kern.

"Nothing," Kern said.

"Me, neither," Hayden said.

Jack Tatum and Tim Anderson were in North Carolina, where a road trip intended to end on the beaches of Fort Lauderdale had stopped. It took awhile for their agent, Tony Razzano, to find Tatum to say he'd been chosen 19th, by the Oakland Raiders.

"Where's Oakland?" Tatum asked.

Anderson was next to go. San Francisco took him with the 23rd overall pick. Hayden answered his phone before the very next pick, the 24th overall, to hear: "Leo, this is Bud Grant of the Vikings."

"The Minnesota Vikings?" Hayden asked.

"Where else?" Grant said.

When Jan White became the third pick in the second round, that made five Ohio State players taken in the first twenty-nine picks. Only Southern California with five players in the initial twenty-four picks of the 1968 draft has had more players from one recruiting class taken higher (the University of Miami had five players drafted in the first round in 2002 and six in 2004, but with underclassmen eligible by then, more than one recruiting class was involved).

Throw in tackles Rufus Mayes (14th overall) and Dave Foley (26th overall) from the 1969 draft and there were six first-round picks (and White, the 29th pick) on the national champions. That didn't include Outland and Lombardi Trophy winner Jim Stillwagon (fifth round) or All-American players Ted Provost, Mike Sensibaugh, and Kern.

Mayes and Foley were the only seniors off the 1968 national champions drafted by the pros (Steve Howell, a starting forward on the Ohio State basketball team, was picked in the 10th round by Cincinnati). Chuck Hutchinson, a second-round pick by St. Louis, was the highest of four players selected in the 1970 draft.

The Super Sophomores had thirteen players selected in the 1971 draft.

So they scattered to all corners of the football world and lived a mixed bag of NFL experiences, just as you would expect.

Tatum became the only player with a 1968 national championship ring to earn a Super Bowl ring, winning in 1977 with Oakland. He was voted to three Pro Bowls. With his paralyzing hit on New England receiver Darryl Stingley and his autobiography, *They Call Me Assassin*, his pro career was marked by controversy. He retired in 1980 and lives in Oakland. He was inducted into the College Football Hall of Fame in 2004.

Mayes, originally drafted by Chicago, was traded his second year to Cincinnati and went on to have an eleven-year NFL career. He died in 1990 of bacterial meningitis at the age of 42.

Foley, originally drafted by the New York Jets, moved to Buffalo in 1972. There, he blocked for O.J. Simpson as a member of The Electric Company, the line that turned the Juice loose for an NFL-record 2,003 yards in 1973. Each member was a Big Ten lineman, too, which ended any argument when Simpson talked about West Coast football being superior to the Big Ten. Foley currently runs Foley Benefits Group in Springfield, Ohio.

Brockington became the first NFL running back to rush for more than 1,000 yards in his first three seasons. He was the NFL Offensive Rookie of the Year in 1971 and voted to three consecutive Pro Bowls. In his fourth season in 1974, Brockington ran for 883 yards with Green Bay. The wear of his forceful style and a change in the playbook led to diminished statistics afterward. He retired in 1978. He currently lives in San Diego and works for an insurance company.

Anderson became embroiled in contract problems with San Francisco and signed with Toronto of the Canadian Football League. He became the highest NFL draft pick to sign with a CFL team. He played three years in Canada before returning to San Francisco. He played with the 49ers for two years and with Buffalo for two more. He has a company that builds and remodels houses in the San Francisco Bay Area.

Hayden played with Minnesota in 1971 before moving to St. Louis. By 1974, drug problems overtook his career and he was out of the league.

White played with Buffalo for two seasons and started twenty-seven of twenty-eight games before deciding football wasn't fun anymore and retiring. He is the director of juvenile services in Greene County, Ohio.

Hutchinson played guard for six years for St. Louis and Cleveland before becoming an offensive line coach for Toronto in the CFL. He then moved to the Oakland Invaders of the U.S. Football League and was named its coach in 1984. Four years followed as chief negotiator of the Green Bay Packers. He then became vice president of a Wisconsin cheese company.

Stillwagon, at 6-0 and 220 pounds, was considered too small to be an impact player in the NFL and was a fifth-round pick of Green Bay. He disliked its managerial style, as well as its offer, and signed with Toronto of the CFL. He was a three-time All-Star before retiring due to injuries in 1976. He currently lives in Columbus and runs Stillwagon Enterprises, which is in the employee recognition business. He was inducted into the College Football Hall of Fame in 1991.

Doug Adams, drafted in the seventh round, played four seasons with Cincinnati. He retired in 1975 and became a dentist in Mt. Orab, Ohio. In 1997, he was riding a bicycle when he was hit and killed when struck by a car whose driver had fallen asleep at the wheel. He was 47.

Provost, a seventh-round draft pick, played with Minnesota in 1970 and with St. Louis in 1971. He then played five seasons with Saskatchewan in the Canadian Football League. During off-seasons, he returned to Columbus and began refurbishing old houses. That led to a construction business he still has today.

Jim Otis, drafted in the ninth round by New Orleans, seemed on his way out of the league after three seasons split between the Saints and St. Louis in which he didn't gain more than 211 yards. But he kept believing in himself, as always, and ran for 1,076 yards in 1975. He ended up playing nine NFL seasons and scoring 19 touchdowns. He is a developer in St. Louis.

Sensibaugh, drafted in the 10th round, played for eight seasons with Kansas City and had 27 interceptions. He currently runs a pool company in Missouri.

Larry Zelina was drafted in the eighth round by Cleveland, but injuries cut short his career. He remained close to Ohio State, becoming president of the Varsity "O" Club and co-authoring a book on the national championship season called *Ohio State '68: All the Way to the Top*. He died of a heart attack in 2005. He was 55.

Bruce Jankowski, a 10th-round pick by Kansas City, suffered a career-ending knee injury in 1972. He had a career in sales for a couple of decades in Kansas City, and currently works for a start-up company that helps make wireless phone companies work faster and more securely.

Kern was drafted in the 10th round by Baltimore, a team with John Unitas and Earl Morrall as quarterbacks. He moved to defensive back and played four seasons for Baltimore and Buffalo before the back issues that threatened his athletic career in 1968 forced him to retire. He earned a doctorate from Ohio State before managing the company with rights to sell Nautilus equipment in California. He then returned to Columbus to become a business partner of United States Midwest Bank and currently is a director of the bank's holding company. Kern was elected to the College Football Hall of Fame in 2007.

Nick Roman, who missed the 1968 season with a knee injury, was drafted in the 10th round and played five seasons with Cincinnati and Cleveland. He died in 2003 of a heart attack. He was 55.

Ron Maciejowski was drafted in the 15th round by Chicago, then spent some time in Cincinnati. That meant he was involved with four legendary coaches: Woody Hayes, George Halas at Chicago, and Paul Brown and Bill Walsh at Cincinnati. Maciejowski then took a job with Worthington Industries in Columbus, where he is currently an executive vice president.

Mark Debevec, drafted in the 16th round by Cincinnati, didn't make the team and returned to his family grape farm in Geneva, Ohio, where his father was ill. He soon took over the farm and today Debevec's Vineyards continues to turn out good Ohio wine.

(4)

When he arrived at the Baltimore Colts in the summer of 1971, Rex Kern did a survey of the seventeen rookies in his draft class. Only two had graduated from their college. He was one of them. He began to gain some perspective on his Ohio State experience.

In the following years, as Kern read media accounts of players not graduating, of coaches not caring, of a college athletic system that had broken down at this most fundamental point, he became more curious about Hayes's program. While working for the university in the mid-1970s, Kern researched the graduation rates of football lettermen under Hayes, going back to the coach's first year at the school in 1951.

When he got the figures, he took them down to Hayes. "Coach, I've got some great news for you," he said after one spring practice. He related how 87.6 of all lettermen under Hayes had graduated and another 36.7 percent went on to graduate studies.

Hayes took Kern's news after practice that day and grabbed the right corner of his glasses in contemplation for a few seconds.

"I'll be damned," he said. "I thought it was better than that. We're going to start working tomorrow to make that number higher."

In 2007, the NCAA reported 67 percent of Division I football players graduated from the 2000 class, the most recent year studied. Ohio State football team's graduation rate was 53 percent from 1997-2000, the most recent years reported.

Exactly as promised to parents while he was recruiting, Hayes pushed his boys to their degrees and beyond. Phil Strickland finished his four years of football a quarter short of graduating. He had money for either classes or books. But not both. Hayes heard of Strickland's dilemma and wrote a check for the books.

"We'll just call this an extension of your scholarship," he told Strickland. "If you do not graduate, you owe me this money back. If you do graduate, you owe nothing." Strickland got his degree that quarter in health education.

During his first NFL off-season, Jack Tatum listened to Hayes make a speech in Charlotte, North Carolina, where his parents had moved. Hayes visited Tatum's parents afterward, and in front of them, got Tatum to promise to get his degree. The next off-season, Tatum finished his degree.

Kevin Rusnak sat at his family home in 1972, a couple of years after his Ohio State time was over. His father, a tough man who ran in a tough crowd, answered the phone, listened a moment, and said, "Yes, sir."

There was a pause as he listened. "Yes, sir."

Another pause.

"Yes, sir, I understand."

When he got off the phone, Rusnak asked his father who that was, since he had never heard him talk that way with anyone.

"That was Woody," he said. "You're going back to finish your degree."
Rusnak did, too.

Each time Mike Polaski saw Hayes in the years after his playing days had ended, it was the same conversation. "Mike, did you get your degree yet?" Hayes asked. Polaski said he hadn't. "Well, are you working toward it?" Hayes asked.

Five years after Polaski had left school, the same script. Hayes asked if Polaski had graduated yet, Polaski said he hadn't, then Hayes started in on why he should.

"Whoa, Coach, time out," Polaski interrupted. "Commencement is tomorrow morning. I'll be graduating then." He is now a lieutenant in the Columbus fire department.

Tom Bartley wanted to become a pharmacist but didn't have the grades for Ohio State's College of Pharmacy. He went to Hayes, who called the dean of that college. Bartley was accepted, graduated, and in 1973 took over a business in Waverly, Ohio, that today is called Bartley's Pharmacy.

Bill Long, who left so unhappy, had a tryout with the Baltimore Colts and ran into the same issues with Unitas and Morrall that Kern soon would. With Hayes's help, Long got into Capital University Law School in Columbus. After graduating, he embarked on a twenty-five year career as a lobbyist. He recently has become an advocate of People for the Ethical Treatment of Animals.

At the ten-year reunion, Hayes said to Sensibaugh, "You should be using your math degree."

"You shouldn't have coached," Sensibaugh said back. "You should've been President."

Brockington returned to Ohio State after his rookie NFL season with the intention of finishing his degree, but never found the time or inclination. He remains today one quarter short of his degree.

"We failed John," Hayes told Jim Jones, the brain coach.

In Columbus for Hayes's funeral in 1987, Brockington went to see Jones, who had risen to athletic director. Brockington said it was the first time he had returned in years because he wanted to avoid Hayes's anger about his not graduating.

Such was not unusual.

"Perhaps my favorite experience with Woody occurred several years ago at a reception honoring one of his many championship teams," Ohio State president Edward Jennings wrote Kern in 2002. "While I do not recall which team it was, the reception was at least twenty years after the fact, putting the team members at least in their early forties. During the reception, I noticed that there were about five or six men who would not go near Woody. Indeed, these men made it a point to avoid him if he came close.

"Obviously, this got my curiosity up and so at the close of the reception I asked of a good friend, who was also a team member, why such behavior was exhibited from grown men who were clearly proud of their membership on the team as evidenced by their presence at the reception. Perhaps they had a falling out with Woody during the intervening years. No, said my friend, those men are the players who, to this day, have not graduated and knew without a doubt that Woody would confront them for their having not graduated, in no uncertain terms. Woody would have not only embarrassed them but would have insisted that it was not too late to complete their degree."

Jennings finished: "In many ways he was a throwback to the days when in order to be a football coach, one first had to be a faculty member in the academic community. We would do well to follow his example today."

The story of Bill Pollitt tells this best of all.

(5)

After serving in the army, Pollitt returned to Ohio State as a graduate assistant in 1970. Running the freshman defense in practice against Hayes's varsity offense, he grew to know the coach in a way he hadn't as a player. When Pollitt decided to attend law school, Hayes promised to help.

The problem was Pollitt's grades. Never a disciplined student, his law school test scores were among the lowest 2 percent in the country. "The bottom of the bottom," as he said. Hayes personally attended Pollitt's interview with the dean of the Ohio State Law School, where the average test score among students was 600. Pollitt had a 396.

The dean told Hayes that if Pollitt just had a 500, he could be accepted. But there was no way to take someone with such a low score. Likewise, every law school Pollitt applied to rejected him. Capital University was his final chance. He scheduled an interview. Hayes couldn't attend, but wrote a letter of recommendation.

Pollitt walked into the interview and the assistant dean of the Capital Law School immediately asked, "Are you good with your hands?"

"Give me a knife and I'm hell on a buffet table," Pollitt said, thinking a question-and-answer session was part of the interview process.

"Well, that's good, because you should go to trade school," the assistant dean said. "Plumbers are making $10 an hour. Quite frankly, having looked at your scores, you're wasting our time, and we're wasting yours."

When Pollitt told Hayes the interview hadn't gone well, Hayes "went berserk," he remembered. "He began throwing stuff around, knocking things off his desk. He was banging on tables. He threw a legal pad on the floor." Then he stopped and looked at Pollitt, who began backing up for fear the left hand would be cocked.

"Goddammit, do you want to go to law school?" Hayes then yelled.

Pollitt said he did.

"Will you make it?" Hayes yelled.

Pollitt said he would.

"You'd better," Hayes said. "Because if you screw up, you'll not only screw it up for you. You'll screw it up for every player who comes after you. My word won't mean shit."

Three days later, Pollitt got a letter of acceptance from Capital. With the fear of Woody in him, Pollitt ranked fourth in his class after his first year. He graduated and became a private attorney. When former Ohio State tight end Greg Lashutka was elected Columbus city attorney, he appointed Pollitt a city attorney in 1978. That began his climb inside the public legal system.

Today, Judge H. William Pollitt Jr. presides over Courtroom 12A in the Franklin County Municipal Court in Columbus. In one election, he delivered the campaign line: "I'm the only judge to bring down O.J. Simpson."

Decades later, Pollitt can only surmise what Hayes did to get him into Capital. John McCormac, the dean of the Capital Law School, was a part-time referee who worked the Ohio State spring game. McCormac was out of town that day Pollitt interviewed with the assistant dean at Capital. Hayes somehow convinced McCormac to accept him, Pollitt figures.

"Here I was, a reserve player who didn't help him win anything, and he changed my life," Pollitt said. "Nobody can say anything bad about Woody Hayes in front of me. He gave me an opportunity no one else could have."

(6)

The ironic part is that Hayes's career ended on the kind of play he despised more than Michigan: A pass. Even worse, as Chaump realized immediately from the coach's box in the 1978 Gator Bowl, it was an unnecessary pass.

"We don't throw the ball the years we should have thrown the ball," he said. "Then we can kick a field goal to win the game and we're throwing the ball."

Clemson 17, Ohio State 15. Fourth quarter. Third-and-five. Ball at the Clemson 24-yard line. And Ohio State passes. Woody passes. The call is for the wingback to delay out of the backfield, then circle into the middle on a simple route. It was open, too. Quarterback Art Schlichter threw the ball. But when Hayes made famous the line that three things can happen on a pass, and two of them are bad, he didn't factor into the equation what happened next.

Clemson nose guard Charlie Bauman defied his assignment, dropped into coverage, and found the ball thrown into his chest. He intercepted it, started running, and was tackled in front of the Ohio State bench. A national TV audience saw what happened next, but ABC commentators Keith Jackson and Ara Parseghian apparently missed it. As did Chaump in the press box. He heard fellow assistant Gary Tranquill moan beside him.

"Oh, god, we're finished," Tranquill said. "I just saw Woody take a swing at the kid."

"You're kidding," Chaump said.

Through the years, Hayes had talked of quitting only when his fire died. Or if his health went. Years earlier, Tiger Ellison had asked Hayes if he ever intended to retire.

"Hell, no," Hayes said. "When I do, I'll die on the 50-yard line at Ohio Stadium in front of the usual crowd of 87,000."

"If you do," Ellison said, "I sure hope the score's in your favor."

"If it isn't, I won't," Hayes said.

The score wasn't in his favor in 1978. But he was done. This capped a series of televised spectacles through the years in which Hayes had been the controversial centerpiece. Just in the 1970s, he shoved a camera in the face of a *Los Angeles Times* cameraman before a Rose Bowl game, slugged a Michigan State fan after a game, and punched an ABC cameraman during a Michigan game.

He came from an era where the clenched fist could be a coaching technique, but the one in the Gator Bowl was thrown against an opposing player and seen by a nationwide television audience. At least, people thought they saw it. ABC's Jackson and Parseghian never mentioned it. There was no replay. No sideline reporter. So Jackson and Parseghian, not exactly sure what had happened, continued on as if nothing had.

Hindman saw it, however, and he couldn't ignore it as easily. He talked privately with Hayes after the game. He then tried to find Ohio State president Harold Enarson, who was staying with a friend in Jacksonville. At 3:30 a.m., they finally talked. Hindman then met again with Hayes, who refused to resign and told Hindman to fire him.

Hindman had played for Hayes at Miami, joined his Ohio State staff in 1963, and had benefited from Hayes's lobbying to land the athletic director's job. In what he termed the hardest thing he had to do besides burying his father, he fired Hayes.

On the flight home that morning, Hayes got on the plane's speakers. "This is your coach," he said. "I want to tell you I will no longer be your football coach at Ohio State."

The fallout was loud, bloody, and predictable. One moment in forty-five years of public life became, in many parts of the country, a legacy. Over the next several days, as the fallout drifted across the sports nation, Hayes kept to himself. He called Bauman and didn't apologize but did express his appreciation for the understated manner in which Bauman handled the issue.

Amid the criticism and debate, two letters from common people attempted to tell the other side, the 90 percent that Lyal Clark had discussed years earlier with Mallory.

One, from Tom Brownfield of Houston, Texas, was published in *Sports Illustrated*:

> *In the autumn of 1968, while Ohio State's 'super sophomores' were leading the Buckeyes to an unbeaten season, I was a Marine pilot in the Oakland Naval Hospital, recovering from Vietnam burn injuries. I was invited by Woody Hayes' wife, Anne, who, like her husband, has done many charitable deeds, to join the team in Pasadena, where it was preparing for the Rose Bowl game against USC. There, Coach Hayes gave me one of his Bowl tickets. On January 1, 1969, from a seat on the 50-yard line, next to Mrs. Hayes, I saw Ohio State defeat the Trojans and O.J. Simpson, 27-16. This probably did more for my recovery than any treatment.*

As my son and I left the Cotton Bowl after Ohio State beat Texas A&M this past New Year's Day, an angry Aggie shouted, 'What's a Buckeye, anyway?' The answer: 'It's a winner.' So was Coach Hayes, right to the end.

The second letter was to the *Elyria Chronicle Telegram*. It read in part:

It's a shame, a real shame, that you did not know anything more about Woody Hayes before you wrote about one isolated incident. It is a shame, a real shame, that you didn't have the opportunity to know the Woody Hayes that millions of people know and love.

She described how Hayes drove a few hours from Columbus to cheer her husband at his hospital bedside in 1981 shortly before he died.

That hour was such a joy for Lee and he rallied briefly after that. Lee died on April 16 of that year and those last weeks were made easier because of the outreach of Woody Hayes and others in the coaching field.

It was signed by Eloise Tressel, the widow of long-time Baldwin-Wallace coach Lee Tressel and mother of future Ohio State coach Jim Tressel.

(7)

When he left coaching, Hayes had more victories—238—than any active coach except Alabama's Bear Bryant. He had undefeated national champions in 1954 and 1968. He won thirteen Big Ten titles in twenty-eight seasons. He was coach of the year in 1957, 1968, and 1976. He coached fifty-eight All-American players. His players won three Heisman trophies.

He didn't die quickly after leaving the sideline, as Bryant would. Nor did he fade from view in the manner some might have. He remained a presence in the Ohio State community after his coaching days, never losing his desire to help his players or his school. He kept an office on campus in the ROTC building. In 1982, hundreds of fans, friends, former players, and band members turned out as Stadium Drive was renamed Woody Hayes Drive.

"Hi, Woody," the band yelled before the ceremony.

"Hi, band," Hayes said.

In a 1983 game, he saluted the American flag flying at half-staff for marines killed in Beirut, then turned and dotted the "i" in the marching band's Script Ohio.

In 1986, he delivered the commencement address at Ohio State. "Graduates, Mr. President, friends, and families," he began that speech, "today is the greatest day of my life."

He spoke of his favorite themes. "Something that I use in almost every speech, and that is, 'Paying forward,'" he said. He continued on to his work ethic: "There were smarter people than I. But you know what they couldn't do? They couldn't outwork me."

He dropped some history, including the "Battle of Salamis, 500 years before the birth of Christ," Pearl Harbor, and the Battle of Britain, mentioning how the British general who conducted that desperate battle would be fired.

"Well, there have been a lot of great men fired—MacArthur, Richard Nixon, a lot of them," he said.

The crowd got the message and applauded, just as crowds stood and applauded Hayes at speeches across the country in his retirement. Thirteen months after his Gator Bowl incident, he returned to his Waterloo for a speech to the Jacksonville Quarterback Club. He made no mention of the Bauman incident. He did, however, joke about some recent recruiting scandals involving West Coast teams.

"I kept wondering why it got tougher and tougher to win out there in the Rose Bowl each year," he said. "My gosh, they used 330 ineligible athletes during the '70s."

In retirement, Hayes gave as many as eight speeches a week. In one stretch, he spoke to Iowa tire dealers on Saturday, raccoon hunters in Danville, Ohio, on Monday, Ohio State agricultural students on Tuesday night, and he was in Florida on Wednesday. He kept alive in politics, too. In a 1984 presidential rally in Columbus, he equated the Ohio State football team's need to win "four more games" to make the Rose Bowl to visiting pPresident Reagan's need to win "four more years" and retain the White House.

He wore a tuxedo, led the Columbus Symphony Orchestra in "Stars and Stripes Forever," then compared his directing style to Toscanini's. "Wasn't he the one who used to get mad and throw things and stomp on his baton?" Hayes asked. "He had the so-called 'artistic temperament.'"

He was roasted at a University of Miami fund-raiser by an all-star lineup. Former president and Michigan center Gerald Ford said, "There are a lot of

Woody Hayes fans here tonight. I had a chance to talk with some of them earlier. Even though I'm no longer in office, I still like to get opinions from a minority group."

"Our guest of honor is a man who struts like a peacock, crows like a rooster, but whenever he gets to the bowl, he lays an egg," actor Shirley MacLaine said.

"I learned one heartwarming fact about Woody Hayes's marriage," actor Ann-Margret said. "After all these years, Anne and Woody never go to bed without sharing a romantic glass of wine. I know it's true, because Anne told me she's still going to bed with Cold Duck."

Hayes tapped his love of history in the early 1980s to host the broadcast of six World War II films on WBNS-TV in Columbus. Across his coaching career, his coach's show had been a Saturday night staple on WBNS. Now, in retirement, he provided narration and historical resonance to movies such as *Midway*, *Patton*, *Tora! Tora! Tora!* and *The Desert Fox: The Story of Rommel*.

To provide perspective on Patton, he went to West Point. For Midway, he visited the *U.S.S. Yorktown*. For *The Desert Fox*, he interviewed the son of the general, Manfred Rommel, and discussed him during his commencement address. "I asked him, 'Did your father agree with Hitler's order to stop on May 24, 1940, when they were within forty miles of the English Channel?'" Hayes said. "And he said, 'Wait a minute, Coach. There's something you're not thinking about. My father did not have choices at all. He lived in a dictatorship.'

"That night when I got home, I started wondering why he had become so upset. And then I recalled the last decision his father had made on this earth: the decision to take poison so that this boy and his mother could live. You can appreciate democracy when you look at it that way."

(8)

In the mid-1980s, Kern flew with one of his sons from California to Columbus for an Ohio State game. His son was 5 or 6 and had never met or talked with Hayes. He only knew the coach from all the stories his father told around the dinner table.

As they stepped off the press box elevator before the game, Kern saw Hayes talking with Paul Horning, his good friend and sports writer for the *Columbus Dispatch*. Kern nudged his son.

"Look, there's Woody," he said.

His son took off in a sprint through the press box like a kid going to open a Christmas present. He jumped into Woody's arms, wrapped the coach in a big hug, and gave him a kiss. Hayes sat there, stunned, wondering who this boy was, but hugging him right back.

Here's the point: From all his father's stories, the innate goodness of Hayes came through. This was his conditioned response to finally meeting the friend he had never seen.

Through the years, most all of his players developed an appreciation they sometimes missed in the daily grind. Gillian, who was never particularly close to Hayes in college, couldn't wait to attend the ten-year reunion. He wanted to tell his teammates how so much of what Hayes had preached in school had turned out to be right.

"But at the reunion, everyone had the same observation," he said. "Everyone was saying the same thing. 'The Old Man knew what he was doing.'"

Maybe this is the best testament to Hayes: Most of his players, in ways great and small, think about him on a daily basis. Foley thinks about Hayes handling his adversity in 1966 and his success in 1968 in exactly the same way. *The manner in which people judge you shouldn't affect you*, Foley took from that. *Your work will judge you.*

"As a young kid to witness that, it's a great life lesson," he said. "What it tells you is that adversity isn't the end result. It's just the start. It's a challenge. Get up and get to work."

Dick Kuhn read one of Woody's short-list of books, Sun-Tzu's *Art of War*. He was struck by the line: *A good commander knows his troops must fear him more than the enemies.* That explained the old coach, Kuhn thought.

Jankowski still makes time to talk with some elderly people simply because Hayes impressed upon him the importance of it.

Most of the players remember the promises Hayes made in recruiting them:

1. A great education.
2. The opportunity to play the best college football in America.
3. A chance to make friends for a lifetime.

There was a fourth one left unstated, as they all discovered. That was to be coached by a man who put an imprint on their lives far beyond what any of them could imagine. He wasn't a perfect man. But he was the most remarkable person most, maybe all, have been around. They didn't always agree with what he did. But time has allowed them to see beyond what he did to who he was.

"One of his favorite lines was, 'You either get better or worse but never stay the same,'" Chuck Hutchinson said. "My kids are tired of hearing that from me. There isn't a day that goes by that I don't think of something Woody said or did and how he reacted to different situations. How could any of us ever realize that this was going to be his greatest gift?"

He remained there for his players, too. When he heard Alan Jack had multiple sclerosis, Hayes called the dean of Ohio State's medical school, found out the name of the country's best doctor for handling the disease, and set up an appointment for Jack with that doctor at the Mayo Clinic. Jack didn't need more medical help, but the gesture meant the world to him.

When Stillwagon's mother died in 1980, Hayes showed up unannounced at her funeral. When Zelina's father had cancer, Hayes had his medical records shipped to University Hospital so doctors could offer a second opinion. When Stottlemyer's father was in University Hospital, Hayes showed up unannounced to visit him.

His powers of memory never faltered and never ceased to amaze. When a man approached him after a Cleveland speech, Hayes asked, "You're Larry Zelina's Uncle Paul, aren't you?" They had met, years earlier, once after a game. When Stottlemyer bumped into Hayes in the Milwaukee airport eight years after leaving, the coach asked about his parents—"How're Victor and Gladys doing?" He then tried to recruit Stottlemyer back to Columbus to work.

At the fifteenth year reunion, Hayes told Ed Bender's wife how, one day, he saw a family outside St. John Arena and asked if they wanted a tour. He gave them one, and in the ensuing conversation learned their ninth-grader was in line to replace a running back his staff had recruited at Garfield High in Akron.

"If you replace him, we'll be talking to you in three years," Hayes told the ninth-grader. It was the start of Bender's recruitment to Ohio State. Bender stood in awe that night so many years later. In all his time at Ohio State, it was the first time he had heard Hayes mention the story. Hayes remembered every moment of it correctly, too.

(9)

Over time, Hayes's health deteriorated. He had heart attacks in 1974 and 1985 and a stroke in 1984. He had a pacemaker and suffered from diabetes and high blood pressure. He had his gallbladder removed in 1981 at Ohio State's University Hospital. After complications, a second surgery was necessary.

When Kern called from California to check on him in the hospital, the coach immediately turned the conversation to Kern's ongoing back problems.

"We've got to get you here to see the finest doctors there are," Hayes said, ever the Ohio State fan, overlooking the fact that his latest complications arose from a surgical sponge being left in him.

Kern's final visit with Hayes came shortly after president Edward Jennings christened Woody Hayes Drive. Hayes was frail at this point and walked with a cane. They ate lunch at the Faculty Club, still one of Hayes's preferred spots to discuss academia. When Kern tried to pay, Hayes was still Hayes, refusing to allow him and saying when Kern insisted, "I'll punch you right here."

Kern began the drivve to Hayes's Cardiff Avenue home.

"You want to go down Woody Hayes Drive?" Hayes asked.

The coach and the quarterback made that drive past the stadium where so many of their good days had occurred, on the road that now bore Hayes's name. After driving those several blocks, Kern took him to Cardiff Avenue. He walked with Hayes around the home, to the back stairs, having thought carefully about what he would say next. Kern opened the door. Hayes turned to say goodbye.

"Coach, I just want you to know how much I love you," Kern said.

He leaned in and kissed Hayes on the cheek. Hayes stepped back, somewhat startled by the action. He looked at Kern with softness. It was a moment the quarterback has embraced through the years.

In his public legacy, Hayes was lumped into the same winning-is-everything mode as his football hero, Vince Lombardi.

"I don't think it's possible to be too intent on winning," he had said. "If we played for any other reason, we would be totally dishonest. This country is built on winning and on that alone. Winning is still the most honorable thing a man can do."

But two years before Hayes died, Bob Greene, a Columbus native, Chicago newspaper columnist, and avid Hayes fan, had dinner at the Jai Lai with him.

Near the end of the meal, Greene asked Hayes if anything was more important than winning. Hayes said there was one thing.

"There are some lines by a great orator," Hayes said. "My dad used to quote him. He said it better than I ever could: 'And in the night of death, hope sees a star, and, listening, love hears the rustle of a wing.'"

The line was from the poet Robert Green Ingersoll.

"You see, the important thing is not always to win," he told Greene that dinner. "The important thing is always to hope."

When Hayes died in his sleep at his Upper Arlington home on March 12, 1987, Anne Hayes and their son, Steve, wondered what to put on his tombstone. They figured Ohio State would take care of his football legacy. They wanted his gravesite to be simple and reflect something of the total man they knew. The director of the Mason Memorial Studio opened a desk drawer and showed them a copy of Greene's column. He offered a possibility.

On Hayes's plain tombstone, the Ingersoll quote is inscribed.

"We thought that quote sort of summed him up," Steve Hayes told Greene. "It was one of his favorite quotes, but most people didn't know it. They associated him with football quotes: 'When you get knocked down, get back up.' That was only part of my dad. The real part of him was in those words that he recited to you."

More than 1,400 people attended Hayes's funeral at the First Community Church in Upper Arlington. His signature block "O" baseball cap and a folded American flag lay at the altar.

"He wasn't a Neanderthal, a know-nothing," his friend Richard Nixon said in the eulogy. "He was a Renaissance Man with a sense of history. He was not just a tyrant but an old softie. The last nine years of his life were probably his greatest. He basked in the warm glow of tributes from those who came to know and respect him, and love him."

Flags flew half-mast across Ohio. The Jai Lai put out the sign, "In All The World, There's Only One Woody." Visitors began placing flowers at the 50-yard line in Ohio Stadium, where a memorial service was held a few days later with 15,000 people attending.

"I love you, Woody Hayes," Earle Bruce, who had succeeded him as Ohio State's coach, said in the memorial. "Football loves you. The university loves you. Ohio loves you."

Kern also spoke at the stadium service, and as he flew home to California, struggled over how he and his teammates could honor their coach's life. He kept returning to the theme of Hayes and education. He wrote a letter to his 1968 teammates suggesting they collectively donate $100,000 to set up a scholarship at Ohio State in Hayes's name.

Dave Foley called Kern. He was in the insurance business and suggested a manner of combining cash and life insurance that would have added value. Another letter went out to the team. This one took into account Foley's thoughts and suggested a much higher figure was obtainable. Kern, in fact, called Anne Hayes to tell her, "We're going to raise $1 million."

Later, Anne told Kern she thought he was loony. But she said it after $1.3 million had been raised, adding cash with future life-insurance payouts. In November of 1988, at the twentieth reunion of the team, the Woody and Anne Hayes 1968 National Championship Athletic Scholarship Fund was announced. At midfield, Kern presented Anne with a trophy to commemorate the fund. At the time, it was one of the top twenty gifts in the history of the university and thought to be the largest any single team had given to any school in the country. It remains eligible today to "varsity football players, spouses, and their first- and second-generation children who are pursuing degrees."

Depending on the year, between five and twelve scholarships are awarded annually, totaling about $15,000, said Ron Maciejowski, the liaison between the team and the university regarding the fund.

The Hayes legacy runs in other worthy directions around the university—and city—he loved. There's the Woody Hayes Athletic Center, which shows just how far Ohio State and athletics have traveled. Instead of the eight-station Universal gym that welcomed his players in 1968, the athletic center contains an 8,000-square-foot weight room.

Then there are the academic scholarships in the College of Medicine and for ROTC leadership. The University Sertoma Club in Columbus presents its annual Woody Hayes National Scholar-Athlete Awards as a "living memorial to the coach's dedication to excellence and the community." College students may vie in each of the three divisions for academics, athletics, and community service. In fourteen years, eighty-four students have received the award.

Even the cabin Hayes used for getaways in southeastern Ohio is giving back. It's available to be rented by visitors and the profit goes toward the Anne Hayes Scholarship Fund for Academic Excellence in the School of Social Work.

Anne had her own idea as to where Woody's name should leave a legacy.

She threw her considerable mind and energy into a campaign for a specific professor's chair at Ohio State. Fund-raisers were held. Annual events were organized. Sale of busts of the coach contributed $1,000 toward it.

In 1994, on Anne Hayes's 80th birthday, more than 1,000 people came to a fund-raising dinner where it was announced that more than $1 million had been raised toward the necessary $1.5 million to endow the Wayne Woodrow Hayes Chair in National Security Studies. The chair's mission statement was to make it "home to a high-profiled tenured professor who conducts research and educates a new generation in the issues of national securities studies."

"Woody would consider this the highest accolade of his life," Anne said at her birthday party. In 2001, the chair was completely funded. By then, John Mueller occupied the Woody Hayes Chair and was an Ohio State political science professor. His most recent book, *Overblown*, deals with exaggerations of national security threats, particularly terrorism.

(10)

With time, as the assistants filled out their careers, it became obvious what a star-packed coaching staff Hayes assembled that championship season.

Bill Mallory left Ohio State within weeks of that Rose Bowl win to succeed Schembechler at Miami University in Oxford, Ohio. Hayes had pushed him to Miami officials for the job. After four 7-3 seasons, his Miami team went 11-0, won the Tangerine Bowl, and was ranked Number 17. Mallory then took Colorado, Northern Illinois, and Indiana to bowl games and Top 20 rankings. At Indiana, he was twice named Big Ten Coach of the Year. He retired in 1996 and splits time between Florida and Bloomington, Indiana.

Lou Holtz also left Columbus that winter to take the William and Mary job, and while Hayes was not happy Holtz had stayed just one season, Hayes still made two requests before he left. He wanted Holtz to talk with his replacement about the secondary. And he wanted Holtz to write a chapter for Hayes's upcoming book, *Hot Line to Victory*. When Holtz handed in the chapter, Hayes wrote a check and tried to give it to Holtz, who refused it. Hayes jammed it in Holtz's shirt pocket, ripping the pocket. Holtz took it out and ripped it up.

"Coach, I can tear these up quicker than you can write them," Holtz said. That stopped Hayes. Holtz does have one regret: He wished he had looked at the figure on the check before he ripped it up.

William and Mary was the starting point of Holtz's successful head-coaching career. In thirty-three years as a head coach, he won a national championship at Notre Dame, three Coach-of-the-Year honors, 249 games, and became the only coach in college football history to lead six different schools to bowl games. He was also the only coach to take four schools to Top 20 rankings. He retired in 2004 after six years at South Carolina and became an ESPN analyst. In 2008, he was elected to the College Football Hall of Fame.

Lou McCullough left Ohio State in 1971 to become the Iowa State athletic director. His role with Ohio State football didn't end when he left Columbus, though. He hired fellow assistant Earle Bruce as Iowa State's coach in 1973. McCullough retired in 1982 and died in 2000.

George Chaump left Ohio State after eleven seasons to become running backs coach of the Tampa Bay Buccaneers. He went on to become head coach at both Marshall and Navy before returning to his roots. For the past five years he has been coaching at John Harris High in Harrisburg, Pennsylvania, the school he left for Ohio State in 1968. His team finished second in the state in 2007.

"After the Rose Bowls, and the headlines, and the big stadiums, I'm back to doing what I've always got the most satisfaction from," Chaump said. "That's knowing you're helping out a kid who needs some help."

Hugh Hindman was Ohio State's athletic director from 1977 to 1984, where he became known for firing his one-time coach and boss, Woody Hayes. Hindman died in 1994. He was 67.

Esco Sarkkinen ended a lifelong career with Ohio State upon retiring when Hayes left in 1978. Sarkkinen, an All-Big Ten running back in 1939, would put his ear to Ohio Stadium and tell players he could hear the echo of the crowd chanting, "Let's go, Esco!" In 1946, he began his thirty-two year run as an assistant coach. He died at age 79 in 1998.

Larry Catuzzi coached for three years at Williams College before entering the world of investment banking in 1970. He briefly surfaced in coaching again, becoming a Houston Texans assistant in the World Football League in 1974. He debated joining the Baltimore Colts staff a year later before returning to the investment world in Houston. Catuzzi lost one of his three daughters, Lauren, on Flight 93 in the tragedy of September 11, 2001. He serves on the Board of the Flight 93 Federal Advisory Commission. Lauren's Garden, a memorial to all 9-11 victims, is being completed in Houston.

(11)

Every success story doesn't have a simple plot. In his senior year at Ohio State, Leo Hayden was exposed to drugs. He tried marijuana. By the next year, when he was a first-round pick of the Minnesota Vikings, he was a heroin addict. "It was just that simple," he said. "I came to it with a competitive spirit. If they smoked one joint, I smoked two. If they could finish a joint in three hits, I finished it in two."

For thirteen years, drugs dominated Hayden's life. He lost football, his money, his friends, and his way in life. He descended into a world, he says, of "forging checks, swindling people, selling drugs, and doing whatever I could to support my habit."

He ended up in a Kentucky jail for ten years.

"I got out of that life by the grace of God and Woody," he said.

One day in jail, he called Hayes and asked for help.

"Leo, I'd love to help you, but I can't do anything unless you come back to Ohio," Hayes said.

Upon being released, Hayden returned to Columbus. Jan White, his former teammate who had stayed in contact, helped him. White accompanied him to a meeting with Hayes that began with the coach being the coach, asking what Hayden wanted.

"Just one thing," Hayden said. He took out an 8-by-10 glossy of Hayes. "I want your autograph."

The ice broken, Hayes helped Hayden get a job as a salesman with a Columbus car dealer. He was on his way back into society.

"The people who loved me were the ones there for me," he said.

Soon, Hayden took a job with the Ohio Department of Alcohol and Drug Addiction services coordinating their work in prisons and with juveniles. Today, he lives in Chicago and runs the nonprofit National Center for Violence Interruption in Chicago that specializes in teaching young people how to treat each other.

(12)

They left Ohio State and dispersed into the stream of life. James Gentile has had a private dental practice for the past three decades in Boardman, Ohio. Jerry Tabacca is a periodontist in Columbus. Larry Qualls lives in the Dayton area and is in the publishing business. Gerald King lives in Nokomis, Florida, and works in real estate appraisal. Ted Kurz lives in St. Petersburg, Florida, where he works in private business.

In 1968, Kevin Rusnak returned for football to find he had been demoted from quarterback to a blocking end. Woody was upset that Rusnak was playing baseball in the spring.

"Go over with the tackles," he said.

The next season, his penance complete, Rusnak was welcomed back with the quarterbacks. All the while he played baseball. He became an All-American outfielder. He was drafted in the 11th round in 1970 by the New York Yankees. They misspelled his name, however, and the Philadelphia Phillies got him. He played less than two years in the Phillies organization before having enough. He became a Ford Motors supervisor in Midland, Michigan.

Mike Dale is an exercise physiologist in Pittsburgh. Paul Schmidlin is in the insurance business in Perrysburg, Ohio. Jaren Bombach is an orthopedic surgeon in Columbus. John Sobolewski lives in Great Neck, New York.

Butch Smith, a real estate broker in Columbus for thirty-five years, recently suffered a stroke that paralyzed much of his left side.

David Whitfield sacked Terry Bradshaw twice in the East-West Shrine Game before becoming a commissioned army officer. He went to Fort Sill, Oklahoma, where in 1971 half the class went to Vietnam. His half went to Germany. He now works for the city of Massillon as an equal opportunity director and a recreation supervisor.

Paul Huff, currently retired, owned Columbus Wood Products. Ralph Holloway is a regional sales manager for Worthington Industries, the same place his childhood friend Jack Marsh worked until recently retiring. Bill Hackett lives in Fort Wayne, Indiana, and works in sales in the lawn and garden business.

Brian Donovan, who worked the Debevec family's vineyards one summer in college, started his vineyard in the same area. A decade ago, he sold the vineyard and returned to Columbus where he became a housing inspector.

Jim Oppermann taught the mentally handicapped in Franklin County for six years before getting into construction. For the past twenty-two years, he has owned a company that sells pipe fittings, valves, and fire hydrants.

Steve Crapser owns a technology consulting business near Framingham, Massachusetts. Bruce Smith served in the army until 1975, when he began a career that culminated with him being a manager and director of employee benefits and compensation in the Cincinnati area.

Vic Stottlemyer was drafted into the army upon graduation in 1970, then enlisted in the air force. He piloted refueling and reconnaissance missions over Vietnam in 1972. He never saw Hayes talk to the troops in Vietnam, but met several servicemen who did and were as charmed by him as every recruit. Stottlemyer retired in 2008 after a career flying with United Airlines.

Dave Brungard is retired in Panama City, Florida, after an insurance career in Birmingham, Alabama. Art Burton lives in Dayton. Gary Roush got his master's degree in engineering and went to work in Michigan for General Motors, where he has been for thirty-seven years.

Dick Kuhn worked as a graduate assistant for Hayes before going into sales at Worthington Steel, then starting a business in the late 1970s as a manufacturing representative. When he turned 40, he returned to school, got re-certified as a teacher, and now teaches economics and psychology at Marlington High School near his hometown of Louisville.

Ed Bender returned to his hometown of Akron and took a job as supervisor in a rubber company before moving into human resources. Today, he's a human resource manager for Ralston Foods in Lancaster.

Alan Jack went from the army to become an assistant coach at Denison University. He then went to work for Worthington Steel and today works as an independent steel representative and distributor for a Swiss company.

Bob Trapuzzano taught and coached for seven years in Pennsylvania before starting a general contracting business. For the last several years, he has been buying and renovating homes in Pittsburgh.

Bob Smith was a graduate assistant for Hayes, coached high school football for five years, then for thirty-five years was a general contractor in Kentucky. He recently moved to Newark, Ohio, and, in looking for a doctor, found his teammate, Gerald Ehrsam.

Ehrsam graduated from Ohio State's medical school. Today he practices internal medicine at Licking Memorial Hospital in Newark. Joe Sinkowski is in the garden business in Athens, Ohio.

Ray Gillian got his master's degree in education in 1970 while a graduate assistant for Hayes, then became an assistant coach and assistant professor at East Stroudsburg University. Today he is the vice provost of institutional equity at Johns Hopkins University in Baltimore. Gillian also made up for his lost honeymoon from being married a week before the 1968 season. On his twenty-fifth wedding anniversary, he had a surprise wedding ceremony and exchange of rings with Charell—and added the honeymoon this time.

Jim Coburn played football for the semipro Columbus Bucks after leaving Ohio State before taking a job in the automotive industry near Detroit. Today he works for a company that makes raw materials for cars.

Dirk Worden returned to teach and coach for four years at Lorain Clearview High School. All the while, he tried to rehabilitate his injured knee in hopes of playing in Canada with his brother, Jim. The knee never came around, he began to work construction, and became business manager of the local union. "It was like a team and you had to wear helmets," he said. Today he is executive director in charge of training for several thousand construction workers in Ohio.

John Muhlbach considered attending divinity school after graduating from Ohio State. Hayes was so intent on making it happen that when he received the Walter Camp Coach of the Year award at Yale, he had Muhlbach join him on John Galbreath's private jet for the trip so that Muhlbach could interview at the Yale Divinity School. Muhlbach decided to go a different route and today works in an insurance agency.

Mike Radtke was working in a bank six years after graduating when he took a call from athletic director Hugh Hindman, who had just recommended him to a booster. Radtke got a call from the booster, who wanted to sell his recycling business in five years. Radtke took the job, bought the Columbus business five years later, and still runs it today.

Jim Conroy tore up his knee in practice during the Michigan week of his senior year. He wasn't a starter and didn't play much, but Hayes approached as Conroy sat with his knee packed in ice in the training room.

"I know you want to go to law school," Hayes said. "You've given your all these past four years. I want to thank you for that. You just let me know if there's anything I can do to help get you into a law school."

He started to walk out of the room, then turned back.

"Except for *one* school."

Conroy is a lawyer in the Cleveland area.

Dave Cheney, an All-Big Ten tackle as a senior, wasn't drafted by any NFL team. Hayes offered to make a call and get him into a camp as a free agent. He went to law school at Ohio Northern instead. He became a lawyer and practiced for thirty-three years in Lima before retiring this May. He is now the magistrate of a municipal court.

Dan Aston made the golf team his senior year and ended up making pro golf's Satellite Tour. He moved to Phoenix and died of a heart attack in 2006.

Phil Strickland entered the marines, where he became a pilot and flew for twenty years. He is currently retired in Columbus, where he holds a legacy from that team: a bottle of Thunderbird wine. It was bought for sixty cents in 1969. It has become a standing joke and a lasting keepsake among some African American players of 1968. It will remain sealed until their group is down to a final survivor. The survivor will then salute all of them with it.

Until then, it gets passed around like a Christmas fruitcake. At a recent golf tournament, Bruce Smith offered Strickland two bottles in premiere boxes. When Strickland got home and opened them, one was the bottle of Thunderbird.

"I've got to think how to pass it on now," he said.

Jim Esswein and Bob Grossman, who played in the Ohio State Marching Band that 1968 season, are now part of a small band that can be heard around Columbus still playing Ohio State songs.

Esswein is introduced to the crowd in this manner: "Here's the man who dotted the "i" at the 1969 Rose Bowl."

And forty years later, the applause he heard bowing down to the field keeps coming.

(13)

In the winter of 2006, Jack Tatum called Kern. Even though they hadn't talked in a while, he had a favor to ask. His daughter, Jestynn, was a freshman on the basketball team at Santa Barbara City College in southern California, about an hour from where Kern lived. He wanted to know if Kern could check in on her from time to time. Kern said he'd be happy to do so.

A few days later, Kern and his wife, Nancy, went to a Santa Barbara game. After the game, they talked with Jestynn about her team, her school, and generally about her time away from home. The Kerns had fun meeting her.

The next time Jestynn talked with her father, she had a question.

"How do you know the Kerns again, Dad?" she asked.

He said Rex and he were teammates at Ohio State.

"But, Dad, that's been almost forty years," she said. "Why would they do something like come and see me?"

Therein lay the magic of this team. When Ralph Holloway made wedding plans for the fall of 2008, he asked Tim Anderson to be his best man and Tatum to be in the wedding party.

Butch Smith and Gerald King were partners in a real-estate business.

"I talked to Jim Stillwagon the other day and told him my neck still hurts from him," Jim Roman said. "I get a tic whenever I see the number 68."

Listen to Mike Radtke. When Tom Backhus had heart surgery and needed a place in Phoenix to recuperate, Radtke opened his Phoenix home to him for a month. When Radtke went to visit his eldest son in Kansas recently, he called up Bruce Jankowski for a family get-together.

When Radtke bumped into Phil Strickland on the streets of Columbus one day, they greeted each other with a big hug. When Radtke's nephew was graduating at the University of Dayton, lo and behold, there was Jan White watching his son graduate. Another big hug. And more talk. And talk.

"Will you two sit down and watch the graduation?" their wives finally said.

Every five years, the 1968 team has a reunion. In 1993, at the twenty-fifth year gathering, seventy of seventy-six players returned. More than 2,200 fans bought $75 tickets, with the proceeds going to charity.

Most reunions are more private affairs that sometimes carry even more private moments. Conroy opened his hotel room door the morning after the thirty-fifth anniversary in 2003 to find a plastic bag hanging from the doorknob. In the bag was a trophy. It was the Ernie Godfrey Award, given to the player with the highest freshman grade-point average. Sensibaugh had been given it all those years ago. He recently had discovered Conroy actually had slightly better grades, though as a freshman walk-on, he probably wasn't considered eligible.

"You deserve this," Sensibaugh wrote in a note.

During that same reunion, captains Foley and Worden did something that was a long time in coming. In 1968, after Worden injured his knee in the Purdue game, the coaches realized they needed a defensive captain on the field. They selected Mark Stier.

But Stier wasn't officially recognized that season as a captain of the team or all the intervening years later. During that reunion banquet at the Faculty Club, Foley and Worden surprised Stier. They presented him with the lapel pin and engraved pewter mug that Ohio State captains are always given. His name was also newly listed in each game program, the way all captains and All-American players are.

"It was incredibly meaningful to me," Stier said.

Later that fall, Stier attended his first Captain's Breakfast, the meal in which every captain through the years is invited to eat with the current team on the morning of the homecoming game. Stier has been to each Captain's Breakfast since, too.

Stier was briefly a high school coach in Alliance before taking a job with Worthington Industries. He rose to director of human resources before hearing "God's gentle whisper," as he said. He is now the executive minister at the Westerville Christian Church, where football can be reflected in his work.

"My wife says my sermons are halftime speeches," he said.

When discussing life, he stresses it's reflected not by one moment but by a full season of them. When discussing fear, he talks of the 8-by-10 glossy picture of his Purdue opponent that Ohio State coaches put in his locker before their game.

When discussing that 1968 season, he discusses the bonds that remain forty years later.

"This is the part that kids leaving early from school today for the pros miss out on," he said. "For the money involved, I can't fault them. But when you bail out your sophomore or junior year, you miss the chance to be part of a group who are friends for life. There are the memories you'll never have otherwise, significant memories and friends that have enriched my life."

People always ask: *What was it like to be on that great 1968 team?*

The question is phrased wrong. Jestynn Tatum discovered why on the day she met Rex Kern.

See, they're *still* part of that team.

(14)

Regarding the 1968 season, Mark Stier likes to play the "What If" game.

"What if we'd lost to Illinois?" he wonders. "We'd be remembered as a good team, but not a great one. What if, down 10-0, we'd panicked and lost to

Southern Cal? Would we be as close as we've been all these years?"

On an individual level, perhaps the greatest what-if question doesn't fall to onetime starters like Bill Long or Dave Brungard who were displaced by The Best Class Ever. It might fall to someone who was never even known as a part of that class. Someone like Joe Sinkowski.

Sinkowski was part of Larry Catuzzi's successful East Coast raid. He attended the same Long Island high school and had the same Woody-loving coach—Joe Coady—as Ohio State great Matt Snell. At first, his grades were a problem. But once that was resolved he presented the kind of physical package that forecast him for greatness: 6-3, 254 pounds, a member of his school's 440-yard relay team and a New York state finalist in the super heavyweight wrestling division.

He wasn't just bigger than anyone on Ohio State's defensive line by nearly thirty pounds; he was faster than most of them.

"Special," is the word Catuzzi uses.

That ended in the winter of his freshman year when Sinkowski went home to Carle Place, New York. It started with an argument over a girl at a party. There was a fight. Four guys were on him. A bottle opener was raked across his forehead. An all-out melee broke out, and as he went to the door, a bottle of Gordon's vodka cracked over his head.

His left arm immediately went limp. He lost control of his speech. That was February 27, 1969, and he sat in a hospital bed with nerve damage and a blood clot on his brain until March 13, when the doctors operated.

By then, Sinkowski had lost nearly ninety pounds. Hayes called almost daily. He talked to the doctors. He comforted Sinkowski's mother. Slowly, Sinkowski's health began to improve, as did his speech. But the doctors told him football was out. The risk of injury to his head was too great.

"Woody kept telling me to stay, to get my degree," he said. "But here I was, an ex-jock, not sure who I was anymore."

Five years of wandering and a marriage later, Sinkowski was visiting one of his wife's relatives in Riverside Hospital. The elevator door opened. There was Woody Hayes.

Sinkowski looked at him and smiled.

"Joe . . . Joe Sinkowski," Hayes said.

"Yeah, that's right, Coach," Sinkowski said.

Seeing Sinkowski brought another round of attempts by Hayes to complete the first promise he made to every recruit, and perhaps just as important, made to himself. He told Sinkowski he should graduate. He pressed him. He pushed him. But Sinkowski wasn't the studying type. He still had health issues from the fight, too. He faded from Ohio State's view, but in 1977 he was in the hospital again. Seizures, for which the doctors had no answer.

After five days, Sinkowski said he'd had enough. "If you don't have somebody come in here and tell me what's going on, I'm leaving," he said.

The next morning, Hayes entered the room, bringing breakfast with him.

"Hi, Joe, I'm here to tell you why you're staying right here for these doctors to help you," he said.

"Aw, Coach," Sinkowski said.

Not every story comes with a perfect ending. Sinkowski never played the football he wanted to play because of that vodka bottle, and never got his degree, despite Hayes's encouragement.

He lives in Athens, Ohio. He works in the garden and landscaping business. He's happy. He's having a good life. But once in a while he'll remember those times on the freshman practice field, when Rufus Mayes and Dave Foley would double-team him, cracking him hard, and all of it comes back again. What fun even that was.

"I remember us being out there forever and Woody saying, 'It's not cold out here! Who's cold? Turn on the lights and we'll keep practicing,'" Sinkowski said.

His voice falls. "I had the perfect opportunity," he said. "Woody kept telling me to get the degree. I should've listened to him."

(15)

Several players from the 1968 team had successful runs as coaches. Bill Urbanik, upon graduation in 1970, turned down Hayes's offer to be a graduate assistant. Instead, he took a unique offer to join the staff of a friend, Jack Lengyel, at Marshall University. Thus, Urbanik became part of one of the more dramatic stories in sports, Marshall's first season back from the 1968 plane crash in which seventy-five members of the football team were killed.

Marshall won two games that first season, and also fueled Urbanik's desire to coach. He went from being a defensive line coach at Marshall to Wake Forest, then to the Cincinnati Bengals and the Oakland Raiders.

"I ended up coaching for thirty years with the same style as my teachers," he said. "I was just like Bill Mallory or Woody Hayes. I crucified guys."

Today, Urbanik is a high school teacher and an announcer for Wake Forest football.

Tom Backhus and Randy Hart went from being players under Hayes to becoming graduate assistants at Ohio State, then joined Earle Bruce in 1972 at the University of Tampa. That was the beginning of a twelve-year coaching career for Backhus in which his next stops were Wisconsin and the United States Air Force Academy, where Bill Parcells had his first head coaching job and one day asked to meet with Hayes.

"Woody said it was no problem, and we flew to Columbus and spent a day talking," Backhus said.

Backhus took a job at Notre Dame and was reunited with his former high school coach at Cincinnati's Moeller High, Gerry Faust. That was a bad experience for Backhus, who disagreed with Faust on things as fundamental as practice organization and as significant as game plans. Faust eventually fired his onetime high school captain. Today, Backhus operates the 1,000-acre 4Eagle Ranch near Vail, Colorado.

After Tampa, Hart went to Iowa State with Bruce for three seasons before joining Purdue's staff. In 1982, he rejoined Bruce at Ohio State as its defensive line coach and stayed there until Bruce was fired in 1987. Hart then became the University of Washington's defensive line coach and remains so today. To his collection of national championship and Rose Bowl rings as a player, he has added another national championship and six more Rose Bowl rings as a coach.

Jim Roman coached for twenty-eight years at New Philadelphia High School, on the same field on which Hayes began his own coaching career in 1936. During the 1980 season, one of Roman's players broke his neck and became a quadriplegic. Roman didn't know how to handle his other players. He called Hayes, who told him to get them back into their normal routine, just give them something to do so they wouldn't mope.

That winter, Hayes spoke at a banquet to raise funds for the paralyzed player and another one who had cancer.

"He even wrote a $500 check himself," Roman said.

For more than a decade, through golf outings and auctions, Roman helped New Philadelphia raise money for a new football stadium. In 1999, it was opened as Woody Hayes Quaker Stadium. Today, Roman works at Worthington Industries.

Hart and Urbanik, both coaches, wondered about Hayes's end. There are questions as to whether his erratic behavior was caused by a change in his diabetes medication. Hart and Urbanik wonder the other way. They see his heroes as George Patton, Douglas MacArthur, and Richard Nixon, all of whom were fired.

Did Hayes, some of them wonder, end his career intentionally?

"Just a theory that I wanted to ask him about and I never did," Hart said. "I had a chance, at lunch once, and I just didn't ask. It's one of those regrets I'll always have."

(16)

In the spring of 2000, John Brockington couldn't take the fifteen steps up to his front door without gasping for breath. He began to throw up after getting up in the morning. His legs swelled. He couldn't urinate properly.

Brockington had never smoked, drank, or used drugs in his life. He used to carry orange soda with him to parties. But when he went to the doctor for the first time in seventeen years, the diagnosis was as stunning as it was serious: kidney failure. An enlarged prostate was pinching the tube through which urine passed from his bladder. That caused the urine to flow back into his system, leading to a toxic buildup in his system.

For the next sixteen months, the problem was controlled with medication. But during a Green Bay Packers alumni function in Wisconsin, his flights were grounded—it was September 11, 2001—as they were across the country. He bused to Chicago, then to Columbus, where he visited Ron Maciejowski for a weekend celebrating his Ohio State days.

By the time he returned to San Diego, he was in trouble. He started dialysis treatment immediately and was told he would need a kidney transplant. A desperate search began for a donor. Maciejowski contacted his Ohio State teammates with information on how to reach Brockington's transplant coordinator in San Diego about being a possible donor.

He also called the Varsity "O" Club, with its bank of more than 3,000 names. One 70-year-old letterman contacted Maciejowski, asking how to help.

"Hey, did you hear about Brock?" he said to Kern, who immediately called the kidney transplant coordinator at the hospital.

She sounded exasperated.

"Mr. Kern, do me a favor, please," she said. "Tell your teammates to stop calling. We're overwhelmed with the number of people who are calling on John's behalf. I've never seen anything like this. We couldn't possibly test all of you."

"I walked in one day, and she said, 'Who are all these people?'" Brockington said. He looked at the list of names. Some of them he hadn't seen since college.

Before his teammates were tested, a match was found: his girlfriend, Diane Scott. She had grown up in Wisconsin, a Packers fan. As a Marquette University student, she even remembered watching Brockington play.

But it wasn't until 1993, with both of them living in San Diego, that they met. An employee in a café discovered that Scott was a Packers fan and said Brockington frequented the café. One day, when Brockington came by, the employee introduced the two of them.

Diane's match was the first hurdle. Another one came when doctors looked at her. She was 5-3 and 120 pounds. That meant her kidney would be too small, it seemed. But upon examination her kidney was found to be large enough.

On November 28, 2001, the two were wheeled into adjoining surgery rooms. Scott's kidney was taken out and transplanted into Brockington.

"I'm fine today," he said.

He married Diane in 2003. He also has started the John Brockington Foundation, whose mission is to "narrow the gap between the number of people needing transplants and the number of available organs."

(17)

During the 1968 season, a 15-year-old boy from Berea, Ohio, was captivated by Rex Kern. He imitated the Buckeye quarterback. He combed the newspaper for tidbits about him. In the same manner that Kern was once John Havlicek or Mel Nowell on the sandlots of Lancaster, Jim Tressel became Kern on the fields of his youth.

When Kern's photo was on the cover of the *Cleveland Plain Dealer* holding the Rose Bowl's Most Valuable Player ball in one hand and a Bible in the other, Tressel said, "Maybe I ought to be reading the Bible."

The pull of that Ohio State season had an exaggerated effect on Tressel. His father, Lee, the coach at Baldwin-Wallace, was a Woody Hayes fan. For his college class on football, Lee used the spiral-bound book Hayes wrote after the championship, called *Hotline to Victory*. Hayes wrote it, edited it, proofread it, and published it. Self-reliance, just as Coach Emerson said.

Jim Tressel and his brother Dick weren't the only sons of an Ohio coach in which Hayes's book became their milk of sustenance. In Sandusky, the Gruden brothers, Jim and John, mirrored the Tressels in most every area except the coaching paths taken. They would go the pro route. John, at age 39 in 2002 and with the Tampa Bay Buccaneers, became the youngest coach to win a Super Bowl. Jim was on his staff.

"The perception is that you can be Knute Rockne," John Gruden once said. "You can pull out *Hotline to Victory* that Woody Hayes wrote. The game is about motivation, but execution and performance are the Number One criteria in winning games, just like that book shows."

The Tressel brothers stayed in their father's collegiate game. Dick won 124 games coaching Hamline University in Minnesota and was named the Division III Coach of the Year in 1984.

Jim, named Ohio State's coach in 2001, delivered the Buckeyes' first national title since 1968 when his team beat Miami in the 2003 Fiesta Bowl. Jim Otis's son, Jim Jr., was a sophomore quarterback on the team. Jim Conroy's son, John, was a freshman guard.

"The last two Ohio State championship teams have had a Jim Otis on them," Jim Otis Sr. said. "I hope Jim Tressel doesn't have to wait until a third Jim Otis comes along."

There were other connections to '68 that weren't lost on Tressel. Two of Jim Roman's players at New Philadelphia were part of the team, linebacker Cie Grant and student trainer Patrick Fuller.

"When they won the game, I was in tears," Roman said.

There was an older connection to 1968 in which the news had not been so positive. In the weeks before Stanford and Ohio State met in the 1971 Rose Bowl, Stanford coach John Ralston passed out *Hotline to Victory* to his coaches.

"Tell Woody thanks for giving us his playbook," Ralston told Jim Stillwagon when they met in a post-season all-star game.

Stillwagon told Hayes, who didn't believe it. Stillwagon insisted. Then he reminded Hayes about one of the history lessons the coach always discussed with his players: German general Erwin Rommel wrote a book about his tactics that Patton read and used in beating *him*.

"You, of all people, should have known the dangers about writing this book," Stillwagon said.

(18)

On a cold and snowy Denver day in 2003, Jack Tatum felt like he was coming down with a cold. By the time he arrived home in Oakland, he was sure of it. He got sick to his stomach and lay down. When he wouldn't get up for several days, his wife, Denise, grew worried. She urged him to go to the hospital. He refused.

Denise called a couple of his Oakland Raiders teammates, Macarthur Lane and Carlton Oates. They came to his home and threatened to carry him to the hospital if he wouldn't go. Tatum got out of bed, went to the emergency room, and was taken immediately into surgery.

He had a staph infection on his foot, which necessitated the amputation of part of it. Diabetes was the cause, the doctors told Tatum. A couple of weeks later, one of his legs was amputated below the knee. These unfortunate events started a series of health issues with Tatum that had Woody Hayes's former doctor, Manuel Tzagournis, reaching out across the country.

"He called and said he wanted me to come back to Columbus and let him look at me," Tatum said. "I didn't know Dr. Tzagournis. And at first I didn't want to fly all the way there."

Finally, with his health deteriorating, Tatum saw Tzagournis. He cleaned out Tatum's arteries. He discovered Tatum had suffered an aneurysm. He put Tatum on a diet and a program to restore his health. A fund-raiser was organized by John Hicks, an offensive tackle two classes behind Tatum at Ohio State and also his roommate.

"He had a nice car when he was a sophomore and I was a senior," Tatum said. "That's why I joke I let him be my roommate. We'd take his car during the week and return it to him on weekends so he could fill it up with gas."

Holtz spoke at the fund-raiser. Several 1968 teammates showed up. Out of that, an annual event with the National Diabetes Association was formed for the week of the Michigan-Ohio State game. Hundreds of thousands of dollars have been raised to help in the fight against diabetes.

"Remember what Woody said," Tatum said. "'You can't pay back. Pay it forward.'"

(19)

In late June of 2008, Dave Foley phoned Kevin Rusnak.

"Are you coming?" Foley asked.

Foley was organizing the golf tournament for the fortieth reunion of the Boys of '68. Foley has had three knee operations and his right hip replaced twice. Rusnak takes twelve pills a day to combat arthritis. Which is how, down the line, it went. Kern needs a couple of hours of daily therapy on his back. Tim Anderson had his shoulder rebuilt.

But some things don't change with time, such as Rusnak being late for meetings, practice, and now in answering with his reunion plans. Yes, he told Foley, he was coming and would golf with his old roommate, Ted Kurz.

Stillwagon organized the full weekend event. Maciejowski invited everyone to his home. They had tickets to watch Ohio State's football team play Troy on the playground of their youth. For one more weekend, they'd meet and talk and laugh and remember, and once again, all down the roster, break out Woody stories among brothers who appreciated such things the most.

They're now older than the Old Man when he stood in Smith Hall for that first meeting and told them to look around the room at each other.

"The people here in this room will be your best friends in life," Woody said then.

Four decades later, the Old Man was right again.

"He never really forgave the
world for making him a football
coach instead of a field marshal."
—Jim Murray on Woody

Bibliography

Brondfield, Jerry. *Woody Hayes and the 100-Yard War*. New York: Berkley Medallion Books, 1975.

Bruce, Earle. *Earle: A Coach's Life*. Wilmington, Ohio: Orange Frazer Press, 2000.

Ellison, Carolyn J. *Coach the Kid, Build the Boy, Mold the Man: The Legacy of Run and Shoot Football*. Xlibris, 2007.

Greenberg, Steve and Zelina, Larry. *Ohio State '68: All the Way to the Top*. Champaign, Illinois: Sports Publishing, 1998.

Harper, William L. *An Ohio State Man*. Atlanta: Enthea Press, 2000.

Hayes, Woody. *Hotline to Victory*. Self-published, 1969.

Hayes, Woody. *You Win With PEOPLE!* Self-published, 1973.

Holtz, Lou. *Wins, Losses, and Lessons*. New York: Harper Entertainment, 2006.

Hornung, Paul. *Woody Hayes: A Reflection*. Champaign, Illinois: Sagamore Publishing, 1991.

Lombardo, John. *A Fire to Win: The Life and Times of Woody Hayes*. New York: St. Martin's Griffin, 2006.

Menzer, Joe. *Buckeye Madness*. New York: Simon & Schuster, 2005.

Natali, Alan. *Woody's Boys*. Wilmington, Ohio: Orange Frazer Press, 1995.

Park, Jack. *The Official Ohio State Football Encyclopedia*. Sports Publishing LLC, 2003.

Shapiro, Harvey. *Class of '68: A Season to Remember*. Marshall, Indiana: Witness Productions, 1998.

Simpson, O.J. and Axthelm, Pete. *O.J: The Education of a Rich Rookie*. New York: The MacMillan Company.

Snook, Jeff. *What It Means to Be a Buckeye*. Chicago: Triumph Books, 2003.

Tatum, Jack with Kushner, Bill. *They Call Me Assassin*. New York: Everest House, 1980.

Vare, Robert. *Buckeye*. New York: Harper's Magazine Press, 1974.

Index

Z

Zelina, Larry